Does Your Project
Have a Copyright Problem?

Does Your Project Have a Copyright Problem?

A Decision-Making Guide for Librarians

by

MARY BRANDT JENSEN

McFarland & Company, Inc., Publishers
Jefferson, North Carolina, and London

British Library Cataloguing-in-Publication data are available

Library of Congress Cataloguing-in-Publication Data

Jensen, Mary Brandt.
    Does your project have a copyright problem? : a decision-
making guide for librarians / by Mary Brandt Jensen.
        p.   cm.
    Includes index.
    ISBN 0-7864-0282-2 (sewn softcover : 50# alk. paper) ∞
    1. Fair use (Copyright)—United States—Decision making.
2. Librarians—United States—Handbooks, manuals, etc.
I. Title.
KF3020.Z9J45   1996
346.7304'82—dc20
[347.306482]   96-32433
                                                            CIP

Manufactured in the United States of America

McFarland & Company, Inc., Publishers
  Box 611, Jefferson, North Carolina 28640

Brief Table of Contents

Full Table of Contents

Preface

This book was born four years ago when I was invited to Hawaii to conduct a workshop on copyright with Stuart Milligan for the Hawaii Interlibrary Consortium. The librarians who asked for the workshop had asked too many questions to be covered in a one day workshop. As a teacher always faced with too little time to cover the subject matter in class, I knew that I needed to do what I have always tried to do in class—teach these librarians how to analyze any project they might encounter for copyright problems instead of trying to answer questions on specific projects. If I could do that, I would have taught them something that would be valuable for a long time. If I could develop a system for analyzing copyright problems, I could also shorten the time it takes me to answer the myriad of copyright questions that have come to me from all over the world since I began moderating the Internet list cni-copyright.

I managed to develop the first set of questions for the workshop. The rest of the system, the decision charts, and the text for the book probably would never have been developed without a grant that I received from the University of South Dakota Law School Foundation in 1995. I had never seen a book like I wanted to write, and I had no idea how to make it readable. The first drafts were deadly enough to put anyone to sleep and often failed to explain principles that I took for granted after spending years studying copyright law. The grant allowed me to work with Nancy Zuercher, a professor of English at the University of South Dakota, who has taught me much of what I know about using writing as a teaching tool. Nancy spent many hours reading the drafts, pointing out the parts which were unclear, getting me to explain and rewrite the confusing parts, and discussing with me how the reader would use this book. If you find this book useful, much of the credit for usability goes to Nancy Zuercher.

I am also grateful to Donna Sommervold and April Johnson at the University of South Dakota and the University of Mississippi who spent many hours correcting the text and improving the charts. Teresa Maule helped me do the research and indexing. And through it all, Jessica Litman, a professor of copyright law at Wayne State, helped me make sure I didn't misstate or misrepresent the law in my efforts to make it understandable.

I also could not have written the book without the support of my husband, Patrick, who provided much moral support and took over my share of the household so that I could work on the book through many evenings and weekends. I think he will be glad to get his wife back.

Mary Brandt Jensen
Oxford, Mississippi
May 4, 1996

Part I.
Getting to
Know the System

How to Use This Book

This book is designed to help you find and analyze the various copyright issues in any library project. Since it addresses any situation that may arise in a library, it does not read like most books on copyright. Instead of only discussing whether specific projects require the permission of the copyright owner, it discusses each section of the law that might apply to any library project. This allows you to apply the information in the book to projects that may be considerably different from the examples discussed.

The book's organization is designed to help you consider all the appropriate issues and factors even if you have little or no previous knowledge of copyright law. It is easy to jump to conclusions or miss issues if you do not approach copyright problems systematically. The Decision Charts on pages 4 to 12 are the key to figuring out which parts you need to read for any particular problem. Following the Decision Charts and an overview of major areas of copyright issues, Part II contains discussions of the various sections of the law. In addition to this section on how to use the book, Part I contains a section that uses the system to analyze a sample project. Part III contains three additional practice projects with summaries of the analysis for each project. Even if your project is considerably different from these examples, they should help you to understand how to apply the information in Part II to your particular project. The appendices contain statutes, regulations, guidelines and other material referred to in other parts of the book that may be useful in analyzing projects.

It is recommended that you first review all the charts on pages 4 to 12, and in particular the Overview Chart. The charts have been presented together in this section to give the user an opportunity easily to see how they interrelate. Each individual chart appears again with the relevant chapter for the convenience of the user. The Overview Chart will be the starting point to answer any question. To fully understand this systematic approach it is also recommended that you read and follow the lengthy example on electronic reserves that follows this section. (This example was chosen because it is complex and will lead the reader through most of the book.) As you gain understanding on how to move from chart to chart, leaving behind matters that do not relate to your project, you will begin to see what a time-saver the system can be. The charts will direct you to read only the relevant text that you need for your particular project. As you gain familiarity with the charts, this systematic approach can be used to answer quickly a straightforward question or to help you navigate around a thorny problem.

Copyright law is very complex and at times confusing. Sometimes, it may even seem illogical in that it may treat two seemingly similar situations very differently.[1] Because the law is complex and confusing, you need to pay careful attention to legal definitions and statutory clauses. Assuming that words have the same meaning in the law that they ordinarily have outside the law can lead you to the wrong conclusion. Assuming that you understand the plain meaning of a statute without reading the relevant legislative history and case law that interprets the statute can also lead you to the wrong conclusion. At times, neither the law nor the legislative history will provide a definite answer to your questions. This book will tell you what factors to consider. Even when it appears to give a definite answer, do not rely on this book for legal advice. If you need a legal opinion, consult an attorney. If you intend to consult an attorney, it may be helpful to use this book to analyze the potential copyright issues in your project in preparation for your visit with the attorney.

The Charts for the System
(All Ten Collected in One Place)

Those who are just getting acquainted with the system may want to spend time studying the charts so that they may see how the charts interrelate. After the reader becomes familiar with the system, it may not be necessary to consult the full text on some parts of the project.

For the convenience of these users, a collection of the charts is provided on the following pages.

---

1. The confusion or lack of logic usually arises from one or more of three reasons. (1) Congress, the courts, and the other drafters of the law did not anticipate one of the two situations. (2) They anticipated both situations, but unlike the reader, they did not consider the situations to be similar. (3) They anticipated both situations, but differing interest groups had different views on what the correct balancing of copyright interests should be and the law is a compromise between the two positions.

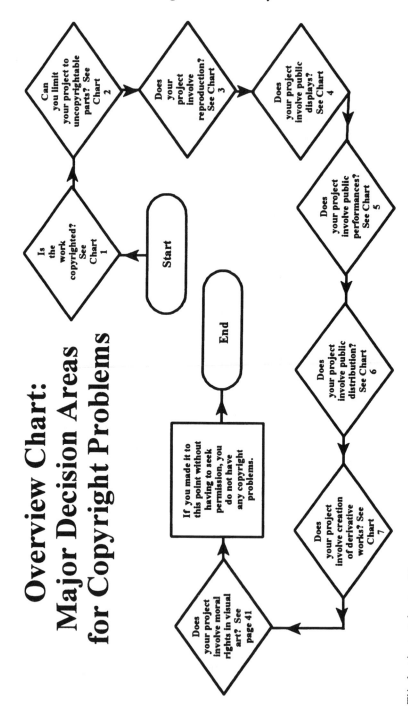

Overview Chart:
Major Decision Areas
for Copyright Problems

Start

Is the work copyrighted? See Chart 1

Can you limit your project to uncopyrightable parts? See Chart 2

Does your project involve reproduction? See Chart 3

Does your project involve public displays? See Chart 4

Does your project involve public performances? See Chart 5

Does your project involve public distribution? See Chart 6

Does your project involve creation of derivative works? See Chart 7

Does your project involve moral rights in visual art? See page 41

If you made it to this point without having to seek permission, you do not have any copyright problems.

End

This chart is repeated on page 36.

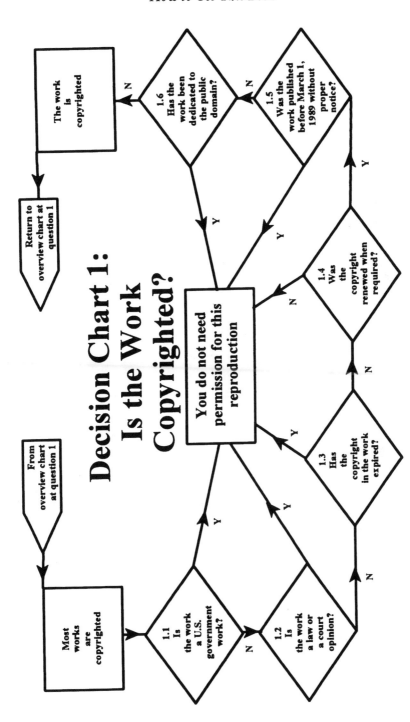

Decision Chart 1: Is the Work Copyrighted?

From overview chart at question 1

Most works are copyrighted

1.1 Is the work a U.S. government work?

1.2 Is the work a law or a court opinion?

You do not need permission for this reproduction

1.3 Has the copyright in the work expired?

1.4 Was the copyright renewed when required?

1.5 Was the work published before March 1, 1989 without proper notice?

1.6 Has the work been dedicated to the public domain?

The work is copyrighted

Return to overview chart at question 1

This chart is repeated on page 46.

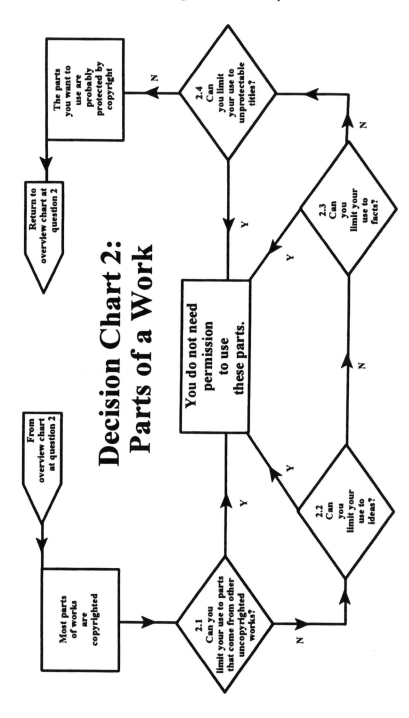

Decision Chart 2:
Parts of a Work

From overview chart at question 2

Most parts of works are copyrighted

2.1 Can you limit your use to parts that come from other uncopyrighted works?

N

Y

2.2 Can you limit your use to ideas?

Y

N

You do not need permission to use these parts.

2.3 Can you limit your use to facts?

Y

N

2.4 Can you limit your use to unprotectable titles?

Y

N

The parts you want to use are probably protected by copyright

Return to overview chart at question 2

This chart is repeated on page 58.

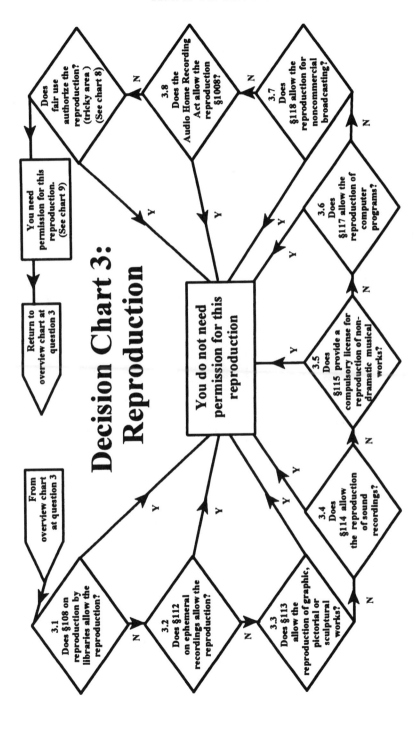

Decision Chart 3: Reproduction

From overview chart at question 3

3.1 Does §108 on reproduction by libraries allow the reproduction?

N → **3.2** Does §112 on ephemeral recordings allow the reproduction?

N → **3.3** Does §113 allow the reproduction of graphic, pictorial or sculptural works?

N → **3.4** Does §114 allow the reproduction of sound recordings?

N → **3.5** Does §115 provide a compulsory license for reproduction of non-dramatic musical works?

N → **3.6** Does §117 allow the reproduction of computer programs?

N → **3.7** Does §118 allow the reproduction for noncommercial broadcasting?

N → **3.8** Does the Audio Home Recording Act allow the reproduction §1008?

N → Does fair use authorize the reproduction? (tricky area) (See chart 8)

Y → You do not need permission for this reproduction

You need permission for this reproduction. (See chart 9)

Return to overview chart at question 3

This chart is repeated on page 62.

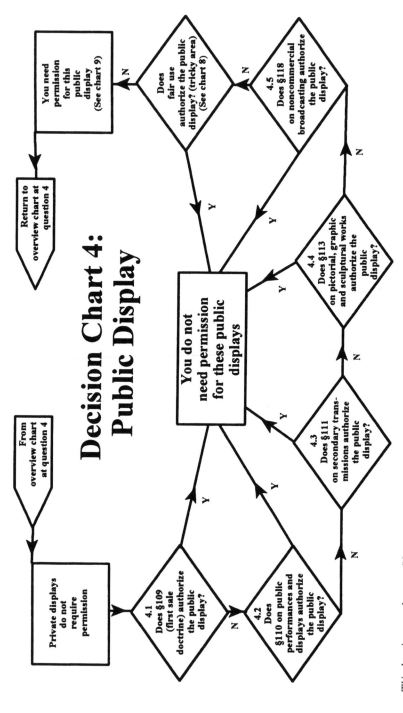

Decision Chart 4: Public Display

From overview chart at question 4

Private displays do not require permission

4.1 Does §109 (first sale doctrine) authorize the public display?

4.2 Does §110 on public performances and displays authorize the public display?

4.3 Does §111 on secondary transmissions authorize the public display?

4.4 Does §113 on pictorial, graphic and sculptural works authorize the public display?

4.5 Does §118 on noncommercial broadcasting authorize the public display?

Does fair use authorize the public display? (tricky area) (See chart 8)

You do not need permission for these public displays

You need permission for this public display (See chart 9)

Return to overview chart at question 4

This chart is repeated on page 78.

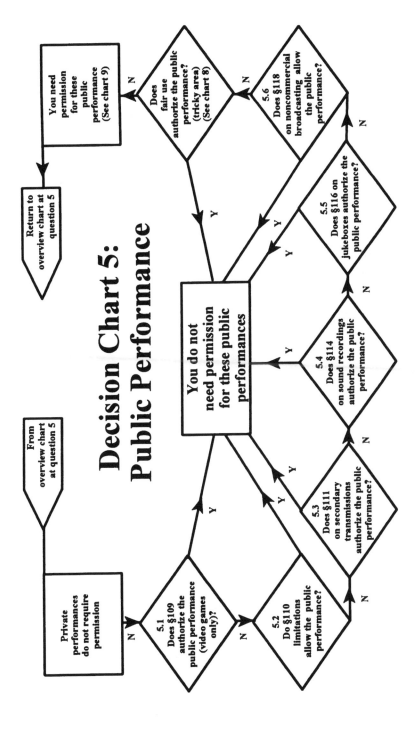

Decision Chart 5: Public Performance

From overview chart at question 5

Private performances do not require permission

5.1 Does §109 authorize the public performance (video games only)?

5.2 Do §110 limitations allow the public performance?

5.3 Does §111 on secondary transmissions authorize the public performance?

5.4 Does §114 on sound recordings authorize the public performance?

5.5 Does §116 on jukeboxes authorize the public performance?

5.6 Does §118 on noncommercial broadcasting allow the public performance?

Does fair use authorize the public performance? (tricky area) (See chart 8)

You do not need permission for these public performances

Return to overview chart at question 5

You need permission for these public performance (See chart 9)

This chart is repeated on page 90.

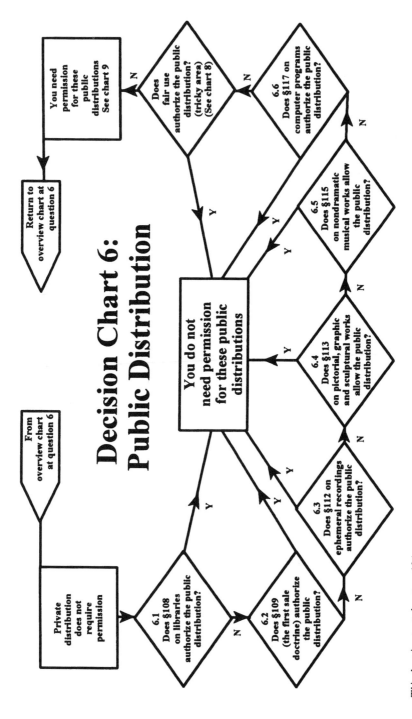

Decision Chart 6:
Public Distribution

From overview chart at question 6

Private distribution does not require permission

6.1 Does §108 on libraries authorize the public distribution?

6.2 Does §109 (the first sale doctrine) authorize the public distribution?

6.3 Does §112 on ephemeral recordings authorize the public distribution?

6.4 Does §113 on pictorial, graphic and sculptural works allow the public distribution?

6.5 Does §115 on nondramatic musical works allow the public distribution?

6.6 Does §117 on computer programs authorize the public distribution?

Does fair-use authorize the public distribution? (tricky area) (See chart 8)

You do not need permission for these public distributions

Return to overview chart at question 6

You need permission for these public distributions See chart 9

This chart is repeated on page 104.

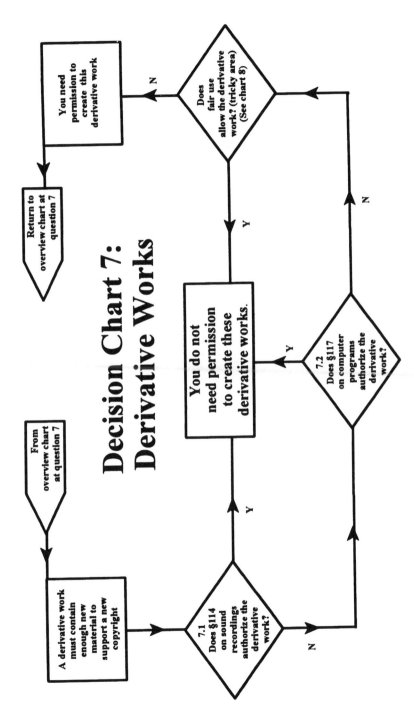

Decision Chart 7:
Derivative Works

From overview chart at question 7

A derivative work must contain enough new material to support a new copyright

7.1 Does §114 on sound recordings authorize the derivative work?

7.2 Does §117 on computer programs authorize the derivative work?

You do not need permission to create these derivative works.

Does fair use allow the derivative work? (tricky area) (See chart 8)

You need permission to create this derivative work

Return to overview chart at question 7

This chart is repeated on page 116.

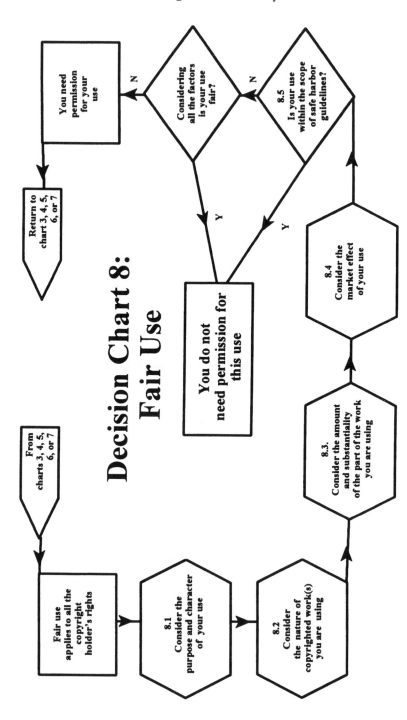

Decision Chart 8:
Fair Use

From charts 3, 4, 5, 6, or 7

Fair use applies to all the copyright holder's rights

8.1 Consider the purpose and character of your use

8.2 Consider the nature of copyrighted work(s) you are using

8.3. Consider the amount and substantiality of the part of the work you are using

8.4 Consider the market effect of your use

8.5 Is your use within the scope of safe harbor guidelines?

Considering all the factors is your use fair?

You do not need permission for this use

You need permission for your use

Return to chart 3, 4, 5, 6, or 7

This chart is repeated on page 120.

Chart 9:
Permission

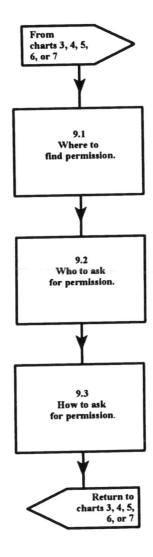

This chart is repeated on page 136.

Applying the System to an Example: An Electronic Reserve Project

This example demonstrates how to use the Decision Charts to guide you in deciding which segments of Part II to consult in analyzing a problem. The detailed analysis suggested by the Decision Charts may seem complicated, but it should make it easier to find new issues and different perspectives than a less systematic approach. This systematic approach can be particularly helpful with complex projects, such as electronic reserve, that have a lot of different copyright issues.

Electronic reserve systems will probably include a variety of works which the law treats differently. (For example, see page 61.) The electronic nature of the system also raises a variety of copyright issues that are not usually involved in projects limited to print technology. While some of the issues raised by an electronic system may not be present in more traditional projects, the structure of the law, and thus the approach of the Decision Charts, does not change.

Since an electronic system raises more copyright issues than a print system, you should expect more potential copyright obstacles. Sometimes you may be able to eliminate some obstacles in a project by modifying your approach to the project. (See for example, page 160.) At other times, the charts may lead you to sections of the law that may not appear to be applicable at first glance, but which may resolve one or more of the obstacles. It may be extremely difficult, if not impossible, however, to modify a project to eliminate some problems. If you cannot eliminate a copyright obstacle, you may have to decide whether the project, or a particular part of it, is worth the effort needed to obtain the permissions that the law requires.

Description of the Project

Before attempting to analyze any project, you will need a good description of the project. For this example, I have combined elements of

14

several different electronic reserve systems that I have either seen or been asked about.

The Newtown College Library has decided that it should set up an electronic reserve collection to better serve its students. There are several ways to set up the system, but the librarians prefer to scan articles and convert the contents to ASCII files using optical character recognition software. They intend to put all the files on a central file server accessible from any PC in the library. Professors are expected to give students a list of assigned readings. Students are expected to go to the library, log on to the system and search for the appropriate material. Once located, students may read the material on the screen or download a copy either to a floppy disk or to a laser printer operated by a vending card. Students who choose to download must provide their own disks and are not charged anything. Students who choose to print will be charged 10 cents a page which is the same charge assessed for self-service photocopying in the library.

Analysis of the Law Following the Decision Charts

The Overview Chart identifies the major areas in which copyright issues arise. It refers you to other charts for more detailed questions in each area. The first area that the Overview Chart refers to is determining whether the works are copyrighted, which is covered in more detail in Chart 1. As the first element in Chart 1 indicates, most works are copyrighted (see page 44), so you should start with the assumption that the works most faculty members will want to have in the electronic reserve system are probably copyrighted. Chart 1 then proceeds through a series of questions to help you decide whether particular works in the electronic reserve system fit into any exceptions to the general rule that most works are copyrighted.

Chart 1 identifies government works as the first category of works that are not copyrighted. Some works that faculty members want to place on reserve may be government works. For example, a world geography professor might ask to have the *CIA World Factbook* added to the electronic reserve collection to assign the sections on specific countries for background reading. This book is produced annually by the employees of the Central Intelligence Agency as part of their duties, so it cannot be copyrighted. Since works produced by employees of the United States government in the course and scope of their duties are not copyrighted, adding them to an electronic reserve system presents no copyright problems. (See page 45.) However, many of the works that faculty members want to put in the electronic reserve system will not be United States government works.

The second question in Chart 1 focuses on laws. Occasionally, faculty members may want to put the text of a statute, regulation or court case in the electronic reserve system. When faculty members select cases and laws to add to the system, however, they will usually be selecting versions produced by private publishers who have added copyrighted material to the basic public domain text of the statute or case. (See page 47.) If only the uncopyrightable text of a statute or court opinion is used, court opinions and laws may be added to the system without encountering any copyright problems.

Question 3 asks whether the copyright on a work you want to use has expired. Using the Duration Timeline on page 49, you can see that works originally copyrighted less than 75 years ago are often still protected by copyright. The U.S. copyright has expired, however, on editions of works published more than 75 years ago. These editions may be added to the system without any copyright problems.

The copyright on some works less than 75 years old may have expired because the copyright was not properly renewed. Question 4 indicates that you could use these works without copyright problems if you could figure out which works had not been renewed. Determining whether a copyright has been renewed, however, can be a time consuming and expensive process. (See pages 50 to 52.) Considering the number of works that are likely to be put into an electronic reserve system, the process is likely to be prohibitively expensive. Thus, you should probably assume that all copyrights were properly renewed and were not forfeited for failure to renew.

Some of the works faculty want to have added to the electronic reserve system may have been published less than 75 years ago but before 1989. Question 5 asks whether works published before March 1, 1989, contain the proper notice. You will need to examine these works to see if they contain proper copyright notices. Works published in the United States before 1989 without proper notice may be added to the system without encountering copyright problems because any copyright that might have existed in these works has been forfeited. The requirements for a proper notice under the 1909 Act are described on page 53. The requirements for a proper notice under the 1976 Act before March 1, 1989, are described on page 54.

Question 6 indicates that you can also use works that have been dedicated to the public domain. The ways in which works may be dedicated to the public domain are discussed on page 55. It is unlikely that you will find many works dedicated to the public domain. Those works that have been dedicated to the public domain, however, may be added to the system without encountering any copyright problems.

You have now come to the end of Chart 1. Some of the works that faculty want to add to the system will fit into one of the exceptions, and thus will not be currently protected by copyright. Many other works that faculty members will want to have added to the system, however, will not fit into any of the exceptions, so you must conclude that they are currently protected by copyright.

Returning to the Overview Chart, it indicates that the next group of issues to analyze concern which parts of a work are copyrighted. You can avoid copyright problems if you can limit your project to uncopyrightable parts of works such as parts taken from public domain works, ideas, facts or titles (see Chart 2). However, what most faculty usually want to put on reserve are verbatim copies of parts of works or entire works. They are often interested in more than just facts and ideas in copyrighted works. Thus it is not possible to restrict a reserve project to just the uncopyrightable parts of copyrighted works. Since we can see this just from looking at Chart 2, we do not need to read Chapter 2.

The Overview Chart lists reproduction as the next major area we need to consider. Because legal definitions often differ from the ordinary meanings of words, you can easily overlook a part of the project that may present a copyright problem if you assume you know the legal definition of a right. This is especially true when you are analyzing a project involving new technologies. The legal definition of reproduction is "reproduc[ing] a material object in which the work is duplicated, transcribed, imitated, or simulated in a fixed form from which it can be perceived, reproduced, or otherwise communicated, either directly or with the aid of a machine or device." (See page 34.)

The first stage of the project involving a reproduction occurs when the library scans the works selected by faculty members to convert them to electronic form. An additional reproduction will probably also occur when a text file is produced from the scanner output using optical character recognition software. Yet another reproduction is likely to occur when the text file from the OCR program is copied onto central disk space on the library's file server. Some people believe that additional copies may be made when portions of documents are transferred to the memory of individual PCs when students are searching for the relevant documents or are reading them on screens. (See page 35.) Students will make additional copies when they download the documents to disks, or when they print the documents. If the facts are altered slightly so that the library puts a copy of the documents in the private space assigned to each student instead of in a common area of a central server, the library will be making even more copies than it makes under the original project facts. It will make a copy of the work for each student to whose space the files are sent.

Unless you find authorization for each of these reproductions in the copyright law, you will have to find or get permission from the copyright holder for them. Chart 3 takes you through the sections of the law which might authorize a reproduction. It identifies §108 as the first section that might help.

The first subsection of §108 governs who may take advantage of its limitations. Section 108 applies to most libraries. (See page 60.) It applies to the library used in this example because the facts specify that the library is open to the public. The facts also state that the only charges related to the project are page charges for printing which are similar to the self-service photocopy charges. The price for printing is fixed low enough that it covers only costs of printing and does not generate a profit for the library. Thus, there is no commercial advantage associated with the reproduction in this electronic reserve example.

Part of §108 applies to all types of works. Other parts do not apply to musical works, pictorial works, graphic works, sculptural works, motion pictures or other audiovisual works. (See page 61.) Most of the works in an electronic reserve system are likely to be literary works to which all of §108 is applicable. However, it is possible that faculty members might want to include works from the excluded categories in the electronic reserve project.

The second and third subsections of §108 allow preservation and replacement copying under certain circumstances. These two subsections will be of little use in authorizing the reproduction that occurs in an electronic reserve project because these subsections are limited to reproduction in facsimile form. The legislative history indicates that the restriction to facsimile form was included so that the subsections would not authorize conversion to machine readable form. While it is possible that the images scanned in the process of creating electronic copies of works might satisfy the requirement for facsimile reproduction, the ASCII text files that are actually added to the system are clearly not in facsimile form. (See page 63.)

The remainder of §108 applies to reproduction for library patrons. Upon first impression, it would appear that these subsections might authorize at least some of the copying involved in the electronic reserve project, because at least some of the copying is for patrons. Unlike subsections (b) and (c), these subsections are not limited to reproduction in facsimile form. However, subsections (d) and (e) are limited to no more than one article or selection per patron at a time. Furthermore, libraries are not authorized to provide copies of the same work to different students under these subsections if the requests are related. And the legislative history clearly indicates that Congress considered assigned readings for the same class to be related. Thus, subsections (d) and (e) of §108 do not authorize reserve reproduction in either the electronic or the nonelectronic environment. (See page 66.)

Subsection (f) may be applicable to part of the reproduction that occurs in this example. It protects a library from liability for contributory infringement if a patron makes an infringing copy on unsupervised reproducing equipment in the library. Since the computers that the students use in the library to read, download and print material from the electronic reserve collection could be considered unsupervised reproducing equipment, this subsection might protect a library from liability for the copying that students do if the library complies with all the requirements of the subsection. (See page 68.) But this subsection applies only to copying done by patrons on unsupervised equipment located in the library. It will not authorize any copying done by library employees in the process of building the system or while delivering material to patrons.

Section 112 is the next section that Chart 3 refers to. The ephemeral recording limitation in §112 applies only to reproduction made in connection with a transmission of a performance that the library has a right to make under either a license or another section of the law. At this point in the analysis, we have not yet decided whether the library has a right to make any transmissions of performances. However, even if the library has the right to transmit performances in connection with the electronic reserve project, §112 is unlikely to authorize any of the reproductions associated with this project.

Section 112 limits

    a. how many copies can be made,

    b. what purposes the copies can be used for,

    c. to whom the copies can be transferred, and

    d. how long the copies may be kept.

    (See pages 69 to 71.)

Subsection (a) limits the number of copies to one copy; subsection (b) to thirty copies, subsection (c) to one copy, and subsection (d) to ten copies. All of the subsections say or imply that no further copies can be made from the copies authorized by §112. If a library either directly or indirectly authorized or encouraged the making of additional copies from its original one to thirty copies, the library would lose its protection under §112. Our analysis thus far indicates that at least three copies of each work are likely to be made in the process of preparing the electronic files and putting them in the system. If a copy is made by the library computer each time it transmits a copy to the memory of a student's PC (see page 35), the library could easily exceed the maximum of 30 copies. Even if the copies loaded into computer memory do not count as reproductions because they are not fixed or if the copies are made by students rather than the library, the entire §112 privilege could be lost when the thirty-first copy is downloaded to a student's disk or printed. Since classes often exceed 30 students, the number of copies might frequently exceed 30.

Copies made under §112 can be used only for archival purposes or for purposes of authorized transmissions. While the copies that are made in the process of loading works into the system and transmitting the works to the memory of students' PCs could be said to facilitate transmissions, the copies made when students download or print are not used solely for purposes of transmission. Nor are they used solely for archival purposes.

Those parts of §112 that allow the transmitting organization to make more than one copy or to transfer possession of the copies only allow the transmitting organization to share the copies with other organizations that have a right to transmit public performances of the work. So unless the students have a right to transmit public performances, which is unlikely, §112 does not cover the copies made by the students or copies transferred to students.

Subsection (c) says that a copy may be kept for transmission purposes for no longer than six months. Subsection (b) allows an organization to keep the copy for transmission purposes for seven years. Subsection (c) limits retention to one year. Subsection (d) has no time limitation, but is limited to copies of performances designed for handicapped audiences. While all of these time periods are long enough to cover a single semester if the other requirements were met, several of them are too short to permit repeated use over several terms.

Thus it would appear that §112 is unlikely to authorize the reproductions associated with an electronic reserve system even if the library has a right to transmit public performances of the works in the system.

According to question 3, §113 is the next section which might authorize a reproduction. Most of the works in the electronic reserve system will be literary works rather than pictorial, graphic or sculptural works. Section 113 does not apply to literary works. Even if the system contains pictorial or graphic works, §113 will not authorize the reproductions associated with their use in the system because §113 only authorizes reproduction in connection with advertising or commenting upon a work or in news reporting. The reproduction associated with electronic reserve does not fall into any of these categories. (See page 72.)

Question 4 identifies §114 as the next possibility. The only reproduction authorized by §114 is reproduction of sound recordings in the context of educational broadcasting. The authorization is only available to public broadcasting stations. This limitation is not applicable to the electronic reserve example because electronic reserve does not involve an educational broadcast by a public broadcasting entity. (See page 72.)

Chart 3, question 5 refers us next to §115. It is unlikely that §115 would authorize any of the reproduction connected with an electronic reserve system because most of the musical sound recordings that faculty are likely to want to put on reserve are prerecorded. In order for §115 to authorize the reproduction, a new recording of a nondramatic musical work would have to be made. (See page 73.)

Section 117, which is the next section in Chart 3, is of little use in the electronic reserve setting either. First, it applies only to computer programs. Very few of the works that faculty want to put on reserve will meet the definition of a computer program. Second, it only authorizes reproduction for archival purposes and reproduction that is necessary to use a computer program in a computer. (See page 74.) The electronic reserve system is clearly not limited to archival purposes. Loading a computer program into a networked system, like the one described in this example, is not an essential step in using most programs since the programs could be loaded into an individual machine used by patrons.

Question 7 leads us to §118. Like §114, the only reproduction authorized by §118 is reproduction in the context of educational broadcasting. The authorization is only available to public broadcasting stations. This limitation is not applicable to the electronic reserve example because electronic reserve is not an educational broadcast by a public broadcasting entity. (See page 75.)

Section 1008, the Audio Home Recording Act, the subject of question 8, prohibits copyright infringement suits based on noncommercial reproduction of musical sound recordings by consumers using a digital or analog recording device. It will not cover any of the reproduction involved in the electronic reserve project because none of the computers used to make copies in the project will meet the definition of a digital or analog recording device. The Audio Home Recording Act is also limited to musical sound recordings. (See page 76.)

The final possibility that Chart 3 refers to is fair use. Fair use analysis is complicated enough that Chart 3 refers us to Chart 8. Section 107 on fair use is the section of the Copyright Act that libraries rely on to authorize the reproduction associated with photocopied reserve materials. Since fair use is not limited to any particular technology, it is applicable to the electronic reserve example. Deciding whether scanning material for print reserve purposes is a fair use is not very different from determining whether photocopying would be permitted for reserve purposes. In deciding whether scanned reserve readings are a fair use, each factor listed in §107 must be considered.

The first factor listed in Chart 8 is the purpose and character of the use. (See pages 119 to 125.) The purpose of the use presents little or no problem in an academic or school library. The purpose is nonprofit teaching, an approved purpose under §107. Other libraries may have similar collections whose purpose is not specifically mentioned in §107. Nevertheless, if the library is a nonprofit library and the scanning is done to facilitate purposes such as research, scholarship, education, news reporting, comment or criticism, the purpose of the use will weigh in favor of a finding of fair use.

The character of the use presents a somewhat greater problem. The particular character of this use, conversion to a machine readable form and posting to a potentially large audience, could get out of hand and quickly lead to unfair uses. But the other factors should mitigate the potential for abuse.

The second factor identified by Chart 8 and the statute is the nature of the work. The nature of the copyrighted works depends upon what will be scanned. The nature of journal articles would probably not present a problem, since limited copying of journal articles for reserve has long been considered a fair use.[2] On the other hand, if pages from a consumable workbook were scanned, the nature of the copied work would present a problem. The nature of other works designed especially for the education market, such as textbooks, might also pose a problem, since by definition any uncompensated

---

2. See "Gentlemen's Agreement," *J. of Documentary Reproduction* 2 (1939): 31; "Reproduction of Materials Code," *A.L.A. Bull.* 35 (1941): 84.

copying of this type of work by educational institutions cuts into the primary market for the work.

The amount and substantiality (see Chart 8, factor 3) of the copying is very important. If whole books are scanned, the likelihood of infringement rises dramatically. Even when journal articles, which are much shorter than books, are scanned, this factor may weigh against a finding of fair use. The *Texaco* opinion made it clear that journal articles should be treated as independent works. What matters is how much of the article, not how much of an issue of a journal, is used. If a whole article is scanned, the amount of the work used in proportion to the whole is 100 percent. When only portions of works, such as chapters from books, are scanned, this factor is less likely to weigh against a finding of fair use. (See pages 128 to 130.)

There are two sets of guidelines that may be of assistance in determining the amount that may be copied for both print and electronic reserve systems. Neither set of guidelines sets maximum limitations.

The *Guidelines for Classroom Copying in Not-for-Profit Educational Institutions* (see Appendix B) set out bright line minimum standards for making multiple copies for classroom use. These guidelines do not directly address reserve systems, but they do address multiple copies for classroom use. Since reserve copies are usually used for the same purposes as multiple copies for classroom use and fewer copies are made by the institution when works are put on reserve than when copies are given to every student, any amount that could be copied under the guidelines ought to be permitted in a reserve system.

The *Classroom and Reserve Use Guidelines (ACRL/ALA)* (see Appendix E) directly address copying for reserve purposes. Unlike the *Guidelines for Classroom Copying*, the ACRL/ALA guidelines do not use numerical bright line rules. Instead the ACRL/ALA guidelines state that the amount should be reasonable in relation to

  a. the total amount of material assigned for the whole term,
  b. the subject matter and level of the class,
  c. the number of students enrolled,
  d. the difficulty and timing of assignments,
  e. the number of other courses which may assign the same material, and
  f. the effect on the market for the work.

The effect on the potential market for or value of the work is the fourth factor listed in Chart 8. It is very important to the scanned reserve reading scenarios. If the scanning effectively substitutes copies for additional purchases of or subscriptions to a work, then there is a definite detrimental effect on the value of the work. For example, if a university has a satellite program on a remote military base, then it should not use scanned materials as a substitute for opening a basic branch library. On the other hand if distant learners are watchers of telecourses broadcast over the entire state, then the use would not be substituting for a possible branch library or for multiple sub-scriptions. The economic impact on the holders of the copyright would be much less. Even when the copies do not substitute for purchases of or sub-scriptions to works, the reproduction involved in electronic reserve may neg-atively affect the market. After the Second Circuit decision in the *Texaco* case, it may be necessary to consider the effect of lost license fees on the copyright holder. Lost license fees are likely to be particularly important if electronic copies are retained in the system longer than a single semester. (See pages 131 to 132.)

The fifth element in Chart 8 says that we must balance all four factors. The balance of the fair use factors will vary in electronic reserve situations depending upon the individual facts concerning each item in the system. The first factor will always weigh in favor of a finding of fair use, but how the other factors weigh for each individual work will vary with electronic reserve just as they vary with print reserve. The one difference is the very strong temptation to keep electronic copies at the end of the semester for later use. Any time any copies, print or electronic, are kept and used on reserve again, the fair use argument gets considerably weaker.

Except for possible insulation from liability under §108(f) for unsuper-vised student copying on library computers, the only section which might authorize any of the reproduction involved in the electronic reserve project is §107 on fair use. Fair use will probably authorize some of the reproduction involved in electronic reserve, but it is unlikely to authorize any reproduction in an electronic reserve system that exceeds what fair use would authorize in a traditional photocopy-based reserve system. At the end of Chart 8, we return to where we were in Chart 3. Fair use was the last element in the reproduc-tion chart, so we return to the Overview Chart to see if there are any more major areas that we need to address. Public displays in Chart 4 are the next area.

Public displays of the works may occur at several points in the project. When any part of the work appears on a computer screen, a display occurs. (See page 35.) Displays could occur when a work is being scanned if the soft-ware displays the results of the scan on a screen for inspection by the opera-tor. If the library chooses to inspect the output of the optical character recog-nition software to correct errors before the file is put in the central computer, displays will probably occur in the editing process. Some parts of the docu-ments are likely to be displayed when students search the system to locate the appropriate documents. Additional displays will occur if students choose to read the documents online. If material being printed scrolls across the screen as it is printed, displays may also occur during printing.

These displays only present copyright issues if they are public displays. The facts for this example indicate that all of the computers connected with the project are located in the library. The library is a public place. (See page

37.) Therefore, every time a part of a copyrighted work appears on a computer screen in this project, a public display will probably occur.

If the facts are modified so that students are able to access the library's server from computers in their homes, it could be argued that some of the displays are not public. The argument may be even stronger if the library chooses to put copies of the reserve documents in students' private mail space on the central file server instead of requiring the students to retrieve the documents from a central area available to all students. However, if the documents are loaded into an area of the library's server accessible to more than one student, the displays would probably remain public. Even if the students accessed the server from computers in their homes, the displays would be public because the displays would be transmitted to several members of the public at different times. (See page 38.)

Unless you find authorization for each of these public displays in the copyright law, you will have to find or get permission from the copyright holder for them. Chart 4 lists the sections that might authorize a public display.

Section 109, the first section in Chart 4, gives the library the right to display publicly the copy it owns or any copy which it lawfully makes. If a copy was lawfully made, §109 gives the owner of the copy the right to display it directly or by projection of no more than one image at a time to "viewers present at the place where the copy is located." (See page 79.) Display over a computer network, however, is not likely to be either direct display or display by projection. Furthermore, it is highly unlikely that an electronic reserve system would limit its displays to no more than one image at a time. Several students or patrons would probably be allowed to view different images simultaneously.

Section 110, which is the second section mentioned in Chart 4, is the section most likely to cover displays. Subsections (1) and (2) cover displays conducted by educational institutions. Subsection (5) covers reception by the general public.

The questions presented by §110(1) are where the display or performance occurs and whether the electronic reserve situation satisfies the face-to-face requirement. If the display occurs on the library's central computer, then it probably occurs in a place devoted to instruction.[3] If the display occurs on a student's own screen or another screen located off campus, §110(1) is much less likely to cover the situation. (See page 81.)

The face-to-face requirement of §110(1) was designed to prevent subsection (1) from covering performances and displays that are transmitted. Section 101 defines "transmit" as communicating the work "by any device or process whereby images or sounds are received beyond the place from which they are

---

3. H.R. Rep. No. 1476, 94th Cong. 2d Sess. at 82 (1976) states that a library is a similar place. The library's computer is part of the library, a natural extension of its physical existence, and thus should also be considered to be a similar place.

sent." With remote users, the place from which the materials are sent is the library's computer, and the place where the materials are received is the remote user's terminal. A remote user would not be remote if her terminal were not beyond the library's computer, and thus the material is transmitted. It is extremely unlikely that the instructor will always be physically present in the same general area as the students when the students access electronic reserve materials. Thus, §110(1) is not likely to cover the electronic reserve situation. (See page 81.)

Subsection (2) is much more likely to allow public displays in the electronic reserve situation. It authorizes public displays of all types of works as a regular part of systematic instructional activities of nonprofit educational institutions or government bodies. Reserve material is usually used as part of the systematic instructional activities of educational institutions. Since the display and or performance is a necessary part of that use, it also occurs as part of systematic instructional activities. The display is directly related to and of material assistance in comprehending the content of the transmission. The student cannot read the material if it is not displayed on his screen. And special circumstances, such as distance from the main campus or the need for access to a computer to use the material, may prevent attendance of the viewers in classrooms or normal places of instruction. Thus even if the place of display, such as the student's terminal or PC, is deemed not to be a normal place of instruction under subsection (1), subsection (2) covers the situation. (See pages 81 to 83.)

Although §110(2) may authorize the public display that occurs when the library transmits the display, it does not authorize the additional public display that occurs when a student receives the display. Section 110(5) allows the public reception of transmitted displays if the display is received on a single receiving device of the kind commonly used in private homes. While the legislative history discusses only radios and televisions, the actual language of the statute is much broader. Personal computers have become quite commonplace in the home, and they are capable of receiving transmissions from other computers to which they are connected. Thus they meet the requirements of subsection (5). The only restrictions imposed by subsection (5) are that no direct charge can be made to see or hear the transmission and that the transmission cannot be further transmitted to the public. Therefore, when the library has a right to transmit a display from its computers, §110(5) authorizes the remote users' reception of the transmitted display. (See pages 83 to 86.)

Of course the application of all subsections of §110 is contingent upon the copy in the library's computer being lawfully made under copyright law. Section 110 does not justify making the electronic copy to post on the library's computer; it simply sanctions the public displays that may result from such postings. The library has to rely upon §107 on fair use to sanction the making of the copy to put on the central server.

Since subsections (2) and (5) together authorize all of the public displays connected with the electronic reserve project, you do not need to go through the rest of Chart 4. Return to the Overview Chart and consider question 5, public performance.

If the collection is limited to textual materials and no sound equipment is used, public performances will be highly unlikely. However, public performances may occur in electronic reserve systems if audio or video works are included in the collection. Public performances may also occur with textual materials if computers equipped with sound cards are used to read the material aloud as would occur with special terminals for the visually impaired. (See page 39.)

Chart 5 leads you through the possible exemptions for public performances. Section 109 is the first. The only public performances authorized by §109 are public performances of coin-operated video games. Section 110 is the second.

Subsection (1) of §110 is inapplicable to public performances involved in electronic reserve for the same reasons that it is inapplicable to public displays involved in electronic reserve. (See page 24.) Subsection (2) of §110 is limited to performances of nondramatic literary and musical works. It does not cover performances of dramatic literary, dramatic musical works or audiovisual works, so it will not cover all of the public performances that would occur in an electronic reserve system. (See page 92.) Subsection (3) applies only to performances as part of religious services. (See page 94.) Subsection (4) does not cover any performances that are transmitted. (See page 94.)

Subsection (5) allows the public reception of transmitted performances if the performance is received on a single receiving device of the kind commonly used in private homes. When we considered this subsection for displays, we decided that when the library has a right to transmit a display from its computers, §110(5) authorizes the remote users' reception of the transmitted display. (See page 25.) It would permit remote users' to receive transmitted performances for the same reasons.

Subsections (6) and (7) cover performances for county fairs and music stores. They are of no help here. Subsection (8) can only be used by an authorized radio carrier, a noncommercial broadcast station or a governmental body. Public libraries, or libraries in public schools or colleges might be considered government bodies. If so, then subsection (8) would authorize the performances that occur when handicapped students use sound boards in computers to read nondramatic literary works on reserve aloud. But it would not authorize any other performances that might occur with students who are not handicapped or with dramatic, musical or audiovisual works.

Subsection (9) can only be used by an authorized radio carrier, so it could not be used for an electronic reserve system. Section 110(10) applies only to veterans and fraternal organizations, so it is not applicable either.

Chart 5 identifies §111 as the third possible section that might exempt a public performance. Most of §111 does not apply to libraries. Those subsections which might be applicable to libraries apply only when a library retransmits a signal received from outside the library. (See pages 99 to 100.) This situation does not occur in this electronic reserve example. It might be applicable if a library relied on online databases as part of its electronic reserve system.

The fourth section listed in Chart 5 is §114. Section 114 makes it clear that the copyright in a sound recording does not usually include the exclusive right to public performance. However, the exception to this general rule is that the copyright holder of a digital sound recording has the exclusive right to perform the recording by means of a digital transmission. Given the digital nature of an electronic reserve system, the sound recordings that the library would like to put in the system are likely to be digital sound recordings. The whole focus of the Digital Performance Right in Sound Recordings Act of 1995 was on performances that occur in the context of electronic systems, so any performance that occurs in the electronic reserve system is likely to be covered by the Act. The exception for noninteractive free performances would not apply because the electronic reserve system is interactive.

The rights of the copyright holder in the underlying work are separate from the rights of the copyright holder in the sound recording and are not affected by §114. The copyright holder in the underlying work usually has the right to prohibit public performances, including the playing of the sound recordings of the work. Thus if the Newtown College Library had a right to put copies of a sound recording in the electronic reserve system, §114 would not affect the right of either the owners of the copyright in the sound recording or the owners of the copyright in the underlying work to prohibit the library from performing the recording publicly as part of the system. (See page 100.)

The §116 jukebox license, the sixth section in Chart 5, applies only to public performances of nondramatic musical works on coin-operated jukeboxes. The electronic reserve project does not use jukeboxes, so §116 will not authorize any of the public performances in the project. (See page 101.)

Chart 5 next refers us to §118. Section 118 will not authorize any of the public performances involved in the electronic reserve project for two reasons. First, only organizations which meet the definition of public broadcasting entities contained in 47 U.S.C. §397 may take advantage of §118. Very few libraries meet this definition. Second, §118 applies only to published nondramatic musical, pictorial, graphic and sculptural works. It does not apply to literary works. (See page 101.) Many works in the electronic reserve project will be literary works.

Finally, Chart 5 refers us to Chart 8 again, to consider the application of fair use to public performances. Most of the reasoning applicable to determining whether the reproductions involved in the electronic reserve project could be considered fair use also applies to determining whether the public performances involved in the project could be considered a fair use. The first three factors, the purpose and character of the use, the nature of the works, and the amount and substantiality of the portion of the works used is the same. (See pages 21 to 22.)

However, the analysis of the fourth factor, the effect on the market is different for public performance issues than it is for reproduction issues. Public performance rights are generally marketed separately from reproduction rights, so you have to focus specifically on the market for performance rights instead of the general market for copies of the works in the reserve system.

For nondramatic literary works, the public performance market is usually much smaller than it is for audiovisual works. So most copyright holders in nondramatic literary works have done nothing to develop the market and are not in a position to provide public performance licenses quickly or easily. According to the *Texaco* case, when a copyright holder does nothing to take advantage of a market and thus makes it difficult for license fees to be collected, the loss of potential license fees has little or no negative effect on the market for or value of a copyrighted work.

Although the market for performance licenses in nondramatic literary works is relatively undeveloped, markets for performance licenses in dramatic, musical, and audiovisual works are well developed. Despite the presence of a developed market, several other factors tend to indicate that any impact that an electronic reserve system might have on the market for public performance rights would be very small. The cost of public performance licenses usually varies depending upon the size of the expected audience, the number of expected performances, the length of time the license covers and the amount of money the licensee expects to collect. If reserves are closely tied to specific classes, the size of the expected audience will often be small. It is unlikely that most students will perform the assigned works more than once or twice, so the number of performances would also be small. If the material is removed from the system at the end of the term, the amount of time covered would also be relatively short. Most of these factors would suggest that the electronic reserve project would have little negative market impact on established public performance license markets.

On balance, it appears that the fourth factor is slightly more likely to weigh in favor of finding that public performances are a fair use than that reproductions are a fair use in the electronic reserve context. Thus in cases where fair use is likely to authorize the reproductions necessary to put a work in the system in the first place, it is also likely to authorize the public performances that occur in the use of the electronic reserve system. (See pages 130 to 132.)

When we return from Chart 8 to Chart 5, it refers us back to the Overview Chart for the next major issue area which is public distribution.

Public distributions do not occur when a copy of a work is displayed on a patron's screen for the same reason that no public distribution occurs when a television image appears on a screen. No copy changes hands. Whether public distributions occur when a user downloads or prints a copy from an electronic system is a question open to debate. (See page 40.) Since some of the case law may support the argument that public distributions do occur and the National Information Infrastructure Working Group on Intellectual Property has recommended that the law be amended to support this position, it may be useful to figure out whether limitations in the law might authorize any distributions that might occur in downloading and printing. Chart 6 will lead us through these limitations.

Chart 6 directs us to §108 first. Section 108 authorizes libraries to publicly distribute any copies authorized under §108. (See page 105.) It does not authorize any other public distributions, however. Earlier in the analysis of this example, we determined that §108 did not authorize any of the reproduction that is a part of this project. (See pages 17 to 19.) So §108 will not authorize any of the public distribution that might be associated with this project.

Chart 6 lists §109 next. Section 109(a) authorizes the owner of any copy or phonorecord lawfully made under the Copyright Act to transfer possession of that particular copy. This provision authorizes a library to lend any copy that it was authorized to make under any other section of the law. However, §109 only authorizes distribution of a particular copy the library owns or has made under another section of the law. It does not authorize any form of distribution that requires the making of an additional copy. Both downloading and printing require the making of an additional copy, so §109 would not authorize possible public distributions in this project. (See page 108.)

The third section that Chart 6 refers us to is §112. Section 112 only implies a limited right of distribution for copies made under it. It does not authorize any other public distributions. (See page 110.) Since we decided that §112 did not authorize any of the reproduction involved in the electronic reserve project (see page 19), it will not authorize any of the public distribution that might be involved in the project.

Section 113, the fourth section referred to by Chart 6, only authorizes public distribution for copies made under it. It does not authorize any other public distributions. (See page 112.) Since we determined that §113 did not authorize any of the reproduction involved in the electronic reserve project (see page 20), it will not authorize any of the public distribution that might be involved in the project.

The fifth section listed in Chart 6 is §115 which also only authorizes public distribution for copies made under it. It does not authorize any other public distributions. (See page 113.) Since we decided that §115 did not authorize any of the reproduction involved in the electronic reserve project (see page 20), it will not authorize any of the public distribution that might be involved in the project either.

Chart 6 lists §117 next. Like sections 108, 112, 113, and 115, §117 only authorizes public distribution for copies made under it. It does not authorize any other public distributions. (See page 114.) Since we determined that §117 did not authorize any of the reproduction involved in the electronic reserve project (see page 20), it will not authorize any of the public distribution that might be involved in the project.

The final possibility listed in Chart 6 is fair use which refers us to Chart 8 again. Most of the reasoning applicable to determining whether the reproductions and public performances involved in the electronic reserve project could be considered a fair use also applies to determining whether the public distributions involved in the project could be considered a fair use. The first three factors, the purpose and character of the use, the nature of the works, and the amount and substantiality of the portion of the works used is the same. (See pages 21 to 22.) However, the analysis of the fourth factor, the effect on the market, is different for public distribution issues than it is for reproduction and performance issues. When a copy of a work is distributed to someone else, it is far less likely that the person to whom the copy is distributed will buy a copy of the work or pay a license fee to get a copy. Thus, the potential market for the work is negatively affected. The effect does not necessarily mean that the distribution is not a fair use. In situations where electronic reserve is used to substitute for making a photocopy of material for every class member, the effect of the electronic reserve system on the market would be no greater than the effect of making all the photocopies. (See pages 130 to 132.) If the making and distributing of photocopies to all the students in the class would be a fair use, then any distribution that might occur through an electronic reserve system is also likely to be a fair use. However, distribution that exceeds what would be fair use in the context of classroom photocopying is not likely to be considered fair use in an electronic reserve system. You must be careful at this point not to get caught up in circular reasoning. The various rights of the copyright holder are separate and independent. Although we have concluded that fair use would justify any electronic reserve distribution that would substitute for the fair use distribution of photocopies to classes, that does not mean that fair use authorizes electronic reserve reproduction that would substitute for classroom photocopies. We have to remember that earlier in our analysis, we determined that more reproductions had to be made to get the material into and out of the electronic reserve system than a paper based reserve system. Those extra copies could have an impact on the fair use analysis leading to a different result than you might reach when making photocopies for a class.

Next we return from the end of Chart 6 to the Overview Chart where we have to consider whether the project involves the creation of derivative works. It is possible that the conversion of a work from a nonelectronic format to an electronic format could be construed to be the creation of a derivative work. But it is more likely that a court would find that format conversion is more like reproduction than it is like translation in that it adds nothing creative or new to the work. If nothing new is added to the work that would support a new copyright, then no derivative work is created. (See page 41.)

It is also possible that the database which holds all the electronic readings might be considered a collective work itself. If the database is viewed as a collective work, then it would be a derivative work based on all of the included works. So we should go through Chart 7 to see if any section might authorize these potential derivative works.

Section 114, the first section listed in Chart 7, limits the copyright holder's right to prepare derivative works based on the sound recording to the right to rearrange, remix or otherwise alter the actual sounds on the recording. This means, for example, that the copyright holder in a sound recording can prohibit the making of bootleg copies of her own recording but cannot prohibit other people from imitating her recording. However, faculty members are not likely to want imitations of sound recordings in the electronic reserve system nor are librarians likely to want to go to the effort of rerecording sound recordings for the system. And the owner of the copyright in the underlying work may have the right to prohibit any type of derivative work including imitations, because the imitations are still reproductions of the underlying work. This limitation is not likely to authorize the creation of the derivative works involved in an electronic reserve project.

Chart 7 sends us to §117 next. Section 117 is applicable only to computer programs. This project involves the creation of derivative works based on works other than computer programs, so §117 will not authorize any of the derivative works involved in this project. (See page 115.)

The last section referred to in Chart 7 is §107 on fair use. So we need to go through Chart 8 a fourth time. Most of the reasoning applicable to determining whether the reproductions, public performances, and public distributions involved in electronic reserve projects could be considered fair uses also applies to determining whether the derivative works involved in the project could be considered a fair use. The first three factors, the purpose and character of the use, the nature of the works, and the amount and substantiality of the portion of the works used is the same. (See pages 21 to 22.)

The analysis of the fourth factor, the effect on the market, is the only factor that may be different for derivative work issues than it is for reproduction, public performance, and public distribution issues. Derivative work rights are generally marketed separately from reproduction rights and public performance rights, so you need to focus on the market for selling derivative work rights. The derivative work rights needed to create electronic reserve databases are likely to be similar to those needed to compile anthologies. Many publishers have developed licenses for this type of reproduction and exploit the market frequently, so you may have to consider the loss of license fees in your analysis. If the reserve system becomes large enough and complete enough to substitute for the purchase of other textbooks, it may also negatively affect the primary market for some included works. If however, the system does not go beyond the bounds of traditional reserve and classroom photocopying that would be considered fair uses, then the effect on the market is not likely to rise to a level that would prevent a finding of fair use. (See pages 130 to 132.) After we finish the analysis of fair use as it applies to derivative works, we return to the Overview Chart to consider moral rights, the last of the copyright holder's exclusive rights.

If the reserve collection is limited to textual works, then moral rights would not be involved because moral rights apply only to specific works of visual art. Moral rights are also inapplicable to audiovisual works. However, if limited edition paintings, drawings, prints or photographs were converted to electronic form and placed on reserve, moral rights might be involved. The conversion to electronic form would have to distort the work in a way that was prejudicial to the artist's reputation for moral rights to apply. (See page 41.) Since it seems unlikely that works which meet the statutory definition of visual art would be included in an electronic reserve system or that their inclusion would damage the reputation of the artist if they were included, this analysis assumes that no moral rights are involved in the project.

Except for the public display questions, most of the copyright questions in electronic reserve come down to a question of whether fair use authorizes the use. And for most of the rights, the fair use analysis was very similar to that used for photocopy-based reserve systems. If the scope of the electronic reserve system does not exceed the scope of what would be allowed under fair use in a photocopy-based system, fair use is also likely to permit the uses of copyright rights involved in an electronic reserve system. However the nature of electronic systems is such that libraries are likely to want to extend electronic reserve systems beyond the scope of what fair use permits in a photocopy-based system. Libraries are likely to want to retain and reuse material from semester to semester. They are also likely to want to put a larger number of journal articles and other items into the system. They may even want to include whole books. The more the electronic system moves away from the constraints that have controlled the scope of photocopy-based reserve systems, the less likely fair use is to permit the use of all the copyright rights involved in the system. When the use of rights exceeds that permitted by fair use, the library will need to find or obtain permission to use materials in an electronic reserve system. Obtaining permission from the copyright holder is discussed in Chapter 9 which includes a sample permission letter for electronic reserve on page 142.

Part II.
The Decision Charts

Introduction—
The Overview Chart

Copyright law grants authors certain property rights in their intellectual and artistic works to encourage authors to produce more works for the benefit of society. In the United States, the primary source of copyright law is the Copyright Act of 1976. This Act has been amended several times since 1976 and interpreted by many court decisions. Chapters 1 through 8 discuss the various sections of the Act that are most likely to affect library projects. All of these sections are not relevant to every problem. The Decision Charts at the beginning of Part I will help you select the most relevant sections for each project.

If the works that you will be using in your project are not copyrightable or copyrighted, you obviously will not have any copyright problems. Over the years, changes in copyright law have made it more difficult to figure out whether a work is copyrighted. Chapter 1 discusses the sections of the law that will help you decide whether a particular work or category of works is likely to be copyrighted.

Copyright gives a copyright holder five basic rights. These are the right to reproduce the work in copies or phonorecords, the right to publicly display the work, the right to publicly perform the work, the right to publicly distribute copies of the work, and the right to create derivative works.[4] Anyone may use a copyrighted work without copyright problems if the use does not entail any reproduction, public display, public performance, public distribution, or adaptation of the work. Authors of works of visual art also have a limited right to prevent any intentional distortion, mutilation, or modification of their work which would be prejudicial to their reputation. In addition, they have a limited right to prevent destruction of a work of recognized stature.[5]

Reproduction means "reproduc[ing] a material object in which the work is duplicated, transcribed, imitated, or simulated in a fixed form from which

---

4. 17 U.S.C. §106 (1995).
5. 17 U.S.C. §106A (1994).

it can be perceived, reproduced, or otherwise communicated, either directly or with the aid of a machine or device."[6] Hand copying is reproduction. Photocopying is reproduction. Typing or scanning a work into a computer becomes reproduction as soon as the file is saved. Digitizing a work is reproduction when the image is stored. Taking a photograph of a work is reproduction of that part of the work that appears in the photograph. Making a backup copy of an audiotape, a videotape or a computer disk is reproduction. Converting an audiotape, a videotape, or a computer file from one format to another is reproduction. Printing something from a computer screen or file is reproduction. Downloading something from a computer is reproduction. Recording someone singing a song is reproduction of the song. Some experts and at least one court believe that copying a work into a computer's memory is also reproduction,[7] but this is probably an incorrect interpretation of the law.[8] It is easy to see why the reproduction right is the most common manner in which people encounter copyright problems. Chapter 3 discusses the limitations on the copyright holder's right to control reproductions of his works.

A work is displayed every time a copy of it is shown "either directly or by means of a film, slide, television image, or any other device or process."[9] The House Report expands upon this definition saying that

> "display" would include the projection of an image on a screen or other surface by any method, the transmission of an image by electronic or other means, and the showing of an image on a cathode ray tube, or similar viewing apparatus connected with any sort of information storage and retrieval system.[10]

Showing individual images from a motion picture or audiovisual work out of sequence is also a display.[11]

The copyright holder's control over displays is limited, however, to "public" displays.[12] A work is displayed "publicly" if it is displayed "at a place open

---

6. H.R. Rep. No. 94-1476 at 61.

7. Working Group on Intellectual Property Rights, Information Infrastructure Task Force, *Intellectual Property and the National Information Infrastructure* 65 (U.S. Patent and Trademark Office September 1995) [hereinafter *White Paper*]; *MAI Systems Corp. v. Peak Computer, Inc.*, 991 F.2d 511, 519 (9th Cir. 1993).

8. Letter from Prof. James Boyle, Washington School of Law, American University to Bruce Lehman, Assistant Secretary, Department of Commerce (April 19, 1996) [available on the Internet at http://www.clark.net/pub/rothman/boyle.htm] and sources cited therein; Office of Technology Assessment, *Intellectual Property Rights in an Age of Electronics and Information* 75 n. 62 (Washington, D.C., GPO, 1986).

9. 17 U.S.C. §101 (1995).

10. H.R. Rep. No. 94-1476 at 64.

11. 17 U.S.C. §101 (1995).

12. 17 U.S.C. §106 (1995).

Overview Chart:
Major Decision Areas
for Copyright Problems

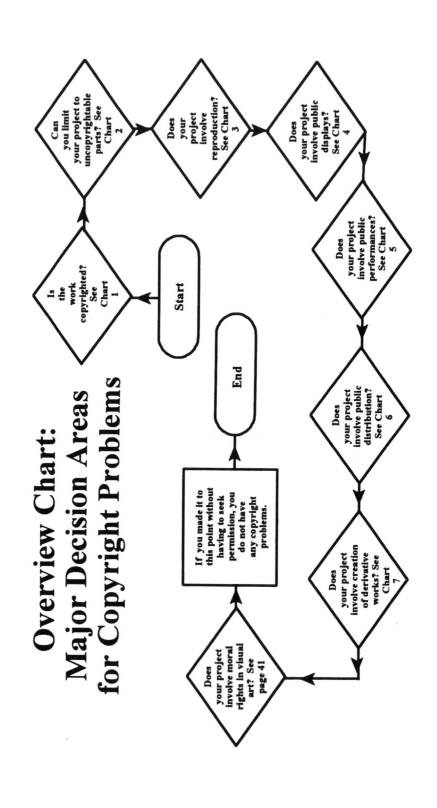

to the public or at any place where a substantial number of persons outside of a normal circle of a family and its social acquaintances is gathered."[13]

A display is also "public" if it is transmitted or otherwise communicated

> to a place [open to the public or where a substantial number of people outside of a normal circle of a family and its social acquaintances is gathered] or to the public, by means of any device or process, *whether the members of the public capable of receiving the performance or display receive it in the same place or in separate places and at the same time or at different times*[14] [emphasis added].

This last clause makes broadcast television, cable television and pay-per-view television public even when received in the privacy of a home.

Many libraries are open to the public. Most libraries that are not open to the public are open to a group larger than a normal circle of a family and its social acquaintances. So displays that occur in libraries will usually fit the definition of public displays. It is possible, however, that some small special libraries might not be considered public places because they are not open to the public and the number of people present in them at any time is likely to be very small.

Some people have argued that displays and performances in private study/viewing rooms in libraries are not public because such displays and performances are analogous to displays and performances in private homes. There are no reported cases that specifically address libraries, and different attorneys have reached different conclusions.[15] A recent trend of cases concerning other locations, however, supports the view that such displays and performances are public.

In *Columbia Pictures Indus. v. Redd Horne, Inc.*,[16] a video store proprietor rented rooms to customers for private viewing of videotapes. The tape players were centrally located and controlled by an employee of the store. The performance of the videotapes was communicated from the centrally controlled tape players to the private rooms where customers viewed the tapes. The court found that because the store was open to the public, these performances of videotapes were public performances.

In *Columbia Pictures Indus. v. Aveco, Inc.*,[17] a video store proprietor rented

---

13. 17 U.S.C. §101 (1995).

14. 17 U.S.C. §101 (1995).

15. *Cf.* Mary Hutchings Reed and Debra Stanek, "Library and Classroom Use of Copyrighted Videotapes and Computer Software," *American Libraries* 17 (Feb. 1986): 120A–D; Debra Stanek, "Videotapes, Computer Programs, and the Library," *Information Technology and Libraries* 5 (March 1986): 42, 47; "Letters," *Information Technology and Libraries* 6 (Sept. 1987): 242–248.

16. 749 F.2d 154 (3d Cir. 1984).

17. 800 F.2d 59 (3d Cir. 1986).

rooms to customers for private viewing of videotapes. Each room contained seating, a videotape player and a monitor. The customers controlled the playing of the tapes from the player in the private room. The court found that because the store was open to the public, these performances of videotapes were public performances.

In *Columbia Pictures Indus. v. Professional Real Estate Investors, Inc.*,[18] a hotel rented rooms to guests which were equipped with VCRs attached to television sets. Guests could rent videotapes in the lobby for private viewing in their rooms. Because the guests controlled access to their rooms and the rooms were a substitute for their homes, the court found that these performances were private performances.

In *On Command Video Corp. v. Columbia Pictures Indus., Inc.*,[19] a hotel rented rooms to guests. The rooms were wired in a way that allowed the viewing of selected videotapes in the rooms at the request of guests. The actual tape players were located in a centrally controlled room in the hotel. Although the court found that the hotel rooms were private places, the performances were nevertheless public performances because the videos were transmitted to members of the public.

This line of cases suggests that all displays and performances in private rooms of libraries are likely to be considered public displays and performances. However, it would also appear that if the displays and performances are controlled from some central location in the library, it is more likely that the displays or performances will be considered public than if they are controlled solely by patrons in the private rooms.

The same definition and reasoning that applies to audiovisual works and viewing rooms in libraries also applies to electronic forms of works and computers in libraries. If a patron accesses an electronic work and causes it to be displayed on a computer screen in a library, a public display probably occurs. In addition, most patrons are members of the public. So if a patron accesses material in a library's computer from anywhere outside the library, a public display probably occurs when the library computer transmits the display to the patron's computer. The display may even be a public display if the patron's computer is located in a private home or office.

Whether a *public* display occurs when the library computer transmits information to a remote user may depend upon where the information is located in the library's computer. Is the patron accessing material in an area of a library's computer that is generally available to other patrons or accessing material sent to an area of the computer that is not accessible to other patrons? Databases and other electronic copies of information stored in areas of

---

17. 800 F.2d 59 (3d Cir. 1986).

18. 866 F.2d 278 (9th Cir. 1989).

19. 777 F. Supp. 787 (N.D. Cal. 1991).

computers accessible to several people (even if only those with valid passwords) appear to meet the criteria of the transmit clause. Several people can receive the information, even though that reception may occur in different places and at different times.[20] On the other hand, areas of computers assigned solely to an individual password do not seem to meet the criteria of the transmit clause if the display or performance occurs while the user is located in a private place. There is no transmission to the public. There is transmission only to a single user.

The next logical question is whether information displayed on a patron's screen is a public display if the information originates from a private area of a computer but is displayed or performed on a screen or other device in an area open to the public or where several people are gathered. For example, a patron could connect to the library's computer from a private home, but might just as easily use a public computer lab or a notebook computer in an airport or hotel lobby. A strict application of the definitions leads to the conclusion that a display in a computer lab or a hotel lobby would be a public display. On the other hand, it is unlikely that more than one or two people would observe the work in such a situation, and the legislative history does not suggest that Congress considered such situations. Chapter 4 discusses the limitations on the copyright holder's control of public displays of his works.

"To 'perform' a work means to recite, render, play, dance, or act it, either directly or by means of a device or process."[21] The legislative history expands upon this definition by stating that the concept of performance

> cover[s] not only the initial rendition or showing, but also any further act by which that rendition or showing is transmitted or communicated ... [A]ny individual is performing whenever he or she ... communicates the performance by turning on a receiving set. ... A performance may be accomplished "either directly or by means of any device or process," including all kinds of equipment for amplifying sounds or visual images, any sort of transmitting apparatus, any type of electronic retrieval system, and any other techniques and systems not yet in use or even invented.[22]

The same definition of "public" is used for performances that is used for displays. (See pages 35 to 39.) Chapter 5 discusses the limitations on the copyright holder's right to control public performances of his works.

Section 106(3) gives the copyright holder the exclusive right "to distribute copies or phonorecords of the copyrighted work to the public by sale or other transfer of ownership, or by rental, lease or lending."

---

20. At least one commentator agrees with this analysis. See Robert L. Oakley, *Copyright and Preservation: A Serious Problem in Need of a Thoughtful Solution* (The Commission on Preservation and Access 1990), 18.

21. 17 U.S.C. §101 (1995).

22. H.R. Rep. No. 94-1476 at 63.

Neither the Act nor the legislative history defines "distribution." A distribution clearly occurs when possession of a physical copy changes from one person to another. However, it is unclear whether a distribution occurs when one person makes a copy electronically accessible and another person acquires possession of a copy by issuing a command to the electronic storage system.[23] Two recent cases concerning bulletin boards suggest that a distribution may occur when a user creates a copy by downloading from a bulletin board.[24] But the language of the statute and the legislative history seems to suggest the opposite conclusion. The statute refers to distributing "copies or phonorecords."[25] The House Report equates the distribution right with the right of publication.[26] Later the Report says that the definition of publication "makes plain that any form of dissemination in which a material object does not change hands—performances or displays on television, for example—is not a publication no matter how many people are exposed to the work."[27] If publication is equal to distribution, and no publication occurs because no physical copy changes hands, then no distribution occurs.

The National Information Task Force on Intellectual Property has recommended that the law be amended to make it clear that public distributions do occur when a copy is transmitted to a user of an electronic system.[28] Since this issue is unclear, it is probably safest to look for authorization in the law for public distributions so you can have the arguments ready if anyone raises the distribution issues.

The distribution right is limited to public distribution. It does not extend to private distribution. While the Copyright Act does not define "public" for purposes of public distribution, it does define "publicly" in the context of displays and performances. "Publicly" means "at a place open to the public or at any place where a substantial number of persons outside of a normal circle of a family and its social acquaintances is gathered."[29] Most libraries serve a group of patrons larger than a normal circle of a family and its social acquaintances. So any distribution that occurs in the context of a library is likely to be public distribution. (For a more detailed discussion of the meaning of "publicly" in the context of displays and performances, see pages 35 to 39.)

The distribution right is not limited to copies originating with the copyright holder or his publisher. It also extends to first public distribution of copies never owned by the copyright holder such as copies made by users from

---

23. *White Paper*, 67–69.
24. *Playboy Enterprises Inc. v. Frena*, 839 F. Supp. 1552 (M.D. Fla. 1993); *Sega Enterprises Ltd. v. Maphia*, 857 F. Supp. 679 (N.D. Cal. 1994).
25. 17 U.S.C. §106(3) (1995).
26. H.R. Rep. No. 94-1476 at 61–62.
27. H.R. Rep. No. 94-1476 at 138.
28. *White Paper*, 213–217.
29. 17 U.S.C. §101 (1995).

copies they have purchased or borrowed.[30] Thus, public distribution probably includes all forms of providing copies of copyrighted works to the public. Chapter 6 discusses the limitations on the copyright holder's right to control public distributions of his works.

"A 'derivative work' is a new work based upon one or more preexisting works, such as a translation, musical arrangement, dramatization, fictionalization, motion picture version, sound recording, art reproduction, abridgment, condensation, or any other form in which a work may be recast, transformed, or adapted."[31] In addition to the material taken from an existing work, the new work must include something new or original contributed by the new author. The amount of new material or work contributed by the new author does not have to be great, but a derivative work must be something more than a mere reproduction of an earlier work. Chapter 7 discusses the limitations on the copyright holder's right to control the making of derivative works from his works.

Section 106A of the Copyright Act gives the author of a *work of visual art* a limited right to prevent distortion, mutilation, modification or destruction of his work. A *work of visual art* means a painting, drawing, print or sculpture or a still photographic image produced for exhibition purposes. The work must be a single or limited edition work for which no more than 200 copies were produced. Each copy must bear the signature or identifying mark of the author or artist. Posters, maps, globes, charts, technical drawings, diagrams, models, applied art, motion pictures, audiovisual works, books, magazines, newspapers, periodicals, databases, electronic information services, electronic publications, merchandising items, advertising, promotional items, descriptive items, coverings, packaging material and containers are specifically excluded from the definition. The artist has the right to prevent any intentional distortion, mutilation or other modification of the work that would be prejudicial to his or her honor or reputation. The artist also has the right to prevent destruction of any work of visual art of recognized stature.[32] The only limitation that applies to moral rights is fair use which is discussed in Chapter 8.

Although the bundle of rights belonging to the copyright holder and the author of a work of visual art are described as exclusive rights, the rights are subject to several limitations. If a particular use of a copyrighted work falls within the scope of one of these limitations, the use is not an infringement of copyright. Many of the limitations are very specific and narrowly drawn, however. A limitation which authorizes one part of a project may not authorize another part of a project. For example, §110, which contains the limitation for

---

30. Melville B. Nimmer and David Nimmer, *Nimmer on Copyright* vol. 2 (New York: Matthew Bender 1996), §8.11[A] at n. 11.

31. 17 U.S.C. §101 (1995).

32. 17 U.S.C. §101 (1995).

educational performances and displays, might authorize the viewing of a video-taped television program in a class. However, it would not authorize the making of a copy of the program so that it could be shown later in a class. Making the copy involves the right of reproduction, and §110 applies only to displays and performances. For this reason it is particularly important to identify and separately analyze each instance of reproduction, public distribution, public display, public performance and production of a derivative work in every project.

Because most of the limitations are specific and narrowly drawn, they may not apply to new technologies as well as they do to older technologies that were well understood at the time the statute was drafted. Sometimes the wording of a limitation may even exclude application to some newer technologies. Although Congress specifically drafted the definition and general rights sections to be adaptable to new technologies, this drafting style did not always carry over to the limitation sections.[33] In addition, many of the limitation sections were the result of political compromise over hotly contested issues. Because of these two factors, the application of the same limitation to what might appear to be analogous situations may not yield logically consistent results. Nevertheless, it is still important to analyze each limitation because the language of even the most specific limitations occasionally provides justifications for certain uses in situations Congress and the lobbyist probably did not anticipate.

For most projects involving new technologies, however, it will be necessary to analyze whether fair use authorizes each portion of the project. And since fair use is an amorphous doctrine which changes depending upon the facts of each case, it will rarely provide clear guidance. Because the boundaries of fair use are so indefinite, it is discussed last in this book, in Chapter 8.

It is an infringement of copyright law to use any of the copyright holder's exclusive rights without permission unless the use is authorized by the copyright law. If the copyright holder's rights are used with permission, however, no infringement occurs. Thus learning how to find or get permission to use the copyright holder's exclusive rights will reduce the number of copyright problems in any project.

A grant of permission to use some or all of the copyright rights is the same thing as a license. All that is usually required to make a license valid is some indication that a person with authority to grant permission has given permission to use the specified rights. Although licenses are not usually required to

---

33. Todd Piccus, "The Small Business Exemption and the Realities of the Home-Electronic Marketplace," *Entertainment and Sports Lawyer* 10, no. 4 (1993): 8, 10; Jessica Litman, "Copyright Legislation and Technological Change," *Oregon Law Review* 68 (1989): 275, 345–346.

be in writing,[34] proving that you have permission to use any of the copyright rights may be difficult without written evidence of the license.

If the work is not protected by copyright, copyright law will not be a problem. If none of copyright's exclusive rights are involved, copyright law will not be a problem. If the limitations authorize all of the uses of exclusive rights in your project, copyright law will not be a problem. If the copyright holder has given permission for the activity involved, copyright law will not be a problem.

If all of the following statements are true, there is a copyright problem.

1. The work is protected by copyright.

2. At least one use of one of the copyright holder's exclusive rights involved in the project is not authorized by any of the limitations.

3. The copyright holder has not given permission for that use.

If you can restructure your project to eliminate all of the uses of the exclusive rights which are not authorized by law or covered by permission, you can avoid the copyright problems.

If there is a likelihood of copyright infringement, consult a lawyer. Do not rely upon your analysis using this book as legal advice. It is a general document and cannot cover all the possibilities. Copyright is a very technical area which frequently requires the advice of counsel. If your university, school system, company or governmental unit already has a lawyer, that person would be a good place to start. However, you should not be surprised if the lawyer for your parent organization cannot answer your question immediately or refers you to another lawyer. This book is designed to help identify potential hidden copyright issues that even attorneys who routinely work with copyright may not deal with on a regular basis.

---

34. Section 204 of the Copyright Act does require that exclusive licenses be written and signed by the copyright holder. An exclusive license is the equivalent of transferring ownership of the part of the copyright described in the license. It gives the licensee the permission to use the rights described in the license and the right to prohibit others from using those rights. A non-exclusive license gives the licensee permission to use rights but does not give the licensee the right to stop others from using the rights described in the license. In some cases, courts have held that state law may require certain licenses to be in writing even though the Copyright Act does not require a writing.

1. Are the Works Protected by Copyright?

Copyright protects all original works of authorship fixed in any stable tangible medium.[35] There are two key elements to the definition of a copyrightable work. The work must be original, and the work must be fixed in a tangible medium.[36] A work is original if it was independently created by the author and possesses a minimal degree of creativity.[37] A work is fixed in a tangible medium if it is stored in any manner that is sufficiently stable to allow it to be perceived, reproduced or communicated for more than a very brief period.[38]

The definition of copyright in the statute is very broad. It makes nearly all works copyrightable. For example, a quick note to a friend or an E-mail message meets the requirements of the definition. A lecture presented by a teacher from brief notes would not be a copyrightable work, however, unless it was simultaneously recorded in some manner. The unrecorded lecture would not meet the fixation requirement. An alphabetical listing of everyone owning a telephone in a given area would not be copyrightable either because it does not satisfy the minimum originality part of the definition. But if both parts of the definition are satisfied, the work is probably copyrighted.

Copyright attaches to a copyrightable work as soon as it is fixed in a tangible medium. As soon as the author saves a work on a word processor or as soon as a tape recorder is turned on to record the words that someone speaks, fixation occurs and copyright attaches. The author is not required to register the work with the Copyright Office or even to attach a copyright notice to the work. The author does not even have to intend to create a copyrighted work.

Given the very broad definition of a copyrightable work and the fact that copyright attaches as soon as the work is fixed, users should assume that nearly

---

35. 17 U.S.C. §102 (1994).
36. H.R. Rep. No. 94-1476 at 51.
37. *Feist Publications, Inc. v. Rural Telephone Service, Co.*, 499 U.S. 340, 345 (1991).
38. 17 U.S.C. §101 (1995).

all works are protected by copyright. The exceptions to this general assumption will be discussed in the next few segments.

1.1 United States Government Works

Works of the United States government are not protectable by copyright.[39] A "work of the United States government" is defined as "a work prepared by an officer or employee of the United States government as part of that person's official duties."[40] Although most government works are easily identifiable, there are a few traps for the unwary. First, the exclusion applies only to works of the United States government. Most works of state governments are copyrightable. Second, if a work is prepared for the United States government by contractors rather than employees of the federal government, the author may retain the copyright in some cases.[41] When a government contractor retains the copyright, the contractor will usually be listed as the author of the work. However, the lack of a notice claiming that the contractor holds the copyright cannot be relied upon after March 1, 1989, as evidence that the contractor did not retain the copyright. (See page 52.) Third, if an employee of the United States government prepares a work but not as part of official duties, the work is copyrightable.[42] Fourth, if a quasi-governmental employee, such as an employee of the Postal Service, prepares a work, it may be copyrightable.[43] Finally, if the government publishes a work created by a private author, the work does not lose its copyright protection.[44]

1.2 Laws

Federal laws, regulations and judicial opinions are not copyrightable because they are works created by federal government employees in the course of their employment. Although most works created by state government employees are copyrightable, state statutes, regulations and judicial opinions are not. State statutes, regulations and judicial opinions cannot be copyrighted because the concept of due process in our Constitution requires free access to the law by all citizens.[45] Although the actual text of state statutes, regulations

---

39. 17 U.S.C. §105 (1994).
40. 17 U.S.C. §101 (1994).
41. H.R. Rep. No. 94-1476 at 59.
42. H.R. Rep. No. 94-1476 at 58.
43. H.R. Rep. No. 94-1476 at 60.
44. *Id.*
45. *Davidson v. Wheelock*, 27 F. 61, 62 (C.C.D. Minn. 1866); *Howell v. Miller*, 91 F. 129, 137 (6th Cir. 1898); *Building Officials & Code Administrators v. Code Technology, Inc.*, 628 F.2d 730, 734 (1st Cir. 1980); *State of Georgia v. Harrison Co.*, 548 F. Supp. 110, 114 (N.D. Ga. 1982).

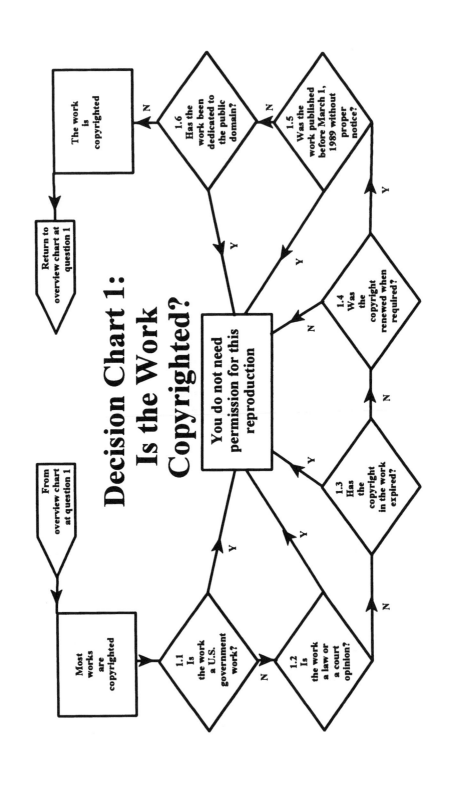

Decision Chart 1:
Is the Work Copyrighted?

From overview chart at question 1

Most works are copyrighted

1.1 Is the work a U.S. government work?

1.2 Is the work a law or a court opinion?

1.3 Has the copyright in the work expired?

1.4 Was the copyright renewed when required?

1.5 Was the work published before March 1, 1989 without proper notice?

1.6 Has the work been dedicated to the public domain?

You do not need permission for this reproduction

The work is copyrighted

Return to overview chart at question 1

and judicial opinions is not copyrightable, any annotations or additional material added to statutes, regulations and opinions by a compiler or publisher is copyrightable.[46]

1.3 Works for Which the Copyright Has Expired

The Constitution allows Congress to grant copyright protection to an author of a work for a limited amount of time. When that time expires, the work enters the public domain.

The term of copyright in the United States has changed considerably over the years. Although each change has lengthened the term of copyright, a work which entered the public domain under an older, shorter term remains in the public domain even when the term of copyright is extended. Thus, it is important to understand the history of the term of copyright in the United States.

The first Copyright Act of 1790 granted protection for 14 years from the date of first publication. The initial 14-year term could be renewed for a second 14-year term which resulted in a total of 28 years of protection.[47] The 1831 Act extended the initial term to 28 years from first publication. The renewal term remained 14 years, so the maximum term of protection under the 1831 Act was 42 years.[48] The 1909 Act left the initial term at 28 years from first publication but extended the renewal term to 28 years for a total of 56 years of protection.[49]

In the late 1950s, Congress began consideration of a major revision of the copyright laws. By 1962, Congress knew that the term of protection under the new act would be longer than the old term. To prevent the copyrights on existing works from expiring under the old law while Congress deliberated, it passed a series of extension acts between 1962 and 1974. These acts extended the renewal term until the new act could take effect.[50]

The 1976 Act has different terms of protection. Which term applies depends upon when the work was created and the type of author.[51]

---

46. *Callaghan v. Myers*, 128 U.S. 617 (1888).

47. Act of May 31, 1790, 1st Cong. 2d Sess., ch. 15.

48. Act of Feb. 3, 1831, 21st Cong. 2d Sess., ch 16.

49. Act of March 4, 1909, ch 320 §23, 35 Stat. 1080.

50. PL 87-668, 89-142, 90-141, 90-416, 91-147, 91-555, 92-170, 92-566, 93-573 and 94-553.

51. Bills which would extend all terms under the 1976 Act by 20 years are currently (1996) being considered by Congress. Many experts think that passage of some sort of extension bill in the near future is almost inevitable. Check an up to date edition of the U.S. Code and all of its supplements for changes to sections 302, 303 and 304 of title 17 before relying on the description of terms under the 1976 Act in this chapter.

1.3 continued If a work was created on or after January 1, 1978, the term of protection ends 50 years after the author dies. If a work created on or after January 1, 1978, has several authors, the term of protection ends 50 years after the last author dies. Anonymous works, pseudonymous works, and works made for hire created after January 1, 1978, are protected for 75 years from first publication or 100 years from creation, whichever occurs first.[52]

If the work was created and published before January 1, 1978, the initial term of protection is 28 years from the date of first publication, and the renewal term is 47 years yielding a maximum period of protection of 75 years.[53]

The provision for works created but not published before January 1, 1978, is complicated but extremely important for old manuscripts, private papers, photographs, slides and any other unpublished works. Many of these works would have been in the public domain if they had been published more than 75 years ago. But because they were never published, they are still protected by copyright.

If a work was created but not published before January 1, 1978, the length of the term of protection depends upon when the author died and whether the work is published before December 31, 2002. Under the 1909 Act, federal law did not protect unpublished works. Unpublished works were protected forever under state common law copyright. The 1976 Act abolished state common law copyright, and extended federal protection to all unpublished works, no matter how old they were.

If the work was created but not published before January 1, 1978, and the copyright holder chooses not to publish the work before December 31, 2002, the copyright will expire either 50 years after the author's death or on December 31, 2002, if the author died before January 1, 1953. If the copyright holder chooses to publish the work on or before December 31, 2002, the copyright will expire either 50 years after the author's death or on December 31, 2027, if the author died before January 1, 1978. If the author of an unpublished work was still alive on January 1, 1978, the copyright term will expire 50 years after his death.

The following example demonstrates how this provision works. John F. Kennedy died on November 22, 1963. Under the 1976 Act, federal copyright law protects his unpublished papers, photographs and home movies. If his heirs do not choose to publish these works by December 31, 2002, they will enter the public domain on December 31, 2013, 50 years after his death. But if his heirs publish any of the works on or before December 31, 2002, the published works will not enter the public domain until December 31, 2027, even though that date is 64 years after his death.

---

52. 17 U.S.C. §302 (1994). See Appendix H at page 210 for a definition of a work for hire.
53. 17 U.S.C. §304 (1994).

If all copyrights were properly renewed, the following duration timeline shows how long copyright lasted at various times during the history of U.S. copyright law.

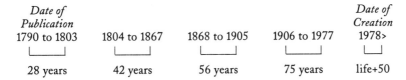

Date of Publication				*Date of Creation*
1790 to 1803	1804 to 1867	1868 to 1905	1906 to 1977	1978>
28 years	42 years	56 years	75 years	life+50

Figure 1. Duration Timeline

The maximum copyright term for all works originally published in the first three periods of this timeline has already expired, so these works are currently in the public domain. Nothing will enter the public domain under the life plus 50 rule until the end of 2028.

Although when publication occurs is no longer as important as it was under the 1909 Act, it continues to have an effect upon the term of copyright for works which were in existence but not published on January 1, 1978. It also continues to have an effect on certain other provisions of the 1976 Copyright Act. (See pages 40, 63, 75, 98 and 125.) The Act defines publication as

> the distribution of copies or phonorecords of a work to the public by sale or other transfer of ownership, or by rental, lease, or lending. The offering to distribute copies or phonorecords to a group of people for purposes of further distribution, public performance, or public display, constitutes publication. A public performance or display of a work does not itself constitute publication [17 U.S.C. §101].

Under this definition, exposure of the work to the public without a material object changing hands is not publication. Thus, displaying a painting in a museum is not publication. Broadcasting a performance on television or providing remote access to a database would not be publication, either although many people might have access to the work. If the television program or database were distributed to the public by renting copies of videotapes or CDs, then a copy would change hands and publication would occur. Publication would also occur if the copyright holder distributed a limited number of copies to distributors who broadcast the information or provided remote access to the public. For example, although a database might not be published if it were available only by remote access from the copyright holder, it would be published if the copyright holder also licensed tapes to libraries to be mounted on their online systems. The database would also be published if the copyright holder licensed a third party database vendor to load the database on its systems for further distribution to the public.

1.4 Failure to Renew the Copyright

Until 1992, works which were not properly renewed immediately entered the public domain at the end of their first term. Effective June 26, 1992, renewal became automatic for all copyrights first secured after January 1, 1964.[54] Since there is only a single term of protection for works created after January 1, 1978, the copyright in these works cannot be forfeited by failure to renew the copyright. Some works first published before 1964 but less than 75 years old, however, may currently be in the public domain because the copyright holder failed to properly renew the copyright. Searching Copyright Office records to determine whether copyrights were properly renewed can be a complex, time-consuming, and expensive process. (See Appendix G.) Thus in most cases, it is better to assume that the copyright was renewed even though 85 percent or more of copyrighted works were not renewed.[55] For many songs and motion pictures, however, the searches have already been done. The following books list songs and motion pictures that have fallen into the public domain because the copyrights were not renewed or for other reasons.

The Mini-Encyclopedia of Public Domain Songs (BZ-Rights Stuff Inc., 1993)
Film Superlist 1950–1959: Motion Pictures in the U.S. Public Domain (Hollywood Film Archives, 1989)
Film Superlist 1940–1949: Motion Pictures in the U.S. Public Domain (Hollywood Film Archives, 1993)
Film Superlist 1894–1939: Motion Pictures in the U.S. Public Domain (Hollywood Film Archives, 1994)

If you decide to do a renewal search for materials other than songs or motion pictures, you will have to find the renewal applications and understand the requirements for a valid renewal, especially the provisions concerning who had the right to apply for renewal at what times.

WHAT RECORDS TO SEARCH

An application for renewal had to be filed in the last year of the first 28-year term of copyright.

Works published before 1950 are governed entirely by the 1909 Act. Under that Act, the 28th year could begin and end in the middle of a year. For

---

54. 17 U.S.C. §304 (1994).
55. Paul Goldstein, *Copyright,* 2d ed. vol. 1 (Boston: Little Brown 1996), §4.9 n. 3.

example, if a work was first published on December 1, 1948, the 28th year began on December 1, 1975, and ended November 30, 1976. Thus, the application had to be filed between December 1, 1975, and November 30, 1976. Although the application had to be filed before November 30, 1976, it might not actually appear in the Copyright Office records for several weeks or months because of delays and workloads in the Copyright Office. Since Copyright Office records are divided by calendar years, you would have to search 1975, 1976 and 1977 to be sure that no renewal records had been filed for this work. Thus, for works published prior to 1950, you must search at least three years of records to make sure no renewal application was filed.

Works published in or after 1950 entered their 28th year after the 1976 Act went into effect. Under this Act, the first term expired at the end of the calendar year in which the end of the 28th year occurred. Thus, the first term of a work first copyrighted on December 1, 1950, ended on December 31, 1978, rather then November 30, 1978. Since the last year of the first term was the calendar year 1978, the renewal application had to be filed during the 1978 calendar year. A renewal application filed in December of 1977 would have been premature and thus ineffectual even though the 28th year of copyright protection began in December of 1977. The application could have been filed any time in 1978. If filed in late December of 1978, it might not have been actually recorded until sometime early in 1979. Thus, for works first copyrighted between 1950 and the end of 1963, you must search at least two years of Copyright Office records.

Currently, Copyright Office records from 1978 to the present are available online. They can be searched on the Internet via the Library of Congress LOCIS system.[56] Thus, it is possible to do an online search for renewals of works first published between January 1, 1950, and December 31, 1963. For works first published before January 1, 1950, manual searches are necessary. In 1996 the Copyright Office charged $20 per hour to search these records.

WHOSE NAME HAD TO APPEAR
ON THE RENEWAL APPLICATION

The renewal term of copyright was actually a second copyright term completely independent from the first term. In most cases, this meant that if an author transferred the copyright to someone else, the new copyright holder did not automatically get the right to renew the copyright.[57] If the transfer

---

56. telnet://locis.loc.gov
57. There were several exceptions to this general rule. The exceptions covered renewal of copyrights in collective works, works made for hire and certain posthumous works. In these cases the copyright holder owned the renewal right even if the copyright holder was not the author. Paul Goldstein, *Copyright,* 2d ed. vol. 1 (Boston: Little Brown 1996), §4.9.

| 1.4 *continued* | specifically mentioned renewal rights or extensions of copy-

right, the new copyright holder got the renewal rights only if the author was alive when the time came to file the renewal application. If the transfer did not mention renewal rights or extensions of copyright, the renewal rights usually belonged to the author or his heirs depending upon whether the author was alive when the time came to file the renewal application. Exactly who owned the renewal right at various times during the year in which a renewal application could be filed, and thus whose name had to appear on the renewal applications, might vary depending upon

 a. whether the author had transferred his renewal rights.

 b. exactly when the author died,

 c. which of the author's heirs were alive at any particular point in the year,

 d. whether the author had a will

 e. who the executors of the will were, and

 f. the laws of inheritance.

1.5 Lack of Proper Notice Before March 1, 1989

Prior to March 1, 1989, a copyright holder could lose his copyright by publishing a substantial number of copies of his work without a proper copyright notice.[58] If someone other than the copyright holder published copies without a proper notice and without authority from the copyright holder, the publication without notice did not put the work in the public domain.

The notice requirement was abolished effective March 1, 1989, when the United States joined the Berne Convention, an international copyright treaty.[59] Publication without a notice or with improper notice after March 1, 1989, may deprive the copyright holder of certain advantages in an infringement suit, but it will not affect the validity of the copyright.[60]

Neither the 1909 or 1976 Acts ever required notice on unpublished copies or phonorecords of works. Publication was what triggered the notice requirement. (See page 49 for a discussion of what constitutes publication.) The law required notices on copies from which a work could be visually perceived. Notices were also required on published phonorecords of sound recordings. However, according to the definitions, soundtracks from motion pictures are copies rather than phonorecords. And since they consist of sounds, they are not copies from which the work can be visually perceived. Thus it

---

 58. *Walker v. University Books, Inc.*, 602 F.2d 859, 863 (9th Cir. 1979); *Beacon Looms, Inc. v. S. Lichtenberg & Co., Inc.*, 552 F. Supp. 1305, 1309 (S.D.N.Y. 1982).

 59. 17 U.S.C. §401 (1994).

 60. Melville B. Nimmer and David Nimmer, *Nimmer on Copyright* vol. 2 (New York: Matthew Bender 1996), §7.02[C][3].

would appear that notices were not required on motion pictures sound-tracks.[61]

The same loophole which eliminated the notice requirement for motion picture soundtracks, also had an effect upon sound recordings of literary and musical works. While a notice was required on sound recordings to protect the sounds in these phonorecords, no notice was required to protect the underlying musical or literary work because the musical or literary work could not be visually perceived from a sound recording. For example, if a sound recording of Martin Luther King's "I Have a Dream" speech had been published without any copyright notices, the lack of notice would have affected the copyright in the sounds but not the copyright in the words of the speech.

Although notice was usually required when copies were publicly distributed, public performance or display of a work did not trigger the notice requirement. Thus while copyright notices frequently appeared on television broadcasts and movies, they were not required to be part of the projected images. Copyright notices were only required when physical copies embodying these audiovisual works changed hands as when videocassettes were rented. Likewise public display of art objects in museums did not trigger the notice requirement because there was no public distribution.

Works published before March 1, 1989, must be divided into two categories for purposes of determining whether they contain a proper copyright notice because the requirements of the 1909 and 1976 acts were different.

NOTICE UNDER THE 1909 ACT

The notice provisions of the 1909 Act were fairly stringent. If a copyright holder published copies of the work with either no notice or an improper notice, the work immediately entered the public domain. In addition, the requirements for the form of the notice were detailed and often technical.

The notice for most works had to contain either the word *Copyright* or the abbreviation *Copr.* or the symbol ©. The symbol ℗ was required on sound recordings in place of "Copyright," "Copr." or ©.

The notice also had to include the name of the copyright holder. When the notice was on maps, art works, art reproductions, scientific and technical drawings, photographs or prints and illustrations, the copyright holder's name could be represented by initials, monograms, marks or symbols on the surface of the work if the full name was given somewhere on the object to which the work was attached such as on the base or on the back. When the work was a printed literary, musical or dramatic work, the notice also had to include the

---

61. *Id.*, §7.06[a].

1.5 continued year in which the work was first published.[62] The date of first publication was also required on sound recordings published after February 15, 1972. The date of first publication was not required, however on pictorial, graphic or sculptural works. Since sound recordings produced before February 15, 1972, were not protected at all under the 1909 Act, the lack of a date or any notice at all had no effect on these sound recordings. Under the 1909 Act, if a work was published with a notice using a date more than one year after the actual date of first publication, the effect was the same as publishing the work with no notice. The work immediately entered the public domain. If a work was published with a notice containing a date before the actual date of first publication, the copyright term ran from the earlier date in the notice. This had the effect of making the copyright term shorter than it would have been if the notice had contained the correct date.

For books, printed publications, newspapers, periodicals and musical works, the Act even specified where the notice had to appear. It had to appear on the title page or the page following the title page for books and other printed publications. For periodicals and newspapers, it had to appear on the title page, the first page of the text or under the title heading. The notice had to appear on the title page or the first page of music for musical works.[63] For all other types of works, the notice could be placed anywhere that was accessible and likely to give reasonable notice of a claim of copyright.[64]

NOTICE UNDER THE 1976 ACT BEFORE MARCH 1, 1989

In many respects the notice requirements under the 1976 Act were less stringent. The technical requirements on where the notice had to be placed on various types of works were eliminated in favor of a general requirement that the notice had to be attached in a manner and location that would give reasonable notice of the claim of copyright.[65] If the notice was omitted or defective on only a relatively small number of copies, the work did not enter the public domain immediately. Instead the copyright holder was allowed to fix the problem within five years by registering the work, correcting the problem on new copies and making a reasonable effort to correct the problem on copies already distributed with either no notice or a defective notice.[66]

The Act still required the presence of the word Copyright or the

---

62. 17 U.S.C. §19 (1909 Act repealed by 1976 Act).
63. 17 U.S.C. §20 (1909 Act repealed by 1976 Act).
64. Melville B. Nimmer and David Nimmer, *Nimmer on Copyright*, vol. 2 (New York: Matthew Bender 1996), §7.10[b].
65. 17 U.S.C. §401(c) (1994).
66. 17 U.S.C. §405 (1994).

abbreviation Copr. or the symbol ©. Instead of requiring the date of first publication only on printed material, however, the 1976 Act required the date of first publication on all published works except pictorial, graphic or sculptural works on greeting cards, postcards, stationery, jewelry, dolls, toys and other useful articles. Finally the rules on how the identity of the copyright holder was to be designated were simplified. On all works, the notice could contain either the name of the copyright holder or an abbreviation or mark by which the name could easily be recognized.[67]

If a work first published before January 1, 1978, was republished between January 1, 1978, and February 28, 1989, with a notice that was proper under the 1909 Act but not under the 1976 Act, the validity of the copyright was not affected by the failure to comply with 1976 Act requirements. Notice on works republished after January 1, 1978, is proper if it complies with the requirements of either Act.

WHAT THE NOTICE COVERS

Although both the 1909 Act and the 1976 Act required a proper copyright notice, neither Act required the copyright owner to specify in the notice which parts of the work were covered by the copyright claim. As long as any part of the work was copyrightable, the copyright owner could put a general copyright notice on the work. Since copyright owners were not required to specify what the notice covered, many authors, editors and publishers made minor changes to public domain works and then added a general copyright notice. Although the copyright covers only the new material added to the public domain work, the user has to figure out what is new and what is old. The only way to be absolutely sure what has been added is to do a careful comparison between the new work and a public domain edition.

1.6 Works Dedicated to the Public Domain

Under the 1909 Act, an author had to take affirmative steps to claim federal copyright protection. The author had to publish the work with a copyright notice on it and comply with certain other formalities. With the passage of the 1976 Act which abolished the publication requirement, authors no longer have to take any affirmative steps to claim copyright protection. It simply attaches when the work is fixed in a tangible medium. Since copyright simply attaches upon creation, the author has to do something to cause the work to fall into the public domain.

---

67. 17 U.S.C. §401(b)(3) (1994).

| 1.6 continued | If a copyright holder does something that clearly indicates an intention to abandon the copyright in the work, then

the work enters the public domain. Prior to March 1, 1989, the most common action that an author took to place a work in the public domain was publication without a copyright notice. But since the notice requirement was abolished in 1989, some other action is now required to put a work in the public domain.

The most common form of dedication to the public domain now is an express statement dedicating the work to the public domain. A statement does not place a work in the public domain, however, if it only abandons part of the copyright. For example, a copyright holder might give the public the right to copy and distribute a work, but not give the public the right to create new derivative works based on the work. The use of a shareware or freeware statement by an author does not place a work in the public domain. A shareware or freeware statement is a form of limited license giving the public the right to use a certain part, but not all of, the copyright bundle of rights. For a discussion of the various parts of a copyright, see pages 34 to 41.

2. Parts of Works

2.1 Parts Taken from Another Work

Copyright protects that part of a work that is original to its author. It does not protect what the author copies from someone else. This is why a copyright in a compilation or derivative work protects only the new material that the compiler or author of the derivative work adds. If the existing material is copyrighted in its own right, it is still protected by copyright. But the copyright in the new derivative or compilation work does not cover the older material included in it. Thus if the copyright expires on an older work contained in a compilation, the copyright in the compilation cannot extend the term of copyright protection for the older work included in the compilation. Similarly if the copyright in the newer compilation expires before the copyright in the older contained works (for example where the compilation copyright was not properly renewed), the fact that the new material in the compilation falls into the public domain does not mean that the older contained work also falls into the public domain. It is still protected by its own properly renewed copyright.

The concept of independent copyright in parts of works is very important for audiovisual works. Even if the main work is in the public domain, a valid copyright in one of the included works might prevent certain uses of the whole work. For example, the movie *It's a Wonderful Life* is in the public domain because the copyright holder did not renew the copyright at the end of the first term. Even though the copyright on the film has expired, a library might encounter difficulty if it decided to show the film publicly for a fee because the copyrights in some of the songs sung in the movie have not expired.

2.2 Ideas

Copyright protects the manner in which a particular author expresses an idea. It does not protect the idea itself.[68] The line between an idea and the way it is expressed is not a bright one. A good example of the how fuzzy the line

---

68. 17 U.S.C. §102(b) (1994).

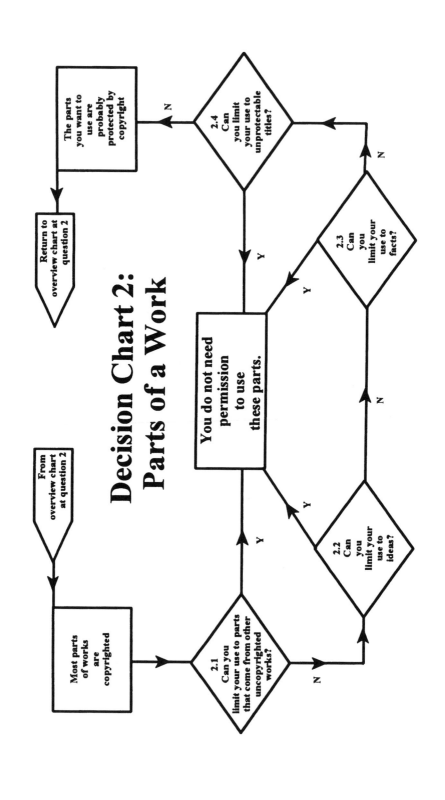

Decision Chart 2:
Parts of a Work

From overview chart at question 2

Most parts of works are copyrighted

2.1 Can you limit your use to parts that come from other uncopyrighted works?

You do not need permission to use these parts.

Return to overview chart at question 2

The parts you want to use are probably protected by copyright

2.4 Can you limit your use to unprotectable titles?

2.3 Can you limit your use to facts?

2.2 Can you limit your use to ideas?

is would be the plot of a television show or movie. The basic idea of a starship captain who pilots a spaceship to explore the galaxy is not copyrightable. Even putting the starship in an organization of planets inhabited by a variety of species and giving it a five-year mission to explore unknown parts of space is probably not enough to rise above idea to expression. But when you add all the personalities that make up the major characters of Captain Kirk, Commander Spock, and Dr. McCoy, and put them on a Constellation class starship, it begins to rise to the level of Gene Rodenberry's particular expression of that idea which is protected by copyright.

2.3 Facts

Facts are also not protectable by copyright. The fact itself is not original to the author. The author may have discovered the fact, but he did not create it. The manner in which the fact is expressed may, however, be protected by copyright. For this reason, if you need to use facts in your project but do not need to use them in the particular form in which they were expressed in a copyrighted work, you should consider rewriting the facts in your own words to avoid copyright problems.

2.4 Titles, Names and Short Phrases

Individual words and short phrases such as names and titles are not copyrightable.[69] They are too short to contain sufficient originality to be protectable. Names of characters are also unprotectable under copyright law. However, both titles and names of characters may be protectable under unfair competition or trademark law.

---

69. *Manufacturers Technologies, Inc. v. Cams, Inc.*, 706 F. Supp. 984, 996 (D. Conn. 1989); *Regents of the Univ. of Minn. v. Applied Innovations Inc.*, 685 F. Supp. 698, 707 (D. Minn. 1987) aff'd 876 F.2d 626, 635 (8th Cir. 1989).

3. Reproduction

3.1 Reproduction by Libraries and Archives—§108

RIGHTS AFFECTED BY §108

Section 108 applies only to the rights of reproduction and public distribution. It will not authorize any public displays, public performances or production of derivative works.

WHO MAY USE §108

Section 108 covers only libraries and archives. It provides no protection to a commercial contractor who contracts with the library to provide reproduction services on the library's premises.[70] Libraries which are considering contracting out photocopying or other forms of reproduction on their premises should consider the implications of this restriction before entering into such a contract.

The §108 limitation is available only to libraries or archives that meet certain criteria. The library must be open to the public or make its collections available to unaffiliated researchers in the field that the library's collection encompasses. Most experts believe that making a library's collection available to unaffiliated researchers through interlibrary loan provides sufficient access for a library to qualify for §108 privileges. If a library lists itself as a nonsupplier on OCLC or any other interlibrary loan system, it probably cannot rely upon interlibrary loan to qualify for §108 privileges.

The reproduction or public distribution by a library under this section must be done without any purpose of direct commercial advantage. Any commercial advantage must be directly related to the reproduction or distribution to disqualify a library from using this section. Corporate libraries and other

---

70. H.R. Rep. No. 94-1476 at 74.

60

libraries in for-profit institutions may use this section if there is no direct commercial advantage associated with the reproduction and distribution itself. Although the district court in *American Geophysical Union v. Texaco*[71] implies in a nonbinding part of the opinion that the protection of §108 may not be available to corporate libraries, both the legislative history[72] and the opinion of most experts clearly indicate that the section is applicable to libraries that are part of for-profit enterprises.[73] An example of a situation in which the reproduction and distribution itself would result in direct commercial advantage would be a document delivery service where the fees charged exceed the actual costs associated with providing the service. Although §108 could not be used to justify reproduction or distribution as part of a for-profit document delivery service, it could still authorize reproduction and distribution that occurs as part of other nonprofit fee based services offered by the library.

WORKS COVERED BY §108

The preservation and replacement copying subsections of §108 apply to all types of works. The remainder of §108 applies to all types of works except musical works; pictorial, graphic or sculptural works; and motion pictures and other audiovisual works. Pictorial, graphic and sculptural works may be reproduced and distributed to patrons, however, if they are illustrations or adjuncts to other types of works. Although most of §108 does not authorize the reproduction and public distribution of most audiovisual works, it contains a special clause that allows libraries to reproduce audiovisual works dealing with news and distribute them to patrons.

The fact that §108 does not authorize copying and public distribution of certain types of works does not mean that all such copying and distribution is prohibited. If the copying and public distribution meets the criteria of another limitation or fair use, it may still be permitted.

PRESERVATION AND REPLACEMENT COPYING

Section 108 contains two subsections that are directly applicable to preservation copying. Subsection (b) gives a library or archives the right to reproduce and distribute a copy or a phonorecord of an unpublished work

---

71. 802 F. Supp. 1, 27–28 (S.D.N.Y. 1992).
72. H.R. Rep. No. 94-1476 at 74–75.
73. Melville B. Nimmer and David Nimmer, *Nimmer on Copyright* (New York: Matthew Bender 1996), §8.03[A][1]; Paul Goldstein, *Copyright* 2d ed. (Boston: Little Brown 1996), §5.2.2[a](1); James S. Heller & Sarah K. Wiant, *Copyright Handbook* (Rothman 1984), 15.

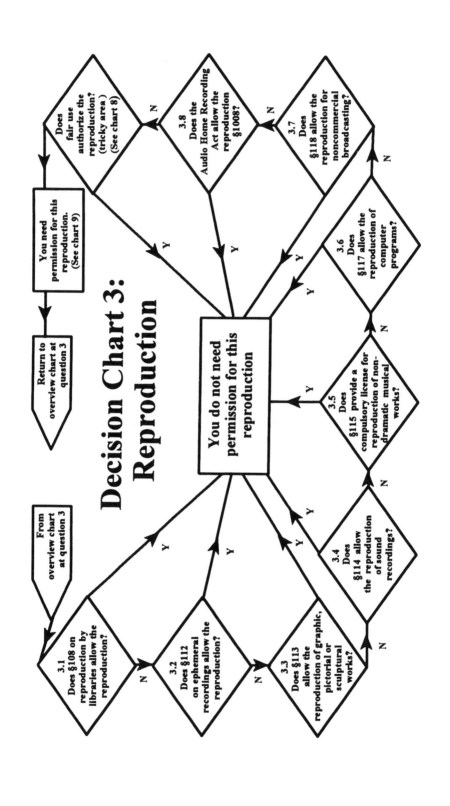

Decision Chart 3: Reproduction

From overview chart at question 3

3.1 Does §108 on reproduction by libraries allow the reproduction?

3.2 Does §112 on ephemeral recordings allow the reproduction?

3.3 Does §113 allow the reproduction of graphic, pictorial or sculptural works?

3.4 Does §114 allow the reproduction of sound recordings?

3.5 Does §115 provide a compulsory license for reproduction of non-dramatic musical works?

3.6 Does §117 allow the reproduction of computer programs?

3.7 Does §118 allow the reproduction for noncommercial broadcasting?

3.8 Does the Audio Home Recording Act allow the reproduction §1008?

Does fair use authorize the reproduction? (tricky area) (See chart 8)

You do not need permission for this reproduction

You need permission for this reproduction. (See chart 9)

Return to overview chart at question 3

duplicated in facsimile form solely for purposes of preservation and security or for deposit in another research library or archives ... if the copy or phonorecord reproduced is currently in the collections of the library or archives.

Subsection (c) gives a library or archives the right to reproduce a copy or a phonorecord of a published work

duplicated in facsimile form solely for purposes of replacement of a copy or phonorecord that is damaged, deteriorating, lost, or stolen, if the library or archives has, after a reasonable effort, determined that an unused replacement cannot be obtained at a fair price.

These subsections contain restrictions which severely limit the kind of preservation activities libraries are permitted to engage in under §108. First, both subsections (b) and (c) are limited to duplicating works in "facsimile form." The statute does not define "facsimile form," but the legislative history states in an example that a manuscript could be photocopied on paper or microfilm, but could not be reproduced in "machine-readable" form for storage in an information retrieval system.[74] Given this example, some copyright holders might argue that the limitation to facsimile form means that §108(b) cannot be used to authorize electronic preservation. But modern forms of electronic imaging fit the dictionary definition of facsimile far better than machine readable formats of the 1960s and 70s. Electronic imaging may be more similar to microfilming than to the machine readable formats known to Congress at the time the example was written. Although electronic imaging might meet the facsimile requirement, scanning and conversion to ASCII characters clearly does not.

All copying sanctioned by §108 is also limited to isolated and unrelated reproduction or distribution of a single copy of the same material. Section 108 may authorize a library which owns a work that needs preserving to make one master copy of the work in facsimile form and to make additional single copies for deposit in other libraries from time to time. It does not, however, authorize a library to make multiple copies of a work that needs preserving in anticipation of requests from other libraries for copies of that work. This can be a problem for major cooperative preservation projects.

The published or unpublished status of the work to be copied also affects the extent of preservation copying rights under §108. Subsection (b) applies only to unpublished works. Subsection (c), which applies to published works, authorizes preservation copying **only if**

a) the work is already damaged, deteriorating, lost or stolen **and**
b) the library, after a reasonable effort, has determined that an unused replacement is not available at a fair price.

---

74. H.R. Rep. No. 94-1476 at 75.

| 3.1 *continued* | Both of the conditions in subsection (c) substantially reduce the number of situations in which §108 authorizes preservation copying of published works.

The provision does not apply to a work until *after* it has started to deteriorate, has been damaged or is lost or stolen. Many librarians would prefer to make a security copy before anything happens to the original. However §108 does not authorize such security copying which means that a library may have to locate another institution with an undamaged copy to exercise its rights under this limitation.

Although many librarians bemoan the high cost of new copies, there is nothing in the language of the statute, the legislative history or any of the case law that would suggest that the full cost of a new copy currently available through commercial markets is not a fair price for a replacement copy. Section 108(c) was designed to give libraries a mechanism to replace or repair out-of-print works. It was not designed to limit the profits that a copyright holder could make from selling additional copies when copies need replacing before the copyright expires.

COPYING FOR PATRONS

Subsections (d) and (e) cover copying at the request of a user. These subsections are not limited to facsimile form and so could include copying by conversion to electronic form or to any other format. Several conditions apply to user requests made under subsections (d) and (e).

Copies made under subsections (d) and (e) must be made at the request of a user and must become the property of the requesting user. A library may not make or keep a copy for its collection or the use of other users under these subsections.

Subsections (d) and (e) contain specific limitations on how much information may be reproduced and distributed to a user at one time. Only a single copy may be provided to a user. A user may request a single article or other contribution to a copyrighted collection or periodical issue. Or the user may request a small part of any other copyrighted work to which §108 applies. A library may provide a copy of an entire work (or a substantial part of a work) to a user under §108 **only if** the library has first determined based on a reasonable investigation that a copy cannot be obtained at a fair price. This limitation does not necessarily mean that there are no other conditions under which the copyright law would authorize a library to reproduce and distribute more information to a user. But any request which exceeds these limits must be authorized under another section or the library must obtain permission from the copyright holder, usually by paying a royalty.

All copies made and distributed under subsections (d) and (e) must contain a copyright notice. In addition libraries must display copyright warning notices at the place and on the forms they use to take requests from patrons. Section 108 obviously contemplates a situation in which users come to a library in person to request copies. In recent years, however, many libraries have expanded their outreach services and accept requests for copies by mail, phone, fax and E-mail. Unless the library answers each request by sending the user a standard form and requiring the user to fill it out, it may be almost impossible to comply with both the letter and the spirit of the law and regulations concerning notice. The Copyright Office regulations concerning §108 require the following notice to be displayed where orders are taken and printed on order forms.[75]

NOTICE
WARNING CONCERNING
COPYRIGHT RESTRICTIONS

The copyright law of the United States (Title 17, United States Code) governs the making of photocopies or other reproductions of copyrighted material.

Under certain conditions specified in the law, libraries and archives are authorized to furnish a photocopy or other reproduction. One of these specific conditions is that the photocopy or reproduction is not to be "used for any purpose other than private study, scholarship or research." If a user makes a request for, or later uses, a photocopy or reproduction for purposes in excess of "fair use," that user may be liable for copyright infringement.

This institution reserved the right to refuse to accept a copying order if, in its judgment, fulfillment of the order would involve violations of copyright law.

Figure 2: §108 Notice

The notice which must be displayed where orders are taken has to be printed on heavy paper or other durable material in at least 18 point type. Obviously, if patrons do not come to the library, they will not be able to see such a displayed notice, although the library would be in technical compliance if it placed such a notice next to the phone, the fax machine and the computer where E-mail is received.

---

75. 37 C.F.R. §201.14 (1995).

3.1 *continued* The regulation concerning the notice on order forms requires the notice to be printed on the front of the form or next to the space for the patron's name. It must be printed in the same size type as the rest of the form or in at least 8 point type if the rest of the form is in 8 point or smaller type. Although a library could technically comply with the law by transferring all requests received to a form containing the proper notice, the patrons are unlikely to ever see this notice unless they fill out their own forms.

Given these difficulties, it would be wise to supplement the notices required by §108 with additional notices on the material sent to the patron. The notices that technically comply with the law should not be eliminated, however, even if patrons rarely see them because without technical compliance the library may lose the benefits of §108.

SYSTEMATIC COPYING

All of the rights of reproduction and distribution under §108 extend only to isolated and unrelated reproduction or distribution of a single copy or phonorecord on separate occasions. Section 108 rights do not extend to systematic reproduction or distribution of multiple copies or phonorecords of the same material. The fact that the copies may be made over a period of time for different individuals does not automatically mean that the reproduction and distribution is isolated and unrelated. If copies of the same material are made for members of a specific group, they may be related, and therefore, not authorized by §108.

The Senate Report, in discussing §108, makes it clear that class readings are not isolated and unrelated. "If a college professor instructs his class to read an article from a copyrighted journal, the school library would not be permitted, under subsection (g), to reproduce copies of the article for the members of the class."[76] This statement, along with the clause in §108(g) which refers to "whether or not intended for aggregate use by one or more individuals or for separate use by the individual members of a group," suggests that the Senate never intended §108 to be used in the reserve situation. Reserve copying should be analyzed using the fair use criteria.

The Senate Report gives the following examples of systematic reproduction.[77]

> 1. A library with a collection of journals in biology informs other libraries with similar collections that it will maintain and build its own collection

---

76. S. Rep. No. 473, 94th Cong., 1st Sess., at 70 (1975).
77. *Id.*

and will make copies of articles from these journals available to them and their patrons on request. Accordingly the other libraries discontinue or refrain from purchasing subscriptions to these journals and fulfill their patrons' requests for articles by obtaining photocopies from the source library.

2. A research center employing a number of scientists and technicians subscribes to one or two copies of needed periodicals. By reproducing photocopies of articles the center is able to make the material in these periodicals available to its staff in the same manner which otherwise would have required multiple subscriptions.

3. Several branches of a library system agree that one branch will subscribe to particular journals in lieu of each branch purchasing its own subscriptions, and the one subscribing branch will reproduce copies of articles from the publication for users of the other branches.

INTERLIBRARY LOAN COPYING

Section 108 is probably best known as the section of the copyright law that regulates interlibrary loan. Section 108 (d) and (e) specifically give libraries the authority to fill requests for copies from users at other libraries. Subsection (g)(2), however, makes it clear that the right to make copies for patrons from other libraries is not unlimited. Systemic copying is not authorized. Despite the restriction against systematic copying, interlibrary arrangements which do not substitute for subscriptions or purchases by the borrowing library are specifically authorized.

Congress asked the Commission on New Technological Uses of Copyrighted Works (CONTU) to develop guidelines to assist libraries in determining when photocopying reaches a level that substitutes for subscription or purchase and is, therefore, not authorized by §108. The CONTU guidelines are reproduced in Appendix A. The guidelines cover the most common type of interlibrary loan requests—photocopies of journal articles less than five years old. The introduction to the guidelines specifically says that the guidelines offer no guidance on when copying of articles more the five years old rises to a level that substitutes for a subscription. Although the guidelines were developed specifically for photocopying, they can also be applied to other means of reproduction and delivery of journal articles such as telefax and electronic delivery.

PATRON USE OF LIBRARY EQUIPMENT

If a library encourages or assists patrons in infringing copyrights, the library could be liable for contributory infringement. Section 108(f)(1) protects

3.1 continued   libraries from liability for contributory infringement when patrons misuse reproducing equipment provided by the library. It states:

> Nothing in this section—
> (1) shall be construed to impose liability for copyright infringement upon a library or archives or its employees for the unsupervised use of reproducing equipment located on its premises: Provided, That such equipment displays a notice that the making of a copy may be subject to the copyright law.

Although the section was primarily aimed at photocopiers, the language is broad enough to include all types of equipment, including computer and audio-video equipment, which can be used unsupervised by patrons. Such equipment might include personal computers equipped with printers, disk drives, CD-ROM drives, scanners, VCRs, audiotape recorders and digital audio-tape equipment. It is probably also broad enough to encompass ports on the library's network to which patrons can connect their own computer equipment.

Libraries should remember, however, that the notice requirement is not restricted to photocopiers either. Notices should be placed on public access audio, video, and computing equipment in libraries. Ways should also be found to display similar notices when a patron connects to the computers or networks that the library uses to house its electronic works.

While §108(f)(1) may immunize libraries from liability for unsupervised infringing copying, it does not protect the library when a library employee does the actual copying or when the equipment the patron uses for copying is supervised. Although neither the statute, the legislative history nor the case law defines how much supervision is enough to cause a library to lose the protection of §108(f)(1), supervised copying probably requires at least sufficient involvement by the library staff to have the opportunity to observe the types of material being copied. Libraries often supervise the use of their audio-visual and computer equipment far more than they supervise the use of their photocopiers. If a library supervises the use of such equipment by patrons, such as by providing monitors in its computer labs, it should make sure that staff members supervising such equipment are well educated about all provisions of the copyright law that might be applicable to reproduction by patrons.

RELATIONSHIP BETWEEN FAIR USE AND §108

Both the language of §108 and the legislative history make it clear that some uses not authorized by §108 may still be authorized by fair use. The legislative history specifically says that fair use may allow some uses of musical, graphic and audiovisual works which are not authorized by §108.

Fair use and the decision in *Williams & Wilkins v. U.S.*,[78] however, should not be relied upon to extend interlibrary copying and public distribution beyond the limits of the CONTU guidelines. In *Williams & Wilkins*, several medical publishers sued the National Library of Medicine and the National Institutes of Health claiming that their massive photocopy services exceeded fair use. The trial court found that the copying exceeded fair use. The Court of Claims, on appeal, refused to hold that the copying exceeded fair use, but what it did say was very equivocal. In short, the court said that it would not stop this copying and distribution while Congress was deliberating a major revision of the Copyright Act. If this type of copying is not fair use, then Congress should say so. The Supreme Court split four to four and so affirmed the Court of Claims decision without an opinion. This kind of affirmance does not carry the same weight as a majority affirmance. Congress's response was §108 and the CONTU guidelines.

MODIFICATION OF §108 BY CONTRACT

Subsection (f) contains a provision that allows a copyright holder to eliminate any or all of the rights that §108 gives to libraries. It states that "Nothing in this section … in any way affects … any contractual obligations assumed at any time by the library or archives when it obtained a copy or phonorecord of a work in its collections." The legislative history states that this provision was intended to allow copyright holders to make manuscripts and other works available to libraries with the understanding that they would not be reproduced.[79] Thus copyright holders can (and often do with electronic works) place contractual limitations upon the library's right to reproduce or redistribute the work to the public as a condition of selling, licensing, or donating a copy for the library's collection.

3.2 Ephemeral Recordings Limitation — §112

Section 112 generally applies only to the reproduction right although it may imply authorization of public distribution in very limited circumstances. It applies only in conjunction with an authorized transmission of a performance or display of a work. Although it was designed primarily for radio and television broadcasters, in certain circumstances it might allow a library to make a copy of a performance or display that the library has the right to transmit.

---

78. 487 F.2d 1345 (Ct. Cl. 1973) aff'd by an equally divided Supreme Court, 420 U.S. 376 (1975).
79. H.R. Rep. No. 94-1476 at 77.

| 3.2 *continued* | If a library has a right to transmit a performance or display of a work under a license or because there is no performance right in the work (see page 100), §112(a) gives the library the right to make one copy of the transmission if it complies with several conditions. Section 112(a) does not apply to motion pictures and other audiovisual works. The library may retain the copy but cannot distribute it to anyone else. The library cannot make any more copies from the copy. The library must destroy the copy within six months of the date it was first transmitted to the public unless the library is preserving the copy exclusively for archival purposes. Within the first six months after the copy is made, the library may use the copy to transmit again to the public in its own service area provided that the library uses its own transmitting facilities.

Section 112(a) applies only if the library acquired the right to transmit the display or performance under a license or assignment of the copyright. If a library or other organization has a right to transmit a performance or display under the educational broadcast exemption (see page 101), §112(b) governs the right to make copies of the transmission. Section 112(b) is much broader than §112(a). It allows the transmitting organization to make up to 30 copies whereas subsection (a) limits the organization to only one copy. These copies may be used for further transmissions to the public that meet the requirements of §110(2). These copies may also be transferred to other educational institutions or government bodies who meet the requirements for educational transmissions under §110(2). The copies may be kept and used for further educational transmissions for seven years after the initial transmission. Each future transmission has to meet all the requirements of §110(2), however. When the seven years have expired, all but one copy must be destroyed. The organization that made the copies may keep one copy solely for archival purposes after the seven years have expired. Since §110(2) applies only to performances of nondramatic literary and musical works or displays of works, §112(b) applies only to displays of works or performances of nondramatic literary and musical works. It does not apply to performances of dramatic works or audiovisual works.

Section 112(c) allows a governmental body or other nonprofit organization to make a copy of a sound recording or a transmission containing a performance of a musical work of a religious nature for a person or organization that has a license to transmit the performance. The library cannot charge either directly or indirectly for making and distributing the copy. All copies except one archival copy must be destroyed within one year from the date the program was first transmitted to the public.

Section 112(d) permits a governmental body or other organization authorized to transmit a performance to the handicapped under §110(8) to make no more than ten copies of the transmission. (See page 98 for a discussion of §110[8].) The organization may allow another governmental body or nonprofit organization entitled to transmit the performance to the handicapped to use one of the ten copies. The copies may only be used by organizations entitled to make transmissions under §110(8). No further copies can be made from the first ten copies. The copies can be used only for purposes of making transmissions under §110(8) or for archival, preservation or security purposes. An organization that allows another organization to use copies made under this section cannot charge for the use.

Although the legislative history suggests that §112 was designed primarily to allow reproduction of copies that would facilitate radio, television and close circuit video and sound transmissions, there is nothing in the language of the statute that restricts it to such applications. It could relate to other transmissions as well including transmissions related to the use of computers and electronic works. There is, however, a curious sentence in the House Report which might limit application of §112(b) in relation to computers and electronic works. In discussing the relationship between §110(2) and §112(b), the report says that an ephemeral recording made under §112(b) must embody a performance or display that meets all the qualifications for exemption under §110(2). The next sentence states "copies or phonorecords made for educational broadcasts of a general cultural nature, or for transmission as part of an information storage and retrieval system, would not be exempted from copyright protection under §112(b)."[80] This sentence seems to refer to statements in the report concerning §110 which state that general cultural recreational and entertainment activities are not covered by §110(1) and §110(2), and thus are not covered by §112(b). But nothing in the statute or the legislative history says that §110(2) cannot be applied to systematic instructional uses of information storage and retrieval systems. When a restriction is not apparent in the language of a statute, courts are often reluctant to create one by expanding on a comment in the legislative history that is not actually part of the law.[81] This particular comment appears to have no basis in the statute, so perhaps the courts will not rely upon it.

3.3 Pictorial, Graphic, and Sculptural Works Limitation—§113

Section 113 is rarely of use to libraries. It applies only to pictorial, graphic and sculptural works. It applies only to the reproduction right, the public distribution right, and the public display right. It does not authorize any public performances or preparation of derivative works.

When useful articles embodying copyrighted pictorial, graphic, or

---

80. H.R. Rep. No. 94-1476 at 103.
81. *Edison Bros. Stores, Inc. v. Broadcast Music Inc.*, 954 F.2d 1419, 1425 (8th Cir. 1992).

3.3 continued   sculptural works have been offered for sale or other public
distribution, §113 allows the making, distribution and display
of photographs or pictures of the useful article for the following purposes:

   a. in advertisements;
   b. in commentaries related to the distribution or display of the useful
      articles; and
   c. in connection with news reports.

3.4 Sound Recordings Limitation—§114

Sound recordings recorded before February 15, 1972, are not protected by federal statutory copyright, but they may be protected by state statutes or state common law. The law in this area varies from state to state. Although the sound recording itself is not protected by federal statutory copyright, the underlying literary or musical work may be. The copyright in the underlying literary or musical work may restrict what you can do with the sound recording.

Although the copyright holder generally has the exclusive right to publicly perform a copyrighted work, the copyright holder in a sound recording produced after February 15, 1972, does not usually have the exclusive right of public performance. The Digital Performance Right in Sound Recordings Act of 1995 does give the copyright holder of the sound recording a limited right to control public performances by means of digital audio transmissions.[82] The copyright holder in the sound recording also has the exclusive right to make and publicly distribute copies of the sound recording and to prepare derivative works based on the sound recording.

Section 114(b) limits the sound recording copyright holder's exclusive right to make copies of a sound recording to the right to reproduce the actual sounds on the recording. It does not give the copyright holder the right to prohibit anyone else from copying or performing or recording any underlying musical, literary or other work. This right belongs to the copyright holder of the underlying musical, literary or other work. This means, for example, that the copyright holder of a recording can prohibit the making of bootleg copies of the recording but cannot prohibit other people from imitating the recording. Of course the owner of the copyright in the underlying song, may have the right to prohibit such imitations. (See page 100.)

Section 114(b) also gives public broadcasting entities the right to reproduce sound recordings as part of the process of including the recordings in educational television and radio programs. Most libraries cannot use this right because they do not meet the qualifications of a public broadcasting entity

---

82. PL 104-39, 109 Stat. 336 (Nov. 1, 1995).

which are set out in 17 U.S.C. §118(g). If a library were to meet those requirements, §114(b) would grant the right to reproduce sound recordings as part of educational programs only if copies of the programs are not commercially distributed to the public.

3.5 Compulsory License for Nondramatic Musical Works—§115

Section 115 will rarely be of use to libraries, since libraries seldom make original sound recordings of nondramatic musical works. It might however cover recordings of festivals and other cultural events made by libraries, archives, or museums as part of oral history projects or for similar purposes.

Section 115 allows a person to make a new sound recording of a musical work that has been previously distributed to the public in the U.S. upon payment of a compulsory license fee. It applies only to the right of reproduction and the right of public distribution. It does not authorize any public displays, public performances or the preparation of any derivative works.

The compulsory license applies only to nondramatic musical works. The license applies primarily to the recording of new performances of a musical work. In addition, new phonorecords made under the compulsory license can only be distributed to the public for private use, not for further public use.

Section 115 usually does not authorize the duplication of another person's recording of a musical work. If you want to duplicate an existing recording of a musical work, you will need permission to duplicate the sounds as well as authorization to record the underlying musical work. If the recording you want to reproduce was made after February 15, 1972, you must obtain permission from the person who holds the copyright in the sound recording. Since sound recordings were not protected by copyright prior to February 15, 1972, there are no copyright holders in these old sound recordings. Nevertheless, under §115, you must still obtain permission from the person who had the license to produce the original sound recording.

3.6 Computer Program Limitation—§117

Section 117 applies only to computer programs. Computer programs are defined as "set[s] of statements or instructions to be used directly or indirectly in a computer in order to bring about a certain result."[83] This definition does not cover other literary works or any other type of work stored on media that can be read by a computer. It covers only the programs that cause the computer

---

83. 17 U.S.C. §101 (1995).

3.6 continued to do something. Thus, §117 does not apply to sound recordings on compact discs. Nor does it apply to the part of CD-ROMs that contain literary works or sound recordings. It applies to the files on the CD-ROM containing the software that allows the computer to use the data, but not to the data files themselves.

Section 117 applies to the rights of reproduction, public distribution and the right to make derivative works. It does not apply to the rights of public performance and display.

Only the *owner* of a copy of a computer program can take advantage of the rights in this section. Whether a program distributed under a shrink-wrap license for a one time fee is sold or licensed is a question open to debate. At least one court has treated such transactions like a sale and applied §117.[84] If a court finds that the program was distributed under a license and the distributor or copyright holder retained ownership of the copy, the user will not have any §117 rights.

The owner of a copy of a computer program has the right under §117 to make another copy for archival purposes only. An archival copy is a backup copy. It serves no other purpose than to replace or repair the original should something go wrong. If you make another copy and put it on a machine that you use at different times than your primary machine, that copy is not used solely for archival purposes. If you loan the other copy to a friend while a copy is still installed on your hard drive, the loaned copy is not used solely for archival purposes. Although copies for these purposes may be authorized by some software licenses, they are not authorized by §117.

Librarians may make a single backup copy of a computer disk that comes with a book if the disk contains only computer programs and the copy is used only to replace or repair the original if it is damaged or lost. If the disk contains data rather than programs, §117 may not cover the situation, but it is possible that other provisions of the law may apply. The archival rights contained in §117, however, clearly do not apply to audiovisual works and sound recordings.

The words "another copy" may imply that only one backup copy at a time is authorized. Whether one or more archival copies are authorized, all archival copies must be exact copies. They may be transferred with the original copy or destroyed. But the original owner may not retain backup copies after transferring ownership of the original copies to someone else.

Section 117 also gives the owner of a copy of a computer program the right to make a new copy or adaptation as part of an essential step in using the program on a machine. This section probably gives the owner of a copy of an IBM program the right to make the changes necessary to run the program on a

---

84. See *Vault v. Quaid Software Ltd.*, 847 F.2d 255 (5th Cir. 1988).

MacIntosh computer or on a machine running Unix. This section would give the owner of a copy of a program the right to transfer it from 5.25" disks to 3.5" disks or to install the program on a single hard drive.

Copies of adaptations may not be transferred or otherwise distributed to anyone else. They must be destroyed when the right to possess the original ends.

3.7 Noncommercial Broadcasting Limitation—§118

Section 118 rarely applies to libraries because it applies only to public broadcasting entities which are defined to be noncommercial educational broadcast stations under 47 U.S.C. §397. Very few libraries meet this definition.

This section applies only to published nondramatic musical, pictorial, graphic and sculptural works. It does not apply to dramatic works, literary works or audiovisual works.

This section provides for a compulsory license under which public broadcasting entities may reproduce, publicly perform or publicly display covered works in the process of producing and transmitting noncommercial educational programs. A public broadcasting entity may produce and transmit a program containing performances or displays of published nondramatic musical works and or published pictorial, graphic, or sculptural works. The entity may also reproduce copies of the program, if the copies are distributed only for purposes of other broadcasts by noncommercial educational broadcast stations. Arbitration panels convened by the Librarian of Congress set the fee, but copyright holders and educational broadcasters can agree to different rates and can agree to rates covering works not covered by this section.

3.8 Audio Home Recording Act—§1008

Section 1008, often referred to as the Audio Home Recording Act, prohibits a copyright holder from suing for copyright infringement because of a consumer's noncommercial use of a recording device to make either digital or analog copies of musical recordings.

The Audio Home Recording Act applies only to the reproduction right. It does not authorize public distribution, public performances or public display of works. Nor does it authorize the creation of any derivative works.

Section 1008 applies to any noncommercial digital or analog reproduction of musical recordings by a consumer using a digital or analog recording device. Neither the Audio Home Recording Act nor the legislative history define who a consumer is. *Black's Law Dictionary* defines a consumer as a user

3.8 continued of a final product or one who purchases, uses, maintains, or disposes of products. The consumer protection laws define a consumer as a buyer of a consumer product. Libraries meet either of these definitions. In discussions on the CNI-COPYRIGHT listserv in the spring of 1994, law professors were divided on the issue of whether copies made by nonprofit libraries could be considered noncommercial copies made by a consumer under §1008. Courts could go either way, but at present, there does not appear to be anything in the statute or the legislative history to prevent libraries from using the section to authorize copying of musical recordings.

To benefit from §1008, the consumer must make the recording using either a digital or analog recording device. A digital or analog recording device is any device of a type commonly distributed to individuals that is designed primarily for making sound recordings. The statutory definition excludes professional model recorders, dictating machines, answering machines and other devices designed primarily for recording nonmusical sounds.

The Audio Home Recording Act applies only to musical works. Unlike many other sections applicable to musical works, it makes no distinction between dramatic musical works and nondramatic musical works. The Act specifically excludes sound recordings of literary works, computer programs, and audiovisual works.

Since the Audio Home Recording Act compensates copyright holders through royalties collected on recording equipment and blank media, it allows copying for much broader purposes than many other sections of the copyright law. The only limitation on the purpose of copying is that it must be for noncommercial purposes. Since archival or backup copying is usually for noncommercial purposes, this section probably allows libraries to make backup copies of audiotapes and CDs containing musical works. It would not, however, authorize a library to make backup copies of talking books, because the Act specifically excludes sound recordings of literary works.

Another important aspect of §1008 is that it protects libraries from potential liability as a contributory infringer when patrons make copies of musical recordings borrowed from the library. It would also protect a library from liability for contributory infringement if a patron used equipment provided by the library to make a noncommercial copy of a musical recording.

4. Public Display

4.1 First Sale Doctrine and Transfers of a Particular Copy—§109

RIGHTS AFFECTED BY §109

Section 109, often called the first sale doctrine, is primarily applicable to the rights of public distribution and public display. Although one subsection, discussed on page 89, applies to the public performance of video games, most of §109 does not apply to public performances.[85] Section 109 does not authorize any reproduction of copyrighted works. Nor does it authorize the production of any derivative works.

WHO MAY USE §109

Most of the rights granted by §109 apply only to owners of copies and phonorecords. Subsection (d) specifically states that the rights granted by the main subsections do not apply to lawful possessors of copies who do not actually own those copies. This means the people who rent, lease, borrow, or license copyrighted works cannot take advantage of most of the provisions of §109. Transactions involving shrink-wrap licenses are sometimes considered sales rather than licenses, and thus may not result in the loss of §109 rights. However, the use of a license that must be signed by the licensee can make the purchaser a possessor rather than an owner of the copy and thus eliminate all §109 rights.

If the copyright holder chooses to lease or license a copy of a copyrighted work to a library, the library has no §109 right to publicly distribute or display the work without the copyright holder's permission. Since many electronic works are currently licensed rather than sold, libraries may need permission from the copyright holder to further distribute such works to the public unless another limitation on the distribution right is applicable.

---

85. *Columbia Pictures Industries v. Redd Horne, Inc.*, 749 F.2d 154, 160 (3d Cir. 1984); *Columbia Pictures Industries v. Aveco*, 800 F.2d 59, 64 (3d Cir. 1986).

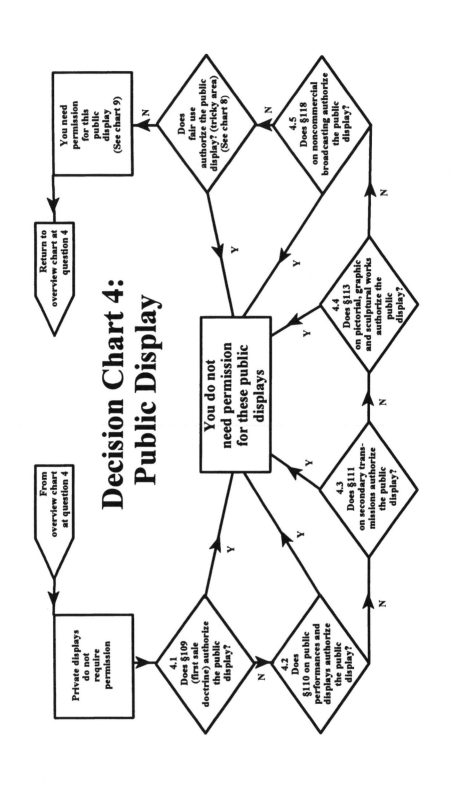

Decision Chart 4: Public Display

From overview chart at question 4

Private displays do not require permission

4.1 Does §109 (first sale doctrine) authorize the public display?

N →

4.2 Does §110 on public performances and displays authorize the public display?

N →

4.3 Does §111 on secondary trans-missions authorize the public display?

N →

4.4 Does §113 on pictorial, graphic and sculptural works authorize the public display?

N →

4.5 Does §118 on noncommercial broadcasting authorize the public display?

N →

Y

You do not need permission for these public displays

Does fair use authorize the public display? (tricky area) (See chart 8)

Y

N →

Return to overview chart at question 4

You need permission for this public display (See chart 9)

N

WORKS COVERED BY §109

The general provisions of §109 apply to all categories of copyrighted works. However, additional subsections limit the rights granted by the general subsections for sound recordings of musical works and computer programs. The final subsection also contains additional provisions for coin-operated versions of video games and video game cartridges.

DIRECT PUBLIC DISPLAY UNDER §109

Subsection (c) of §109 authorizes the owner of a particular lawfully made copy to display the copy either by direct display or by means of "projection of no more than one image at a time, to viewers present at the place where the copy is located." Thus, a library can publicly display an original copy or a copy lawfully made under another section such as §107 or §108.

Section 109 does not give a library the right to publicly perform a copy which it has lawfully made. The distinction between a performance and a display is important, especially for audiovisual works which usually must be performed to communicate their contents to users. (See pages 35 and 39 for a discussion of what constitutes a public display or a public performance.)

The §109 right to display is also confined to viewers present at the place where the copy is located. Transmission to remote viewers is not authorized under §109(c).

The applicability of this section to displays of electronic works is likely to be extremely limited. First, many electronic versions of works are licensed, not sold, and thus, the library does not own the copy of the work being displayed. Second, direct display is of little use since electronic copies cannot be perceived without the aid of a machine and they often must be transmitted from a server to a terminal. Third, the limitation is restricted to display by means of projection of no more than one image at a time, to viewers present at the place where the copy is located. The section does not extend to displays where the image is transmitted by any method including a computer system.[86] The legislative history indicates that "place where the copy is located" should be interpreted broadly to include situations where the "viewers are present in the same physical surrounding as the copy, even though they cannot see it directly."[87] It is unlikely, however, to include projection through a computer to viewers located in different buildings or further way. Furthermore, the one image at a time restriction would not allow two patrons at different terminals to look at the same or different parts of the work simultaneously.

---

86. H.R. Rep. No. 94-1476 at 80.
87. *Id.*

4.2 Display Exemptions in §110

RIGHTS AFFECTED BY §110

§110 applies only to the rights of public performance and public display. It does not authorize any reproductions, public distributions or the production of any derivative works. Some subsections authorize public performances of only some types of works while authorizing public displays of all types of works. So it is important to understand the distinction between a performance and a display. See pages 35 and 39 for a discussion of what constitutes a display or performance.

WHO MAY USE §110

Section 110 is divided into ten subsections. Each subsection is a separate limitation which is available only to the types of users listed in that particular subsection. Some subsections apply only to nonprofit educational institutions or specific types of nonprofit organizations while others may be available to anyone including commercial establishments. Examine each subsection carefully to determine whether your library meets the requirements of the subsection.

WORKS COVERED BY §110

Some subsections of §110 apply to all types of works. Other subsections apply only to nondramatic literary or musical works. Several subsections apply only to nondramatic musical works. One subsection is even specific to nondramatic musical works of a religious nature. It is very important not to combine or confuse the various subsections. Each subsection is a separate limitation and each applies only to the types of works specified in that particular subsection.

FACE-TO-FACE TEACHING EXCEPTION—§110(1)

Section 110(1) allows public performances and displays of a work during face-to-face teaching activities in a classroom or similar place devoted to instruction in a nonprofit educational institution. This subsection applies to both performances and displays. It also applies to all types of works, including dramatic literary and musical works, audiovisual works, and pictorial, graphic, and sculptural works.

This subsection is extremely important to teachers. It is also important to libraries in nonprofit educational institutions because a library in an educational institution is a similar place devoted to instruction.[88] By analogy to this and other examples in the legislative history, the library's computers and computer systems are probably also similar places of instruction. Section 110(1) has no applicability to libraries that are not part of nonprofit educational institutions.

The public performances and displays authorized by subsection (1) are limited to performances and displays that occur during face-to-face teaching activities. The performance or display must be part of a teaching activity. Teaching activities encompass a variety of activities related to systematic instruction, but they do not include activities which are primarily related to recreation and entertainment.[89] Face-to-face teaching does not require the instructor and the students to be able to see each other, but it does require their simultaneous presence in the same general area.

The legislative history also indicates that the term "face-to-face" is intended to exclude performances and displays that are transmitted. Since information stored in a retrieval system usually must be transmitted from the main computer to the user's terminal to be displayed on the screen, most uses of such systems will not occur in a face-to-face setting even if the use is part of teaching activities. In the limited situation where the material to be displayed or performed is located on a computer in the same building or general area as the instructor and the students and the use is part of regular teaching activities, §110(1) might authorize the public display and performance. An example of such a situation might be a class conducted in a CD-ROM lab at a college library to teach students to use the library's CD-ROM databases.

EDUCATIONAL AND GOVERNMENT TRANSMISSION EXCEPTION—§110(2)

Transmitted performances and displays are covered by §110(2) which is considerably more restricted than §110(1). A performance or display is transmitted if images or sounds are communicated beyond the place from which they were sent.[90] The legislative history says that the definition of transmission is

> broad enough to include all conceivable forms and combinations of wired or wireless communications media, including but by no means limited to radio and television broadcasting as we know them. Each and every method by which the images or sounds comprising a performance or display are picked up and conveyed is a "transmission...."[91]

---

88. H.R. Rep. No. 94-1476 at 82.
89. H.R. Rep. No. 94-1476 at 81.
90. 17 U.S.C. §101 (1995).
91. H.R. Rep. No. 94-1476 at 65.

| 4.2 *continued* | The use of closed circuit television and sound systems clearly involves transmissions. Several examples in the legislative history also make it clear that transmissions often occur in the use of electronic forms of works.

Section 110(2) is limited to performances of nondramatic literary and musical works. It does not authorize performances of dramatic literary works, dramatic musical works, or audiovisual works. Since computer programs are nondramatic literary works, §110(2) would apply to transmitting performances of computer programs. However, it would not apply to performances of dramatic literary works, dramatic musical works or audiovisual works stored in electronic media. Section 110(2) applies to displays of all types of works. The significance of the distinction between performances and displays is that subsection (2) does not authorize the sequential[92] showing of images from an audiovisual work or the recitation, playing, dancing or acting out of dramatic works, pantomimes, or choreographic works. It would authorize a transmission showing selected still images from an audiovisual work, especially if they were out of sequence, because that would be a display.

Transmissions of performances and displays are authorized under §110(2) only for nonprofit educational institutions and governmental bodies. It does not authorize transmissions by any other entities. So only libraries in nonprofit educational institutions and governmental libraries can use §110(2).

In order for this subsection to authorize the performances and displays, the performances and displays must be a regular part of systematic instructional activities. The legislative history states that

> The concept of "systematic instructional activities" is intended as a general equivalent of "curriculums," but it could be broader in a case such as that of an institution using systematic teaching methods not related to specific course work. A transmission would be a regular part of these activities if it is in accordance with the pattern of teaching established by the governmental body or institution.[93]

Since doing research and consulting all types of works is a regular part of most educational activities, many transmitted performances and displays in libraries of nonprofit educational institutions would probably meet this condition. However, in governmental libraries, performances and displays that are part of systematic instructional activities are likely to be a much smaller percentage of the transmissions of performances that the library is likely to want to engage in. Performances or displays related primarily to entertainment or

---

92. The nonsequential showing of images from an audiovisual work is a display, and thus, is permitted. 17 U.S.C. §101 (1995).
93. H.R. Rep. No. 94-1476 at 83; S. Rep. No. 94-473 at 75.

recreation, for example, would not be authorized under this subsection because they would not be a part of systematic instructional activities.

The performance or display must also be directly related to the teaching content of the transmission. When the transmission is the result of using electronic forms of information, the performance or display will probably be directly related to the teaching content of the transmission because electronic information cannot be observed or comprehended without a display or a performance.

Section 110(2) also limits where or who the recipients of the transmission can be. The user, who is the recipient of the transmission, must be in a classroom or similar place of instruction such as a library. It is possible that the library or institution's computer itself is a similar place of instruction so that §110(2) might authorize transmission to any terminal directly connected to or located in the same general area as the main computer. (See page 81.) Similar place of instruction probably does not extend to computers located in homes or offices connected to the library's computer via modems or wide area networks rather than directly.

Section 110(2) authorizes transmissions to persons to whom the transmission is directed because their disabilities or other special circumstances prevent their attendance in classrooms or similar places of instruction. The legislative history indicates that this provision covers telecourses aimed at students who are unable to attend daytime classes because of daytime employment, distance from campus, or another intervening reason.[94] Since the reasons for the transmission of information from a computer to remote users are so similar to telecourses, transmission of computer displays or performances to remote patrons affiliated with nonprofit educational institutions and government bodies is probably also covered by this clause. This reasoning probably cannot be extended to cover transmission to nearby people who simply find it inconvenient to come to the library, such as transmission to students in dorm rooms.

The third clause of §110(2)(C) permits transmission to officers and employees of governmental bodies as part of their official duties or employment. This clause may authorize transmission of displays and performances to employees of governmental institutions using governmental libraries, but it does not extend to other patrons of governmental libraries such as members of the public using government sponsored libraries.

HOME RECEIVING DEVICE EXCEPTION—§110(5)

Subsection (5) of §110 permits the public reception of a transmitted performance or display on a single receiving device of a kind commonly used in

---

94. H.R. Rep. No. 94-1476 at 84.

4.2 continued private homes, unless a direct charge is assessed to see or hear the transmission or the transmission is retransmitted to the public.

Early decisions under the 1976 Act used a three-part test to determine whether an organization's equipment met the requirement of "a single receiving apparatus of a kind commonly used in private homes." First the organization had to show that the reception system was of a type commonly used in private homes. Second, the organization had to show that the performance or display was not "further transmitted" to the public. Finally the organization had to show that it was a small commercial establishment.[95] Under these cases, courts often found that organizations could not use the home receiving device exemption. Factors that tended to prevent an organization from using the exemption included using more than four speakers,[96] concealing the speakers in the ceiling or walls,[97] concealing the wiring in the ceiling or walls[98] placing the speakers more than 35 feet from the receiver,[99] having more than 1055 square feet in the area where the transmission could be seen or heard,[100] and having a substantial source of revenue from which to pay license fees.[101] The first four factors were usually related to whether the receiving apparatus was of a type commonly found in private homes. The location and length of the

95. *Hickory Grove Music v. Andrews*, 749 F. Supp. 1031, 1037 (D. Mont. 1990); *International Korwin Corp. v. Kowalczyk*, 855 F.2d 375, 378 (7th Cir. 1988); *Gnossos Music v. DiPompo*, 13 U.S.P.Q.2d 1539, 1542 (D. Me. 1989).

96. *St. Nicholas Music Inc., v. D.V.W., Inc.*, CIV No. C-84-0307W, 1985 WL 9624, 1 (D. Utah Feb. 20, 1985); *Rodgers v. Eighty Four Lumber Co.*, 617 F. Supp. 1021, 1023 (W.D. Pa. 1985); *Little Mole Music v. Mavor's Supermarket No.4*, 12 U.S.P.Q.2d 1209 (N.D. Ohio 1988); *International Korwin Corp. v. Kowalczyk*, 855 F.2d 375, 377 (7th Cir. 1988); *Gnossos Music v. DiPompo*, 13 U.S.P.Q.2d 1539 (D. Me. 1989); *Crabshaw Music v. K-Bob's of El Paso Inc.*, 744 F. Supp. 763, 767 (W.D. Tex 1990).

97. *Lamminations Music v. P & X Markets, Inc.*, No. C-84-6840-WWS, 1985 WL 17704, 1 (N.D. Cal. Apr. 24, 1985); *Little Mole Music*, 1988 WL 167243, 6; *Merrill v. Bill Miller's Bar-B-Q Enterprises*, 688 F. Supp. 1172, 1174 (W.D. Tex. 1988); *Kowalczyk*, 855 F.2d 375, 377; *Gnossos Music*, 13 U.S.P.Q.2d 1539; *Hickory Grove Music*, 749 F. Supp. at 1037.

98. *Little Mole Music*, 12 U.S.P.Q.2d 1209, *Merrill*, 688 F. Supp. at 1174; *Kowalczyk*, 855 F.2d at 378; *Gnossos Music*, 13 U.S.P.Q.2d at 1542; *Hickory Grove Music*, 749 F. Supp. at 1037 (D. Mont. 1990).

99. *Broadcast Music Inc. v. United States Shoe Corp.*, 678 F.2d 816, 817 (9th Cir. 1982); *Hampaline House Publishing Corp v. Sal and Sam's Restaurant*, CIV A No 84-1296, 1985 WL 9451, 1 (E.D. LA Jan. 11, 1985); *Lamminations Music*, 1985 WL 17704, 1; *Merrill*, 688 F. Supp. at 1174.

100. *Sailor Music v. Gap Stores, Inc.*, 668 F.2d 84, 86 (2d Cir. 1981); *St. Nichols Music*, 1985 WL 9624, 1; *Lamminations Music*, 1985 WL 17704; *Rodgers v. Eighty Four Lumber Co.*, 617 F. Supp. at 1174; *Gnossos Music*, 13 U.S.P.Q.2d 1542; *Crabshaw Music*, 744 F. Supp. at 767.

101. *Sailor Music*, 668 F.2d at 86; *United States Shoe*, 678 F.2d at 817; *Lamminations Music*, 1985 WL 17704; *Merrill*, 688 F. Supp. at 1174.

speaker wires were often considered both in determining what type of apparatus was being used and in determining whether the performance was "further transmitted." The size of the establishment and its available income were used to determine whether the organization was a small commercial organization.

Recently, a number of courts have rejected this three-tiered approach, focusing more on the actual language of the statute and less upon the wording of the legislative history.[102] These courts do not consider the commercial status and profits of an organization to be relevant at all. The physical size of the establishment is also down played, although if sound can be heard at high quality over a very large area, it still tends to suggest that the equipment has been augmented beyond what is commonly found in private homes. The physical size of an establishment is no longer relevant for its own sake, however. While a number of speakers, ceiling mounts and concealed wiring may suggest a system is different from that commonly found in homes, these factors no longer automatically disqualify an organization from using the §110(5) exemption. The courts specifically note that ceiling speakers, speakers in multiple rooms and some concealed wiring are now commonly found in private homes. If other factors, such as the model of receiver used, are of a type commonly found in private homes today, they can outweigh factors that earlier courts relied on heavily to find that the receiving device was of a commercial type. Thus it appears that as home technology develops, §110(5) will permit the use of more advanced technology.

While the case law and legislative history for this subsection discuss only radios and televisions, the actual language of the statute is much broader. Personal computers have become quite commonplace in the home, and they can receive transmissions from other computers to which they are connected. Thus they may meet the requirements of subsection (5).

The only restrictions imposed by subsection (5) are that no direct charge can be made to see or hear the transmission and that the transmission cannot be retransmitted to the public. Both restrictions, however, are important. If a library charges patrons for database searches, it cannot use this subsection to authorize the public display that occurs when the search results are displayed on a terminal in a public place. If a library wishes to rely on this subsection to authorize the public displays that occur when patrons do remote searching, the library must also take steps to see to it that patrons do not retransmit the displays. Patrons could easily retransmit the information after downloading by including the information in an electronic mail message to a list or another person.

---

102. *Broadcast Music, Inc. v. Claire's Boutiques, Inc.*, 949 F.2d 1482 (7th Cir. 1990); *Edison Bros. Stores, Inc., v. Broadcast Music, Inc.*, 954 F.2d 1419 (8th Cir. 1992); *Cass County Music Co. v. Muedini*, 821 F. Supp. 1278 (E.D. Wis. 1993).

4.2 continued A combination of the restriction against retransmission and the fact that local area networks and direct connections to wide area networks are rarely found in private homes may also mean that §110(5) may not authorize displays associated with networked computers even though it might authorize the same displays on stand alone computers and computers equipped with modems. Modems and CD-ROM drives are becoming quite commonplace in private homes, however, so many library applications using these devices may be authorized by §110(5). In time, as wireless networks, computer cable connections and other forms of direct networking become more common in private homes, §110(5) may authorize the reception of many more transmissions of displays and performances that are part of library operations.

The biggest future limitation on the use of §110(5) is that it might give a library the right to display information transmitted by someone else, but it does not give a library the right to originate a transmission or retransmit information. Thus it will be more important for providing access to off-site materials than for providing access to material that the library actually houses.

4.3 Secondary Transmissions Limitation—§111

Section 111(a)(1) is unlikely to be applicable to libraries because it applies only to residential institutions and hotels.

Section 111(a)(2) permits the retransmission of a broadcast signal if all the conditions of §110(2) on educational transmissions are met. (See page 81.) It applies only to libraries in educational institutions.

Section 111(a)(3) exempts passive carriers from liability for copyright infringement resulting from their retransmissions of other transmissions. Passive carriers are organizations like the telephone company that have no control over the content of the retransmissions or over who receives the retransmissions. It is not generally applicable to libraries.

Section 111(a)(4) applies to satellite carriers who provide private home viewing. It is not generally applicable to libraries.

Section 111(a)(5) exempts certain secondary transmissions made by governmental or other nonprofit organizations. Since most libraries are nonprofit organizations, they are eligible to retransmit information from remote sources if they comply with the other requirements of §111(a)(5). The exemption usually applies only when the library retransmits a primary transmission intended for the public. The retransmission must be made without any purpose of direct or indirect commercial advantage. The library may only charge a sufficient amount to cover the actual and reasonable costs of retransmission.

Section 111(b) usually prohibits a library from controlling who receives the retransmissions. A library may control who receives its retransmissions only when it is rebroadcasting a broadcast of a station licensed by the FCC, and the library is acting as a station that is required by the FCC to retransmit the primary station's transmissions. In such cases the library is not permitted to alter the primary station's signal. This usually means that if a library wants to take advantage of §111, it cannot control who has access to its secondary transmissions. In short, it must allow any member of the public to have access.

The remainder of §111 applies only to cable systems which are defined as "a facility, located in any State, Territory, Trust Territory, or Possession, that in whole or in part receives signals transmitted or programs broadcast by one or more television broadcast stations licensed by the Federal Communications Commission, and makes secondary transmissions of such signals or programs by wires, cables, or other communications channels to subscribing members of the public who pay for such a service." Most libraries do not engage in services that meet the definition of a cable system.

4.4 Pictorial, Graphic, and Sculptural Works Limitation—§113

Section 113 is rarely of use to libraries. It applies only to pictorial, graphic and sculptural works. It applies only to the reproduction right, the public distribution right, and the public display right. It does not authorize any public performances or preparation of derivative works.

When useful articles embodying copyrighted pictorial, graphic, or sculptural works have been offered for sale or other public distribution, §113 allows the making, distribution and display of photographs or pictures of the useful article for the following purposes:
   a. in advertisements;
   b. in commentaries related to the distribution or display of the useful articles; and
   c. in connection with news reports.

4.5 Noncommercial Broadcasting Limitation—§118

Section 118 rarely applies to libraries because it applies only to public broadcasting entities which are defined to be noncommercial educational broadcast stations under 47 U.S.C. §397. Very few libraries meet this definition.

This section applies only to published nondramatic musical, pictorial, graphic and sculptural works. It does not apply to dramatic works, literary works or audiovisual works.

This section provides for a compulsory license under which public broadcasting entities may reproduce, publicly perform or publicly display covered works in the process of producing and transmitting noncommercial educational

4.5 *continued* | programs. A public broadcasting entity may produce and
transmit a program containing performances or displays of
published nondramatic musical works and or published pictorial, graphic, or
sculptural works. The entity may also reproduce copies of the program if the
copies are distributed only for purposes of other broadcasts by noncommercial educational broadcast stations. Arbitration panels convened by the Librarian of Congress set the fee, but copyright holders and educational broadcasters can agree to different rates and can agree to rates covering works not
covered by this section.

5. Public Performance

5.1 First Sale Doctrine and Transfers of a Particular Copy—§109

Section 109, often called the first sale doctrine, is primarily applicable to the rights of public distribution and public display. Although one subsection applies to the public performance of video games, most of §109 does not apply to public performances.[103] Subsection (e) of §109 authorizes the owner of a coin-operated video game to publicly perform that game. Video games distributed on diskettes and designed for use in general purpose computers, however, are not covered by this limitation.

5.2 Performance Exemptions in §110

RIGHTS AFFECTED BY §110

Section 110 applies only to the rights of public performance and public display. It does not authorize any reproductions, public distributions or the production of any derivative works. Some subsections authorize public performances of only some types of works while authorizing public displays of all types of works. So it is important to understand the distinction between a performance and a display. See pages 35 and 39 for a discussion of what constitutes a display or performance.

WHO MAY USE §110

Section 110 is divided into ten subsections. Each subsection is a separate limitation which is available only to the types of users listed in that particular

---

103. *Columbia Pictures v. Redd Horne, Inc.*, 749 F.2d 154, 160 (3d Cir. 1984); *Columbia Pictures Industries v. Aveco*, 800 F.2d 59, 64 (3d Cir. 1986).

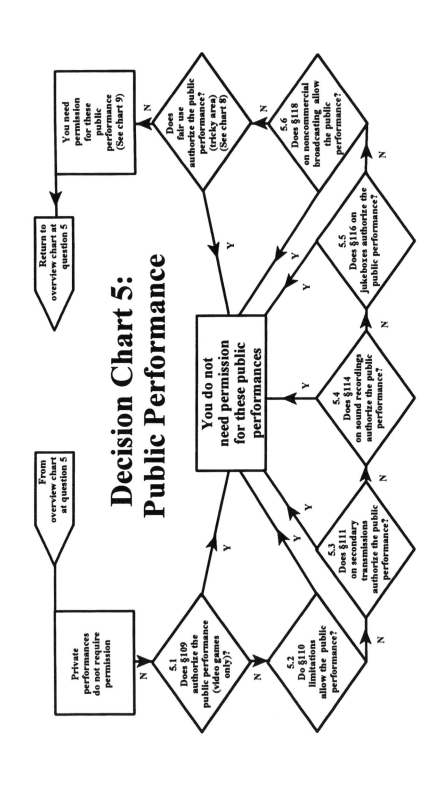

Decision Chart 5:
Public Performance

From overview chart at question 5

Return to overview chart at question 5

You need permission for these public performance (See chart 9)

Private performances do not require permission

5.1 Does §109 authorize the public performance (video games only)?

5.2 Do §110 limitations allow the public performance?

5.3 Does §111 on secondary transmissions authorize the public performance?

5.4 Does §114 on sound recordings authorize the public performance?

5.5 Does §116 on jukeboxes authorize the public performance?

5.6 Does §118 on noncommercial broadcasting allow the public performance?

Does fair use authorize the public performance? (tricky area) (See chart 8)

You do not need permission for these public performances

subsection. Some subsections apply only to nonprofit educational institutions or specific types of nonprofit organizations while others may be available to anyone including commercial establishments. Examine each subsection carefully to determine whether your library meets the requirements of the subsection.

WORKS COVERED BY §110

Some subsections of §110 apply to all types of works. Other subsections apply only to nondramatic literary or musical works. Several subsections apply only to nondramatic musical works. One subsection is even specific to nondramatic musical works of a religious nature. It is very important not to combine or confuse the various subsections. Each subsection is a separate limitation and each applies only to the types of works specified in that particular subsection.

FACE-TO-FACE TEACHING EXCEPTION — §110(1)

Section 110(1) allows public performances and displays of a work during face-to-face teaching activities in a classroom or similar place devoted to instruction in a nonprofit educational institution. This subsection applies to both performances and displays. It also applies to all types of works, including dramatic literary and musical works, audiovisual works, and pictorial, graphic, and sculptural works.

This subsection is extremely important to teachers. It is also important to libraries in nonprofit educational institutions because a library in an educational institution is a similar place devoted to instruction.[104] By analogy to this and other examples in the legislative history, the library's computers and computer systems are probably also similar places of instruction. Section 110(1) has no applicability to libraries that are not part of nonprofit educational institutions.

The public performances and displays authorized by subsection (1) are limited to performances and displays that occur during face-to-face teaching activities. The performance or display must be part of a teaching activity. Teaching activities encompass a variety of activities related to systematic instruction, but they do not include activities which are primarily related to recreation and entertainment.[105] Face-to-face teaching does not require the instructor and the students to be able to see each other, but it does require their

---

104. H.R. Rep. No. 94-1476 at 82.
105. H.R. Rep. No. 94-1476 at 81.

5.2 continued simultaneous presence in the same general area.

The legislative history also indicates that the term "face-to-face" is intended to exclude performances and displays that are transmitted. Since information stored in a retrieval system usually must be transmitted from the main computer to the user's terminal to be displayed on the screen, most uses of such systems will not occur in a face-to-face setting even if the use is part of teaching activities. In the limited situation where the material to be displayed or performed is located on a computer in the same building or general area as the instructor and the students and the use is part of regular teaching activities, §110(1) might authorize the public display and performance. An example of such a situation might be a class conducted in a CD-ROM lab at a college library to teach students to use the library's CD-ROM databases.

EDUCATIONAL AND GOVERNMENT TRANSMISSION EXCEPTION—§110(2)

Transmitted performances and displays are covered by §110(2) which is considerably more restricted than §110(1). A performance or display is transmitted if images or sounds are communicated beyond the place from which they were sent.[106] The legislative history says that the definition of transmission is

> broad enough to include all conceivable forms and combinations of wired or wireless communications media, including but by no means limited to radio and television broadcasting as we know them. Each and every method by which the images or sounds comprising a performance or display are picked up and conveyed is a "transmission...."[107]

The use of closed circuit television and sound systems clearly involves transmissions. Several examples in the legislative history also make it clear that transmissions often occur in the use of electronic forms of works.

Section 110(2) is limited to performances of nondramatic literary and musical works. It does not authorize public performances of dramatic literary works, dramatic musical works, or audiovisual works. Since computer programs are nondramatic literary works, §110(2) would apply to transmitting performances of computer programs. However, it would not apply to performances of dramatic literary works, dramatic musical works or audiovisual works stored in electronic media. Section 110(2) applies to displays of all types of works. The significance of the distinction between performances and

---

106. 17 U.S.C. §101 (1995).
107. H.R. Rep. No. 94-1476 at 65.

displays is that subsection (2) does not authorize the sequential[108] showing of images from an audiovisual work or the recitation, playing, dancing or acting out of dramatic works, pantomimes, or choreographic works. It would authorize a transmission showing selected still images from an audiovisual work, especially if they were out of sequence, because that would be a display.

Transmissions of performances and displays are authorized under §110(2) only for nonprofit educational institutions and governmental bodies. It does not authorize transmissions by any other entities. So only libraries in nonprofit educational institutions and governmental libraries can use §110(2).

In order for this subsection to authorize the performances and displays, the performances and displays must be a regular part of systematic instructional activities. The legislative history states that

> The concept of "systematic instructional activities" is intended as a general equivalent of "curriculums," but it could be broader in a case such as that of an institution using systematic teaching methods not related to specific course work. A transmission would be a regular part of these activities if it is in accordance with the pattern of teaching established by the governmental body or institution.[109]

Since doing research and consulting all types of works is a regular part of most educational activities, many transmitted performances and displays in libraries of nonprofit educational institutions would probably meet this condition. However, in governmental libraries, performances and displays that are part of systematic instructional activities are likely to be a much smaller percentage of the transmissions of performances that the library is likely to want to engage in. Performances or displays related primarily to entertainment or recreation, for example, would not be authorized under this subsection because they would not be a part of systematic instructional activities.

The performance or display must also be directly related to the teaching content of the transmission. When the transmission is the result of using electronic forms of information, the performance or display will probably be directly related to the teaching content of the transmission because electronic information cannot be observed or comprehended without a display or a performance.

Section 110(2) also limits where or who the recipients of the transmission can be. The user, who is the recipient of the transmission, must be in a classroom or similar place of instruction such as a library. It is possible that the library or institution's computer itself is a similar place of instruction so that §110(2) might authorize transmission to any terminal directly connected to or

---

108. The nonsequential showing of images from an audiovisual work is a display, and thus, is permitted. 17 U.S.C. §101 (1995).

109. H.R. Rep. No. 94-1476 at 83; S. Rep. No. 94-473 at 75.

| 5.2 continued | located in the same general area as the main computer. (See page 81.) Similar place of instruction probably does not extend |

to computers located in homes or offices connected to the library's computer via modems or wide area networks rather than directly.

Section 110(2) authorizes transmissions to persons to whom the transmission is directed because their disabilities or other special circumstances prevent their attendance in classrooms or similar places of instruction. The legislative history indicates that this provision covers telecourses aimed at students who are unable to attend daytime classes because of daytime employment, distance from campus, or another intervening reason.[110] Since the reasons for the transmission of information from a computer to remote users are so similar to telecourses, transmission of computer displays or performances to remote patrons affiliated with nonprofit educational institutions and government bodies is probably also covered by this clause. This reasoning probably cannot be extended to cover transmission to nearby people who simply find it inconvenient to come to the library, such as transmission to students in dorm rooms.

The third clause of §110(2)(C) permits transmission to officers and employees of governmental bodies as part of their official duties or employment. This clause may authorize transmission of displays and performances to employees of governmental institutions using governmental libraries, but it does not extend to other patrons of governmental libraries such as members of the public using government sponsored libraries.

PERFORMANCES AS PART OF RELIGIOUS SERVICES—§110(3)

Subsection (3) of 110 permits performances of nondramatic literary or musical works and dramatico-musical works of a religious nature during religious services. It does not apply to a library unless religious services are being conducted in the library.

NONPROFIT PERFORMANCES OF NONDRAMATIC LITERARY AND MUSICAL WORKS—§110(4)

Subsection (4) authorizes nonprofit performances of nondramatic literary and musical works under certain conditions provided that the performance is not transmitted to the public. This subsection applies only to nondramatic literary and musical works. It does not apply to audiovisual works or to dramatic literary and musical works.

This exception is also subject to several other restrictions. The performance cannot be transmitted to the public although the public may be present at the

---

110. H.R. Rep. No. 94-1476 at 84.

place where the performance is taking place. The purpose of the performance cannot be direct or indirect commercial advantage. The performers, promoters and organizers cannot be paid, but other staff such as directors and lighting assistants can be paid.

Admission cannot be charged directly or indirectly unless

1. all proceeds, after deducting reasonable costs of production, are used exclusively for educational, religious, or charitable purposes and
2. the copyright holder has not served notice of objection by a signed writing at least seven days before the performance.

This subsection would authorize public readings of nondramatic literary works (such as poetry readings and children's story hour) if no charge were made or if the admission charge benefitted a nonprofit library. It would also authorize musical performances in a local talent show held in a library meeting room if the performances were not of dramatic material. Performances at community theaters probably would not be authorized by this subsection because those performances are usually of dramatic works.

HOME RECEIVING DEVICE EXCEPTION—§110(5)

Subsection (5) of §110 permits the public reception of a transmitted performance or display on a single receiving device of a kind commonly used in private homes, unless a direct charge is assessed to see or hear the transmission or the transmission is retransmitted to the public.

Early decisions under the 1976 Act used a three-part test to determine whether an organization's equipment met the requirement of "a single receiving apparatus of a kind commonly used in private homes." First the organization had to show that the reception system was of a type commonly used in private homes. Second, the organization had to show that the performance or display was not "further transmitted" to the public. Finally the organization had to show that it was a small commercial establishment.[111] Under these cases, courts often found that organizations could not use the home receiving device exemption. Factors that tended to prevent an organization from using the exemption included using more than four speakers,[112] concealing the speakers

---

111. *Hickory Grove Music v. Andrews*, 749 F. Supp. 1031, 1037 (D. Mont. 1990); *International Korwin Corp. v. Kowalczyk*, 855 F.2d 375, 378 (7th Cir. 1988); *Gnossos Music v. DiPompo*, 13 U.S.P.Q.2d 1539, 1542 (D. Me. 1989).

112. *St. Nicholas Music Inc., v. D.V.W., Inc.*, CIV No. C-84-0307W, 1985, WL 9624, 1 (D. Utah Feb. 20, 1985); *Rodgers v. Eighty Four Lumber Co.*, 617 F. Supp. 1021, 1023 (W.D. Pa. 1985); *Little Mole Music v. Mavor's Supermarket No. 4*, 12 U.S.P.Q.2d 1209 (N.D. Ohio 1988); *International Korwin Corp. v. Kowalczyk*, 855 F.2d 375, 377 (7th Cir. 1988); *Gnossos Music v. DiPompo*, 13 U.S.P.Q.2d 1539 (D. Me. 1989); *Crabshaw Music v. K-Bob's of El Paso Inc.*, 744 F. Supp. 763, 767 (W.D. Tex. 1990).

5.2 *continued* in the ceiling or walls,[113] concealing the wiring in the ceiling or walls[114] placing the speakers more than 35 feet from the receiver,[115] having more than 1055 square feet in the area where the transmission could be seen or heard,[116] and having a substantial source of revenue from which to pay license fees.[117] The first four factors were usually related to whether the receiving apparatus was of a type commonly found in private homes. The location and length of the speaker wires were often considered both in determining what type of apparatus was being used and in determining whether the performance was "further transmitted." The size of the establishment and its available income were used to determine whether the organization was a small commercial organization.

Recently, a number of courts have rejected this three-tiered approach, focusing more on the actual language of the statute and less upon the wording of the legislative history.[118] These courts do not consider the commercial status and profits of an organization to be relevant at all. The physical size of the establishment is also down played, although if sound can be heard at high quality over a very large area, it still tends to suggest that the equipment has been augmented beyond what is commonly found in private homes. The physical size of an establishment is no longer relevant for its own sake, however. While a number of speakers, ceiling mounts and concealed wiring may suggest a system is different from that commonly found in homes, these factors no longer automatically disqualify an organization from using the §110(5) exemption. The courts specifically note that ceiling speakers, speakers in multiple rooms and some concealed wiring are now commonly found in private

---

113. *Lamminations Music v. P & X Markets, Inc.*, No. C-84-6840-WWS, 1985 WL 17704, 1 (N.D. Cal. Apr. 24, 1985); *Little Mole Music*, 1988 WL 167243, 6; *Merrill v. Bill Miller's Bar-B-Q Enterprises*, 688 F. Supp. 1172, 1174 (W.D. Tex. 1988); *Kowalczyk*, 855 F.2d 375, 377; *Gnossos Music*, 13 U.S.P.Q.2d 1539; *Hickory Grove Music*, 749 F. Supp. at 1037.

114. *Little Mole Music*, 12 U.S.P.Q.2d 1209, *Merrill*, 688 F. Supp. at 1174; *Kowalczyk*, 855 F.2d at 378; *Gnossos Music*, 13 U.S.P.Q.2d at 1542; *Hickory Grove Music*, 749 F. Supp. at 1037 (D. Mont. 1990).

115. *Broadcast Music Inc. v. United States Shoe Corp.*, 678 F.2d 816, 817 (9th Cir. 1982); *Hampaline House Publishing Corp. v. Sal and Sam's Restaurant*, CIV A No. 84-1296, 1985 WL 9451, 1 (E.D. LA Jan. 11, 1985); *Lamminations Music*, 1985 WL 17704, 1; *Merrill*, 688 F. Supp. at 1174.

116. *Sailor Music v. Gap Stores, Inc.*, 668 F.2d 84, 86 (2d Cir. 1981); *St. Nichols Music*, 1985 WL 9624, 1; *Lamminations Music*, 1985 WL 17704; *Rodgers v. Eighty Four Lumber Co.*, 617 F. Supp. at 1174; *Gnossos Music*, 13 U.S.P.Q.2d 1542; *Crabshaw Music*, 744 F. Supp. at 767.

117. *Sailor Music*, 668 F.2d at 86; *United States Shoe*, 678 F.2d at 817; *Lamminations Music*, 1985 WL 17704; *Merrill*, 688 F. Supp. at 1174.

118. *Broadcast Music, Inc. v. Claire's Boutiques, Inc.*, 949 F.2d 1482 (7th Cir. 1990); *Edison Bros. Stores, Inc., v. Broadcast Music, Inc.*, 954 F.2d 1419 (8th Cir. 1992); *Cass County Music Co. v. Muedini*, 821 F. Supp. 1278 (E.D. Wis. 1993).

homes. If other factors, such as the model of receiver used, are of a type commonly found in private homes today, they can outweigh factors that earlier courts relied on heavily to find that the receiving device was of a commercial type. Thus it appears that as home technology develops, §110(5) will permit the use of more advanced technology.

While the case law and legislative history for this subsection discuss only radios and televisions, the actual language of the statute is much broader. Personal computers have become quite commonplace in the home, and they can receive transmissions from other computers to which they are connected. Thus they may meet the requirements of subsection (5).

The only restrictions imposed by subsection (5) are that no direct charge can be made to see or hear the transmission and that the transmission cannot be retransmitted to the public. Both restrictions, however, are important. If a library charges patrons for database searches, it cannot use this subsection to authorize the public display that occurs when the search results are displayed on a terminal in a public place. If a library wishes to rely on this subsection to authorize the public displays that occur when patrons do remote searching, the library must also take steps to see to it that patrons do not retransmit the displays. Patrons could easily retransmit the information after downloading by including the information in an electronic mail message to a list or another person.

A combination of the restriction against retransmission and the fact that local area networks and direct connections to wide area networks are rarely found in private homes may also mean that §110(5) may not authorize displays associated with networked computers even though it might authorize the same displays on stand alone computers and computers equipped with modems. Modems and CD-ROM drives are becoming quite commonplace in private homes, however, so many library applications using these devices may be authorized by §110(5). In time, as wireless networks, computer cable connections and other forms of direct networking become more common in private homes, §110(5) may authorize the reception of many more transmissions of displays and performances that are part of library operations.

The biggest future limitation on the use of §110(5) is that it might give a library the right to display information transmitted by someone else, but it does not give a library the right to originate a transmission or retransmit information. Thus it will be more important for providing access to off-site materials than for providing access to material that the library actually houses.

COUNTY FAIR EXEMPTION—§110(6)

Subsection (6) covers certain performances during agricultural and horticultural fairs. It is not applicable to libraries.

5.2 *continued* MUSIC STORE EXEMPTION — §110(7)

Subsection (7) allows certain performances of nondramatic musical works as part of the process of selling phonorecords and sheet music. It is generally not applicable to libraries.

EXEMPTIONS FOR THE HANDICAPPED — §110(8) AND §110(9)

Subsections (8) and (9) cover certain performances during transmissions directed at handicapped individuals.

Subsection (8) authorizes performances of nondramatic literary works. It does not apply to dramatic, musical or audiovisual works. The performances must be part of a transmission specifically designed for and primarily directed to blind or handicapped people who are unable to read normal printed material because of their handicap. Performances directed to deaf or other handicapped people who are unable to hear the aural sounds accompanying a transmission of visual signals may also be authorized. The performance must be made without any purpose of direct or indirect commercial advantage. In addition to the other requirements, the transmission must be made through the facilities of a governmental body or a noncommercial broadcast station or someone with a radio subcarrier authorization or a cable system.

This subsection would permit readings of nondramatic literary works over public radio in a program directed primarily at handicapped people. It would also permit readings of nondramatic literary works or signing of nondramatic literary works over a closed circuit system in a public library run by a local government or a governmental educational institution.

If all the conditions were met, it might even authorize the performance part of a system in which a handicapped student connected to a governmental library's computer (or any other governmental computer) by modem could choose a work from the computer and have it read aloud through the computer's speech processor. Some other authorization would have to be found for the performances of works other than nondramatic literary works in such a system, however, because §110(8) is limited to nondramatic literary works.

Subsection (9) permits limited performance on a single occasion of a dramatic literary work published at least ten years before the date of the performance. The performance must occur by or in the course of a transmission specifically designed for and primarily directed to blind or other handicapped persons who are unable to read normal printed material because of their handicap. The performance must be made without any purpose of direct or indirect commercial advantage. In addition, the transmission must be made through the facilities of an authorized radio carrier.

Unlike subsection (8), this subsection applies to dramatic literary works.

It does not apply to dramatico-musical works, musical works or audiovisual works.

The works performed under this section must be at least ten years old. The facilities which may be used for transmissions under subsection (9) are much more limited than the facilities available under subsection (8). Very few if any libraries meet the requirement of an authorized radio carrier.

VETERANS AND FRATERNAL ORGANIZATION EXEMPTION — §110(10)

Subsection (10) permits performances of nondramatic literary or musical works during certain social events organized and promoted by nonprofit veterans and fraternal organizations. It is generally not applicable to libraries, although it might be applicable to performances that occur in a library community room when it is being used by a veterans or fraternal organization for a social event.

5.3 Secondary Transmissions Limitation—§111

Section 111(a)(1) is unlikely to be applicable to libraries because it applies only to residential institutions and hotels.

Section 111(a)(2) permits the retransmission of a broadcast signal if all the conditions of §110(2) on educational transmissions are met. (See page 92.) It applies only to libraries in educational institutions.

Section 111(a)(3) exempts passive carriers from liability for copyright infringement resulting from their retransmissions of other transmissions. Passive carriers are organizations like the telephone company that have no control over the content of the retransmissions or over who receives the retransmissions. It is not generally applicable to libraries.

Section 111(a)(4) applies to satellite carriers who provide private home viewing. It is not generally applicable to libraries.

Section 111(a)(5) exempts certain secondary transmissions made by governmental or other nonprofit organizations. Since most libraries are nonprofit organizations, they are eligible to retransmit information from remote sources if they comply with the other requirements of §111(a)(5). The exemption usually applies only when the library retransmits a primary transmission intended for the public. The retransmission must be made without any purpose of direct or indirect commercial advantage. The library may only charge a sufficient amount to cover the actual and reasonable costs of retransmission.

Section 111(b) usually prohibits a library from controlling who receives the retransmissions. A library may control who receives its retransmissions only when it is rebroadcasting a broadcast of a station licensed by the FCC, and

$\boxed{\textit{5.3 continued}}$ the library is acting as a station that is required by the FCC to retransmit the primary station's transmissions. In such cases the library is not permitted to alter the primary station's signal. This usually means that if a library wants to take advantage of §111, it cannot control who has access to its secondary transmissions. In short, it must allow any member of the public to have access.

The remainder of §111 applies only to cable systems which are defined as "a facility, located in any State, Territory, Trust Territory, or Possession, that in whole or in part receives signals transmitted or programs broadcast by one or more television broadcast stations licensed by the Federal Communications Commission, and makes secondary transmissions of such signals or programs by wires, cables, or other communications channels to subscribing members of the public who pay for such a service." Most libraries do not engage in services that meet the definition of a cable system.

5.4 Sound Recordings Limitation—§114

Sound recordings recorded before February 15, 1972, are not protected by federal statutory copyright, but they may be protected by state statutes or state common law. The law in this area varies from state to state. Although the sound recording itself is not protected by federal statutory copyright, the underlying literary or musical work may be. The copyright in the underlying literary or musical work may restrict what you can do with the sound recording.

Although the copyright holder generally has the exclusive right to publicly perform a copyrighted work, the copyright holder in a sound recording produced after February 15, 1972, does not usually have the exclusive right of public performance. While the copyright holder in a sound recording may not have the exclusive right to publicly perform the sound recording, the copyright holder in any underlying work performed in the sound recording may have such rights and may prohibit others from playing the sound recording publicly. Thus while Whitney Houston may not have the right to prevent others from publicly playing her recording of *I Will Always Love You*, Dolly Parton, as the copyright holder in the song, has the right to prohibit public performances of Whitney Houston's recording.

The Digital Performance Right in Sound Recordings Act of 1995 grants the copyright holder of the sound recording a limited right to control public performances by means of digital audio transmissions.[119] This right applies only to performances that occur as part of audio digital transmissions. It does not apply to analog transmissions or to digital transmissions of audiovisual works.

---

119. PL 104-39, 109 Stat. 336 (Nov. 1, 1995).

Performances which occur as part of transmissions that can be received by any member of the public or for which no fee is charged are exempted from the sound recording copyright holder's control (but not the control of the copyright holder in the underlying work) by §114(d) unless the transmission is part of an interactive service. Interactive digital audio performances are not exempted, however, even if no charge is made for reception. Thus, while a digital radio broadcast picked up by a digital receiver would be exempt, a performance that occurred through the Internet when a user clicked on the link for a particular sound recording would infringe the sound recording copyright even if no fee were charged.[120]

5.5 Jukebox License—§116

Section 116 applies to a library only if the library owns a coin-operated jukebox. It governs licenses which apply only to the public performance right. It does not authorize any reproductions, public displays, public distribution or preparation of derivative works. Section 116 only authorizes public performances on coin-operated jukeboxes.

The jukebox license applies only to recordings of nondramatic musical works. It does not apply to dramatic musical works or literary works even if they are recorded in sound recordings. It does not apply to motion pictures, other audiovisual works or their sound tracks.

This section allows sound recordings to be played on jukeboxes if a license fee is paid. The fee is negotiated periodically between jukebox owners and copyright holders in sound recordings of nondramatic music. If jukebox operators cannot reach an agreement with the copyright owners, the Librarian of Congress may appoint an arbitration panel to settle the dispute.

5.6 Noncommercial Broadcasting Limitation—§118

Section 118 rarely applies to libraries because it applies only to public broadcasting entities which are defined to be noncommercial educational broadcast stations under 47 U.S.C. §397. Very few libraries meet this definition.

This section applies only to published nondramatic musical, pictorial, graphic and sculptural works. It does not apply to dramatic works, literary works or audiovisual works.

This section provides for a compulsory license under which public broadcasting entities may reproduce, publicly perform or publicly display covered

---

120. S. Rep. No. 104-128, 104th Cong., 1st Sess. (1995).

| 5.6 continued | works in the process of producing and transmitting noncommercial educational programs. A public broadcasting entity |

may produce and transmit a program containing performances or displays of published nondramatic musical works and or published pictorial, graphic, or sculptural works. The entity may also reproduce copies of the program, if the copies are distributed only for purposes of other broadcasts by noncommercial educational broadcast stations. Arbitration panels convened by the Librarian of Congress set the fee, but copyright holders and educational broadcasters can agree to different rates and can agree to rates covering works not covered by this section.

6. Public Distribution

6.1 Distribution of Reproductions by Libraries and Archives—§108

RIGHTS AFFECTED BY §108

Section 108 applies only to the rights of reproduction and public distribution. It will not authorize any public displays, public performances or production of derivative works.

WHO MAY USE §108

Section 108 covers only libraries and archives. It provides no protection to a commercial contractor who contracts with the library to provide reproduction services on the library's premises.[121] Libraries which are considering contracting out photocopying or other forms of reproduction and distribution on their premises should consider the implications of this restriction before entering into such a contract.

The §108 limitation is available only to libraries or archives that meet certain criteria. The library must be open to the public or make its collections available to unaffiliated researchers in the field that the library's collection encompasses. Most experts believe that making a library's collection available to unaffiliated researchers through interlibrary loan provides sufficient access for a library to qualify for §108 privileges. If a library lists itself as a nonsupplier on OCLC or any other interlibrary loan system, it probably cannot rely upon interlibrary loan to qualify for §108 privileges.

The reproduction or public distribution by a library under this section must be done without any purpose of direct commercial advantage. Any commercial advantage must be directly related to the reproduction or distribution to disqualify a library from using this section. Corporate libraries and other libraries in for-profit institutions may use this section if there is no direct commercial advantage associated with the reproduction and distribution itself.

---

121. H.R. Rep. No. 94-1476 at 74.

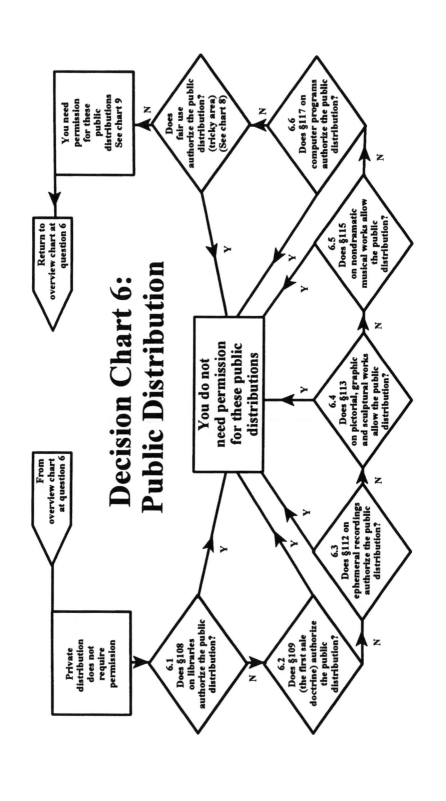

Decision Chart 6:
Public Distribution

From overview chart at question 6

Return to overview chart at question 6

You need permission for these public distributions See chart 9

Private distribution does not require permission

You do not need permission for these public distributions

Does fair use authorize the public distribution? (tricky area) (See chart 8)
N

6.1 Does §108 on libraries authorize the public distribution?
N

6.2 Does §109 (the first sale doctrine) authorize the public distribution?
N

6.3 Does §112 on ephemeral recordings authorize the public distribution?
N

6.4 Does §113 on pictorial, graphic and sculptural works allow the public distribution?
N

6.5 Does §115 on nondramatic musical works allow the public distribution?
N

6.6 Does §117 on computer programs authorize the public distribution?
N

Y

Although the district court in *American Geophysical Union v. Texaco*[122] implies in a nonbinding part of the opinion that the protection of §108 may not be available to corporate libraries, both the legislative history[123] and the opinion of most experts clearly indicate that the section is applicable to libraries that are part of for-profit enterprises.[124] An example of a situation in which the reproduction and distribution itself would result in direct commercial advantage would be a document delivery service where the fees charged exceed the actual costs associated with providing the service. Although §108 could not be used to justify reproduction or distribution as part of a for-profit document delivery service, it could still authorize reproduction and distribution that occurs as part of other nonprofit fee based services offered by the library.

WORKS COVERED BY §108

The preservation and replacement copying subsections of §108 apply to all types of works. The remainder of §108 applies to all types of works except musical works; pictorial, graphic or sculptural works; and motion pictures and other audiovisual works. Pictorial, graphic and sculptural works may be reproduced and distributed to patrons, however, if they are illustrations or adjuncts to other types of works. Although most of §108 does not authorize the reproduction and public distribution of most audiovisual works, it contains a special clause that allows libraries to reproduce audiovisual works dealing with news and distribute them to patrons.

The fact that §108 does not authorize copying and public distribution of certain types of works does not mean that all such copying and distribution is prohibited. If the copying and public distribution meets the criteria of another limitation or fair use, it may still be permitted.

DISTRIBUTION OF COPIES MADE UNDER §108

Section 108 contains a limitation on the distribution right. It says that it is not an infringement for a library to distribute a copy of a work made under the authority of §108. Some experts believe that this means that §108 authorizes any form of distribution, including forms in which the actual delivery

---

122. 802 F. Supp. 1, 27–28 (S.D.N.Y. 1992).

123. H.R. Rep. No. 94-1476 at 74–75.

124. Melville B. Nimmer and David Nimmer, *Nimmer on Copyright* (New York: Matthew Bender 1996), §8.03[a][1]; Paul Goldstein, *Copyright*, 2d ed. (Boston: Little Brown 1996), §5.2.2[a](1); James S. Heller & Sarah K. Wiant, *Copyright Handbook* (Rothman 1984), 15.

6.1 continued requires the making of an intermediary copy (such as telefacsimile and some electronic delivery systems) if the intermedi-
ary copy is not kept. They argue that the effect is the distribution of only a single copy.[125] Other experts disagree, arguing that any form of delivery that
requires the making of more than one copy exceeds the single copy restriction
in §108 and must be authorized by another section or licensed. The view that
§108 permits any form of delivery that results in the delivery of a single copy
to the user is probably the better view. The legislative history indicates that the
Act was designed to be flexible enough to accommodate new technologies.[126]
Thus, any section should be interpreted to permit the use of any technology
unless the language of the section clearly indicates an intention to limit the section to particular technologies. Subsections (d) and (e) of §108 do not use either
the "particular copy" language of §109 (see page 108) or the "facsimile" language
of subsections (b) and (c) of §108 (see page 63), so subsection (d) and (e) should
probably be interpreted to accommodate as many technologies as possible.

RELATIONSHIP BETWEEN FAIR USE AND §108

Both the language of §108 and the legislative history make it clear that
some uses not authorized by §108 may still be authorized by fair use. The legislative history specifically says that fair use may allow some uses of musical,
graphic and audiovisual works which are not authorized by §108.

Fair use and the decision in *Williams & Wilkins v. U.S.*,[127] however, should
not be relied upon to extend interlibrary copying and distribution beyond the
limits of the CONTU guidelines. In *Williams & Wilkins*, several medical publishers sued the National Library of Medicine and the National Institutes of
Health claiming that their massive photocopy services exceeded fair use. The
trial court found that the copying exceeded fair use. The Court of Claims, on
appeal, refused to hold that the copying exceeded fair use, but what it did say
was very equivocal. In short, the court said that it would not stop this copying and distribution while Congress was deliberating a major revision of the
Copyright Act. If this type of copying is not fair use, then Congress should
say so. The Supreme Court split four to four and so affirmed the Court of

---

125. Section 108 does not contain the language found in section 109 referring to a
particular copy, and thus it would appear that this section does not prohibit forms of
distribution that might require the production of an additional copy to convey the
copy to a patron. See David Ensign, "Copyright Considerations for Telefacsimile Transmission of Documents in Interlibrary Loan Transactions," *Law Library Journal* 81
(1989): 805.

126. See *e.g.* H.R. Rep. No. 94-1476 at 47, 51, 52, and 66.

127. 487 F.2d 1345 (Ct. Cl. 1973) aff'd by an equally divided Supreme Court, 420
U.S. 376 (1975).

Claims decision without an opinion. This kind of affirmance does not carry the same weight as a majority affirmance. Congress's response was §108 and the CONTU guidelines.

MODIFICATION OF §108 BY CONTRACT

Subsection (f) contains a provision that allows a copyright holder to eliminate any or all of the rights that §108 gives to libraries. It states that "Nothing in this section ... in any way affects ... any contractual obligations assumed at any time by the library or archives when it obtained a copy or phonorecord of a work in its collections." The legislative history states that this provision was intended to allow copyright holders to make manuscripts and other works available to libraries with the understanding that they would not be reproduced.[128] Thus copyright holders can (and often do with electronic works) place contractual limitations upon the library's right to reproduce or redistribute the work to the public as a condition of selling, licensing, or donating a copy for the library's collection.

6.2 First Sale Doctrine and Effect of Transfer of Particular Copy—§109

RIGHTS AFFECTED BY §109

Section 109, often called the first sale doctrine, is primarily applicable to the rights of public distribution and public display. Although one subsection, discussed on page 89, applies to the public performance of video games, most of §109 does not apply to public performances.[129] Section 109 does not authorize any reproduction of copyrighted works. Nor does it authorize the production of any derivative works.

WHO MAY USE §109

Most of the rights granted by §109 apply only to owners of copies and phonorecords. Subsection (d) specifically states that the rights granted by the main subsections do not apply to lawful possessors of copies who do not actually own those copies. This means the people who rent, lease, borrow, or license

---

128. H.R. Rep. No. 94-1476 at 77.
129. *Columbia Pictures Industries v. Redd Horne, Inc.*, 749 F.2d 154, 160 (3d Cir. 1984); *Columbia Pictures Industries v. Aveco*, 800 F.2d 59, 64 (3d Cir. 1986).

6.2 *continued* copyrighted works cannot take advantage of most of the provisions of §109. Transactions involving shrink-wrap licenses are sometimes considered sales rather than licenses, and thus may not result in the loss of §109 rights. However, the use of a license that must be signed by the licensee can make the purchaser a possessor rather than an owner of the copy and thus eliminate all §109 rights.

If the copyright holder chooses to lease or license a copy of a copyrighted work to a library, the library has no §109 right to publicly distribute or display the work without the copyright holder's permission. Since many electronic works are currently licensed rather than sold, libraries may need permission from the copyright holder to further distribute such works to the public unless another limitation on the distribution right is applicable.

WORKS COVERED BY §109

The general provisions of §109 apply to all categories of copyrighted works. However, additional subsections limit the rights granted by the general subsections for sound recordings of musical works and computer programs. The final subsection also contains additional provisions for coin-operated versions of video games and video game cartridges.

PUBLIC DISTRIBUTION UNDER §109

Section 109(a) authorizes the *owner* of any *copy or phonorecord lawfully made* under the copyright law "to sell or otherwise dispose of possession of that copy or phonorecord." The effect of this language is to give a library the right to publicly distribute any copy lawfully made under any section of the Copyright Act.

The first sale doctrine is extremely important to libraries. Circulation and interlibrary loan functions of libraries necessarily involve public distribution of copyrighted works which might otherwise be an infringement of copyright. Section 109 authorizes circulation and interlibrary cooperation arrangements in which the original copy is lent to a patron or another library without the making of a copy. Unlike the circulation and interlibrary loan reproduction authorized by §108, lending authorized by §109 is not limited to amounts which do not substitute for the purchase of a work. Section 109 permits unlimited lending of an original copy or any copy lawfully made under any other section of the copyright law. Usually, §109 even allows lending for profit or rental of original copies of copyrighted works.

Distribution under §109, however, is confined to delivery of the particular physical copy which was lawfully made. It does not extend to forms of distribution which require the making of additional copies unless the additional reproduction is also authorized under another section. If this were not so, the *particular copy or phonorecord* language of §109 would have no meaning. Thus the *particular copy* language means that §109 may not authorize public distribution by means such as telefacsimile, electronic mail, or other forms of electronic communication that require the production of additional copies in the distribution process.

Once the copyright holder parts with ownership of a particular copy, she usually cannot control further distribution of that particular copy. In recent years, however, the first sale doctrine has, itself, been modified to allow the copyright holder to regain control over further distribution of sound recordings and computer programs.

SPECIAL LIMITS ON TRANSFERS OF SOUND RECORDINGS

Although §109(a) would generally permit the owner of a lawful copy to transfer possession of his particular copy of the work in any manner he chose, subsection (b) prohibits most people from renting, leasing or lending sound recordings of musical works without the express permission of the copyright holder. This provision is generally known as the Record Rental Amendment.

The amendment was targeted primarily at record rental stores, but the library and education communities had to lobby long and hard to preserve their rights to continue to lend musical sound recordings to patrons, teachers and students. Their lobbying resulted in an exception that allows nonprofit libraries and educational institutions to rent, lease or lend musical sound recordings so long as the rental, lease or lending is for nonprofit purposes. The legislative history indicates that Congress intended libraries to be able to charge fees for the lending of musical recordings so long as those fees were merely to cover the costs of lending and were not imposed with the intention of making a profit. The House Report specifically states, however, that Congress did not intend libraries to be able to use record rental to raise funds.[130]

The Record Rental Amendments do not apply to sound recordings sold before October 4, 1984. So anyone who obtained ownership of a sound recording before October 4, 1984, is still free to rent, lease or lend that musical sound recording even if she is doing so for profit. Presently, these provisions are set to expire on October 1, 1997. However, they have already been extended twice and are unlikely to be allowed to lapse in the future.

---

130. H.R. Rep. No. 98-987, 98th Cong., 2d Sess. (1988) at 5.

SPECIAL LIMITS ON TRANSFERS OF COMPUTER
PROGRAMS

Besides prohibiting the rental, lease or lending of musical sound recordings, subsection (b) also prohibits the rental, lease or lending of computer programs. A *computer program* is defined as "a set of statements or instructions to
be used directly or indirectly in a computer in order to bring about a certain
result."[131] This definition does not extend to all material stored in machine
readable form. It only covers programs that cause a computer to do something.
Owners of machine readable copies of works other than computer programs
have the same rights to public distribution as owners of nonmachine readable
copies under the general provisions of §109.

As with the provision prohibiting the rental, lease or lending of musical
recordings, the subsection includes an exception for nonprofit libraries and educational institutions. This exception, though, is more limited. As with musical sound recordings, libraries are permitted to charge fees for the lending of
computer programs if those fees merely cover the costs of lending and are not
imposed with the intention of making a profit. But to rent, lend or lease computer programs, libraries and educational institutions are required to attach
a specific notice to each copy. The text of that notice is included in Appendix F.

SPECIAL PROVISIONS FOR VIDEO GAMES

Video game cartridges and coin-operated video games are specifically
exempted from the computer software rental limitations. Any owner of a lawful copy of a game cartridge or dedicated video game may rent, lease or lend
it even for profit. Video games distributed on diskettes and designed for use
in general purpose computers, however, are subject to the software rental limitations.

6.3 Ephemeral Recordings Limitation—§112

Section 112 generally applies only to the reproduction right although it
may imply authorization of public distribution in very limited circumstances.
It applies only in conjunction with an authorized transmission of a performance
or display of a work. Although it was designed primarily for radio and television broadcasters, in certain circumstances it might allow a library to make and

---

131. 17 U.S.C. §101

distribute a copy of a performance or display that the library has the right to transmit.

If a library or other organization has a right to transmit a performance or display under the educational broadcast exemption (see page 81), §112(b) governs the right to make and distribute copies of the transmission. It allows the transmitting organization to make up to 30 copies. These copies may be used for further transmissions to the public that meet the requirements of §110(2). These copies may also be transferred to other educational institutions or government bodies who meet the requirements for educational transmissions under §110(2). The copies may be kept and used for further educational transmissions for seven years after the initial transmission. Each future transmission has to meet all the requirements of §110(2), however. When the seven years have expired, all but one copy must be destroyed. The organization that made the copies may keep one copy solely for archival purposes after the seven years have expired. Since §110(2) applies only to performances of nondramatic literary and musical works or displays or works, §112(b) applies only to displays of works or performances of nondramatic literary and musical works. It does not apply to performances of dramatic works or audiovisual works.

Section 112(c) allows a governmental body or other nonprofit organization to make a copy of a sound recording or a transmission containing a performance of a musical work of a religious nature for a person or organization that has a license to transmit the performance. The library cannot charge either directly or indirectly for making and distributing the copy. All copies except one archival copy must be destroyed within one year from the date the program was first transmitted to the public.

Section 112(d) permits a governmental body or other organization authorized to transmit a performance to the handicapped under §110(8) to make no more than ten copies of the transmission. (See page 98 for a discussion of §110[8].) The organization may allow another governmental body or nonprofit organization entitled to transmit the performance to the handicapped to use one of the ten copies. The copies may only be used by organizations entitled to make transmissions under §110(8). No further copies can be made from the first ten copies. The copies can be used only for purposes of making transmissions under §110(8) or for archival, preservation or security purposes. An organization that allows another organization to use copies made under this section cannot charge for the use.

Although the legislative history suggests that §112 was designed primarily to allow reproduction of copies that would facilitate radio, television and close circuit video and sound transmissions, there is nothing in the language of the statute that restricts it to such applications. It could relate to other transmissions as well including transmissions related to the use of computers and electronic works. There is, however, a curious sentence in the House Report which might limit application of §112(b) in relation to computers and

6.3 continued electronic works. In discussing the relationship between §110(2) and §112(b), the report says that an ephemeral recording made under §112(b) must embody a performance or display that meets all the qualifications for exemption under §110(2). The next sentence states "copies or phonorecords made for educational broadcasts of a general cultural nature, or for transmission as part of an information storage and retrieval system, would not be exempted from copyright protection under §112(b)."[132] This sentence seems to refer to statements in the report concerning §110 which state that general cultural recreational and entertainment activities are not covered by §110(1) and §110(2), and thus are not covered by §112(b). But nothing in the statute or the legislative history says that §110(2) cannot be applied to systematic instructional uses of informational storage and retrieval systems. When a restriction is not apparent in the language of a statute, courts are often reluctant to create one by expanding on a comment in the legislative history that is not actually part of the law.[133] This particular comment appears to have no basis in the statute, so perhaps the courts will not rely upon it.

6.4 Pictorial, Graphic, and Sculptural Works Limitation—§113

Section 113 is rarely of use to libraries. It applies only to pictorial, graphic and sculptural works. It applies only to the reproduction right, the public distribution right, and the public display right. It does not authorize any public performances or preparation of derivative works.

When useful articles embodying copyrighted pictorial, graphic, or sculptural works have been offered for sale or other public distribution, §113 allows the making, distribution and display of photographs or pictures of the useful article for the following purposes:

  a. in advertisements;
  b. in commentaries related to the distribution or display of the useful articles; and
  c. in connection with news reports.

6.5 Compulsory License for Nondramatic Musical Works—§115

Section 115 will rarely be of use to libraries, since libraries seldom make original sound recordings of nondramatic musical works. It might however cover recordings of festivals and other cultural events made by libraries, archives, or museums as part of oral history projects or for similar purposes.

---

132. H.R. Rep. No. 94-1476 at 103.
133. *Edison Bros. Stores, Inc. v. Broadcast Music Inc.*, 954 F.2d 1419, 1425 (8th Cir. 1992).

Section 115 allows a person to make a new sound recording of a musical work that has been previously distributed to the public in the U.S. upon payment of a compulsory license fee. It applies only to the right of reproduction and the right of public distribution. It does not authorize any public displays, public performances or the preparation of any derivative works.

The compulsory license applies only to nondramatic musical works. The license applies primarily to the recording of new performances of a musical work. In addition, new phonorecords made under the compulsory license can only be distributed to the public for private use, not for further public use. In addition to distributing physical copies of the new phonorecords, the licensee can also use digital transmissions such as transmissions over the Internet to distribute the new recordings.[134]

Section 115 usually does not authorize the duplication of another person's recording of a musical work. If you want to duplicate an existing recording of a musical work, you will need permission to duplicate the sounds as well as authorization to record the underlying musical work. If the recording you want to reproduce was made after February 15, 1972, you must obtain permission from the person who holds the copyright in the sound recording. Since sound recordings were not protected by copyright prior to February 15, 1972, there are no copyright holders in these old sound recordings. Nevertheless, under §115, you must still obtain permission from the person who had the license to produce the original sound recording.

6.6 Computer Program Limitation—§117

Section 117 applies only to computer programs. Computer programs are defined as "set[s] of statements or instructions to be used directly or indirectly in a computer in order to bring about a certain result."[135] This definition does not cover other literary works or any other type of work stored on media that can be read by a computer. It covers only the programs that cause the computer to do something. Thus, §117 does not apply to sound recordings on compact discs. Nor does it apply to the part of CD-ROMs that contain literary works or sound recordings. It applies to the files on the CD-ROM containing the software that allows the computer to use the data, but not to the data files themselves.

Section 117 applies to the rights of reproduction, public distribution and the right to make derivative works. It does not apply to the rights of public performance and display.

Only the *owner* of a copy of a computer program can take advantage of

---

134. PL 104-39, 109 Stat. 344, §4 (Nov. 1, 1995).
135. 17 U.S.C. §101 (1995).

| 6.6 continued | the rights in this section. Whether a program distributed |

under a shrink-wrap license for a one time fee is sold or licensed is a question open to debate. At least one court has treated such transactions like a sale and applied §117.[136] If a court finds that the program was distributed under a license and the distributor or copyright holder retained ownership of the copy, the user will not have any §117 rights.

The owner of a copy of a computer program has the right under §117 to make another copy for archival purposes only. An archival copy is a backup copy. It serves no other purpose than to replace or repair the original should something go wrong. If you make another copy and put it on a machine that you use at different times than your primary machine, that copy is not used solely for archival purposes. If you loan the other copy to a friend while a copy is still installed on your hard drive, the loaned copy is not used solely for archival purposes. Although copies for these purposes may be authorized by some software licenses, they are not authorized by §117.

Librarians may make a single backup copy of a computer disk that comes with a book if the disk contains only computer programs and the copy is used only to replace or repair the original if it is damaged or lost. If the disk contains data rather than programs, §117 may not cover the situation, but it is possible that other provisions of the law may apply. The archival rights contained in §117, however, clearly do not apply to audiovisual works and sound recordings.

The words "another copy" may imply that only one backup copy at a time is authorized. Whether one or more archival copies are authorized, all archival copies must be exact copies. They may be transferred with the original copy or destroyed. But the original owner may not retain backup copies after transferring ownership of the original copies to someone else.

Section 117 also gives the owner of a copy of a computer program the right to make a new copy or adaptation as part of an essential step in using the program on a machine. This section probably gives the owner of a copy of an IBM program the right to make the changes necessary to run the program on a MacIntosh computer or on a machine running Unix. This section would give the owner of a copy of a program the right to transfer it from 5.25" disks to 3.5" disks or to install the program on a single hard drive.

Copies of adaptations may not be transferred or otherwise distributed to anyone else. They must be destroyed when the right to possess the original ends.

---

136. See *Vault v. Quaid Software Ltd.*, 847 F.2d 255 (5th Cir. 1988).

7. Derivative Works

7.1 Sound Recordings Limitation—§114

Sound recordings recorded before February 15, 1972, are not protected by federal statutory copyright, but they may be protected by state statutes or state common law. The law in this area varies from state to state. Although the sound recording itself is not protected by federal statutory copyright, the underlying literary or musical work may be. The copyright in the underlying literary or musical work may restrict what you can do with the sound recording. The copyright holder in a sound recording produced after February 15, 1972, has the exclusive right to make and publicly distribute copies of the sound recording and to prepare derivative works based on the sound recording.

Section 114(b) limits the copyright holder's exclusive right to make copies of a sound recording to the right to reproduce the actual sounds on the recording. It does not give the copyright holder the right to prohibit anyone else from copying or performing or recording any underlying musical, literary or other work. Section 114 also limits the copyright holder's right to prepare derivative works based on the sound recording to the right to rearrange, remix or otherwise alter the actual sounds on the recording. This means, for example, that the copyright holder of a recording can prohibit the making of bootleg copies of the recording but cannot prohibit other people from imitating the recording. Of course the owner of the copyright in the underlying song may have the right to prohibit such imitations. (See page 100.)

7.2 Computer Program Limitation—§117

Section 117 applies only to computer programs. Computer programs are defined as "set[s] of statements or instructions to be used directly or indirectly in a computer in order to bring about a certain result."[137] This definition does

---

137. 17 U.S.C. §101 (1995).

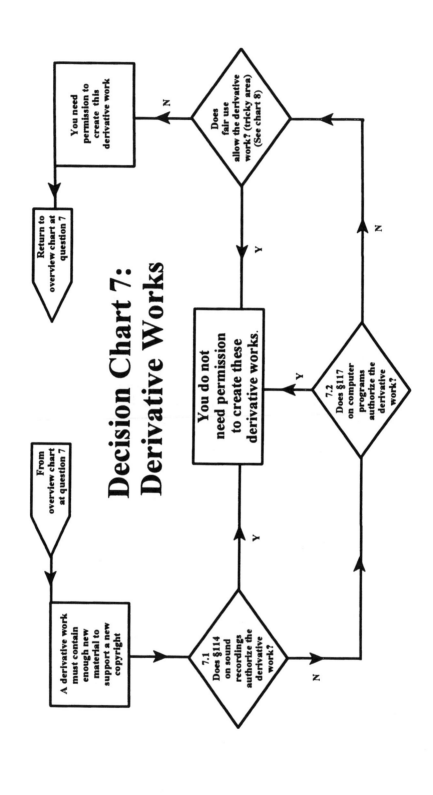

Decision Chart 7:
Derivative Works

From overview chart at question 7

A derivative work must contain enough new material to support a new copyright

7.1 Does §114 on sound recordings authorize the derivative work?

N

7.2 Does §117 on computer programs authorize the derivative work?

Y

You do not need permission to create these derivative works.

Y

Does fair use allow the derivative work? (tricky area) (See chart 8)

N

N

You need permission to create this derivative work

Return to overview chart at question 7

not cover other literary works or any other type of work stored on media that can be read by a computer. It covers only the programs that cause the computer to do something. Thus, §117 does not apply to sound recordings on compact discs. Nor does it apply to the part of CD-ROMs that contain literary works or sound recordings. It applies to the files on the CD-ROM containing the software that allows the computer to use the data, but not to the data files themselves.

Section 117 applies to the rights of reproduction, public distribution and the right to make derivative works. It does not apply to the rights of public performance and display.

Only the *owner* of a copy of a computer program can take advantage of the rights in this section. Whether a program distributed under a shrink-wrap license for a one time fee is sold or licensed is a question open to debate. At least one court has treated such transactions like a sale and applied §117.[138] If a court finds that the program was distributed under a license and the distributor or copyright holder retained ownership of the copy, the user will not have any §117 rights.

Section 117 gives the owner of a copy of a computer program the right to make a new copy or adaptation as part of an essential step in using the program on a machine. This section probably gives the owner of a copy of an IBM program the right to make the changes necessary to run the program on a MacIntosh computer or on a machine running Unix. This section would give the owner of a copy of a program the right to transfer it from 5.25" disks to 3.5" disks or to install the program on a single hard drive.

Copies of adaptations may not be transferred or otherwise distributed to anyone else. They must be destroyed when the right to possess the original ends.

---

138. See *Vault v. Quaid Software Ltd.*, 847 F.2d 255 (5th Cir. 1988).

8. Fair Use

The fair use doctrine, which is codified in §107, applies to all the copyright holder's rights. It is not limited to the reproduction right.[139] For example, the legislative history specifically says that fair use would be relevant to educational broadcasting not covered by §110(2) or §112.[140] The legislative history also mentions use in parodies which involves the performance right.[141]

Although §107 is not limited to reproduction of print works, there is little case law or other guidance applicable to libraries outside the realm of reproduction of print materials. Even in the area of reproduction of print materials, fair use is, at best, a murky doctrine. Fair use rarely provides clear answers, which is why it is discussed after the other more specific limitations in this book. Each problem must be examined on a case by case basis to see what guidance the statute, legislative history, cases, and other material can provide. Fair use remains an equitable doctrine based upon what is reasonable under the circumstances of any particular use.

Although some types of users are allowed greater latitude under fair use than others, fair use is not limited to any particular group of users as many other limitations are. Many of the examples given in the legislative history clearly suggest that nonprofit libraries are among the groups of users treated most favorably by fair use. The nonprofit research purpose of most libraries is only one factor to be considered in fair use analysis, however, and it does not guarantee a finding of fair use. (See pages 119 to 125 for a discussion of how the purpose and character of the use and the user affect fair use analysis.)

Fair use also applies to all types of works. Audiovisual works are not excluded from coverage under §107 as they are under many other sections. The scope of the uses permitted under §107 may vary, however, with the type of work being used. (See pages 125 to 128 for a discussion of how the nature of the work affects fair use analysis.)

---

139. *Harper & Row v. Nation Enterprises*, 471 U.S. 539, 552 (1985); *Salinger v. Random House*, 811 F.2d 90, 95 (2d Cir. 1987).
140. H.R. Rep. No. 94-1476 at 72.
141. H.R. Rep. No. 94-1476 at 65.

Most of the other limitations in the copyright statute were targeted toward specific technologies, and the language is often not flexible enough to adapt to new technologies. The legislative history clearly indicates, however, that §107 is not aimed at any particular technology and was intentionally drafted in broad terms so that it would be flexible enough to accommodate rapidly changing technologies. For example, there are no limitations to facsimile form in §107 as there are for subsections (b) and (c) of §108. This means that §107 might authorize preservation by conversion to machine readable formats when §108 does not.[142]

Although the legislative history says that Congress intended §107 to be flexible enough to accommodate new technologies, it also says that Congress did not intend to either broaden or narrow the doctrine. Congress intended to enact the doctrine into statutory law as it had been developed by the courts. While prior cases are not necessarily binding, such cases and the examples given in the legislative history of §107 do provide some guidance on how the section might be interpreted in particular situations.

The statute provides a list of factors to be considered on a case by case basis in determining whether a particular use is fair. The factors to be considered are

1. the purpose and character of the use;
2. the nature of the copyrighted work;
3. the amount and substantiality of the portion used in relation to the copyrighted work as a whole; and
4. the effect of the use upon the potential market for or value of the copyrighted work.

All the factors are interrelated, and all four factors must be considered for each problem.

8.1 Purpose and Character of the Use

The statute lists criticism, comment, news reporting, teaching, scholarship, and research as favored purposes. These uses are simply examples. The fact that a particular purpose is not on this list does not mean that it will weigh against a finding of fair use. For example, the legislative history discusses several additional purposes that would weigh in favor of finding fair use including conversion of material to a format usable by the handicapped and preservation of endangered films. In fact, the only purpose or character referred to in the statute or legislative history as weighing against fair use is a commercial purpose.

---

142. Getting a court to agree to such an interpretation, however, could be difficult in light of the language in the legislative history to section 108.

Decision Chart 8: Fair Use

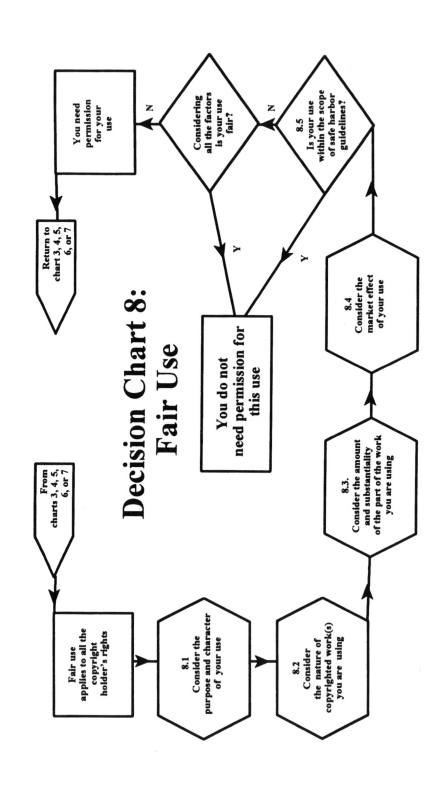

From charts 3, 4, 5, 6, or 7

Fair use applies to all the copyright holder's rights

8.1 Consider the purpose and character of your use

8.2 Consider the nature of copyrighted work(s) you are using

8.3. Consider the amount and substantiality of the part of the work you are using

8.4 Consider the market effect of your use

8.5 Is your use within the scope of safe harbor guidelines?

Considering all the factors is your use fair?

You do not need permission for this use

You need permission for your use

Return to chart 3, 4, 5, 6, or 7

N

N

Y

Y

EDUCATIONAL PURPOSES

The fact that the purpose of the use is educational weighs in favor of a finding of fair use but does not automatically mean that the use is fair. If one or more of the other factors weighs against a finding of fair use, the total balance may shift toward a determination that the use is not a fair use.

In *Encyclopedia Britannica Educational Corp. v. Crooks*,[143] the Board of Cooperative Educational Services of Erie County videotaped several complete films off the air and made copies for several schools in the district for delayed student viewing. The Board did not obtain permission to do the off-air taping or to make the copies. Although the copying was clearly done for noncommercial educational purposes, it was found to exceed fair use because the other factors, particularly the amount and substantiality of the parts of the works used and the number of copies made, weighed so heavily against a finding of fair use.

In *Marcus v. Rowley*,[144] the defendant copied 11 pages of the plaintiff's 35 page copyrighted booklet on cake decorating. The defendant made only 15 copies of her booklet, did not sell the copies, and used the copies only in teaching. Nevertheless the court found that there was no fair use and the defendant had infringed the plaintiff's copyright.

In 1982 nine publishers sued New York University for producing anthologies of portions of copyrighted works for classes. The publishers claimed that despite the educational nature of the reproduction, the copying exceeded fair use. The case was settled before it came to trial. In the settlement NYU agreed to seek permission from the copyright holder for all copying in excess of the *Educational Photocopying Guidelines* set out in the House Report. (See Appendix B.) If the copyright holder did not grant the permission, NYU agreed not to copy unless the university attorney determined that the particular instance of copying was fair use.

The Anne Arundel Public Schools in Maryland reached an agreement in 1984 with the Association of American Publishers over copying of teaching materials and computer software in the public schools. The case never went to court and the exact terms of the settlement were not published, but the school district agreed to put new policies in place and to carry out a program to educate teachers about potential copyright abuse.[145]

COMMERCIAL VERSUS NONCOMMERCIAL PURPOSES

Whether the purpose is commercial or noncommercial is also very important. In a 1984 case,[146] the Supreme Court said that noncommercial uses were

---

143. 447 F. Supp. 243 (W.D.N.Y. 1978).
144. 695 F.2d 1171 (9th Cir. 1983).
145. *Publisher's Weekly* 226 (Dec. 14, 1984): 16.
146. *Sony Corp. v. Universal City Studios*, 464 U.S. 417, 451 (1984).

| 8.1 *continued* | presumptively fair and that commercial purposes were presumptively unfair. To overcome the presumption that a non-commercial use is fair, the copyright holder must prove either that the particular use is harmful to the copyright holder, or that if it should become widespread, it would adversely affect the potential market for the copyrighted work. The copyright holder does not have to prove that the harm has already occurred or that the harm will definitely occur in the future. Proof that the copyright holder will probably be harmed if the use is allowed to continue is sufficient.

Although few cases involving noncommercial uses have been reported since this test was clarified by the Supreme Court in 1984, a couple of cases decided around the same time indicate that it is possible for copyright holders to overcome a presumption in favor of noncommercial uses, especially if all the other factors weigh against a finding of fair use. In 1984, the arch diocese of Chicago paid several million dollars to settle a case concerning photocopying of hymns and sheet music for church choirs.[147] As noted previously, in 1983, an author won a suit against a teacher who made 15 copies of 11 pages from a cake decorating booklet for use in a class.[148]

Although there have been few fair use cases involving completely noncommercial purposes in recent years, there have been a number of cases involving commercial purposes which led to a clarification of the law concerning commercial purposes in a 1994 Supreme Court case. The 1984 case seemed to indicate that commercial purposes were presumptively unfair and that the presumption had to be rebutted with a sufficient showing of other factors weighing in favor of fair use. However in 1994,[149] the Supreme Court backed away from the position that the commercial nature of a use created a presumption against fair use. Instead the Court made it clear that the commercial nature of the use is merely one factor in the entire analysis. A commercial use weighs against a finding of fair use but may be outweighed by other factors. In using the cases as guidance on how the commercial nature of a use affects fair use analysis, it is important to note whether the case was decided between 1984 and 1994. If a case was decided in this period and the commercial nature of the use was the only factor that weighed against a finding of fair use, it might be decided differently today.

On the issue of determining whether a purpose is commercial or noncommercial, the Supreme Court has said "[t]he crux of the profit/nonprofit distinction is not whether the sole motive of the use is monetary gain but whether the user stands to profit from exploitation of the copyrighted material without paying

---

147. See Robert McClory, "Music Publisher Wins $3 Million in Lawsuit Against Chicago See," *National Catholic Reporter* 20 (1984): 25.

148. *Marcus v. Rowley*, 695 F.2d 1171 (9th Cir. 1983).

149. *Campbell v. Acuff-Rose Music, Inc.*, 510 U.S. 569, 114 S. Ct. 1164, 1174 (1994).

the customary price."[150] In determining whether the user stands to profit from the exploitation of the copyrighted material, the focus has usually been on the user who does the copying, not the ultimate end user of the copies. The source of user's profit and whether the use itself generates that profit is extremely important in determining whether the purpose and character of the use as a whole should be considered commercial. Thus a commercial enterprise making copies for schools to use in educational endeavors is less likely to find a safe harbor in fair use than an educational institution making its own copies for the same project. And a commercial firm which makes its profit from making copies for other users is far less likely to find a safe harbor in fair use than a commercial firm which makes its profits from selling new works that copy portions of copyrighted works which criticize the copied works or comment upon them.

In 1979 Basic Books sued Gnonom, a copy shop franchise, for copyright infringement. Gnonom copied and sold anthologies of copyrighted material put together by professors. Gnonom made substantial profits from these activities. The case was settled before it went to trial. In the settlement, Gnonom agreed not to copy materials in excess of the *Educational Photocopying Guidelines* set out in the House Report (see Appendix B) without permission from the copyright holder. Another suit filed in 1981 against the Tyco chain of copy shops was settled on similar terms.[151]

In 1990 several publishers sued Kinko's Graphics Inc. for copyright infringement resulting from Kinko's reproduction of courseware packets compiled by university professors. The court found that Kinko's had infringed the plaintiffs' copyrights and that fair use was not a defense. Kinko's profit motive was an important factor in this decision.[152]

Early in 1992, the Association of American Publishers (AAP) sponsored another suit concerning course packets against Michigan Document Services. The profit-making motive of the defendant was again an important element of the analysis that led the district court to find that the copying was not authorized as a fair use.[153]

---

150. *Harper & Row*, 471 U.S. at 562.

152. Association of American Publishers Press Release, "Copyright Triumphs Again" (June 14, 1994)

152. *Basic Books, Inc. v. Kinko's Graphics Corp.*, 758 F. Supp. 1522, 1531 (S.D.N.Y. 1991).

153. *Princeton University Press, Inc. v. Michigan Document Services, Inc.*, 855 F. Supp. 905 (E.D. Mich. 1994). The District Court opinion was reversed in a surprising opinion at the appellate level, originally reported at 74 F.3d 1512, 1996 WL 54741 (6th Cir. 1996), which was withdrawn when the entire 6th Circuit granted a petition for rehearing en banc, 74 F.3d 1528 (6th Cir. 1996). The en banc decision is expected some time in 1997.

| 8.1 *continued* | PRODUCTIVE VERSUS NONPRODUCTIVE PURPOSES |

The courts often make a distinction between transformative uses and nontransformative uses when they discuss the purpose and character of the use. A transformative use is one that leads to the production of a new work for society's use. Some courts use the terms productive and nonproductive in the place of transformative and nontransformative. Transformative uses are more likely to be deemed a fair use than nontransformative uses. As with the commercial nature of a use, the fact that a use is not transformative does not by itself prevent a finding of fair use.

In *Sony Corp. v. Universal City Studios*, television viewers used video recorders to make copies of television programs to watch later. The lower court found that this practice was not a fair use because it was not a productive use. The Supreme Court, however, found that the videotaping was a fair use even though it did not result in the production of new works because other factors weighed in favor of finding fair use. Nontransformative use is simply one consideration that weighs against a finding of fair use. Two factors outweighed the nontransformative nature of the use in *Sony*. First the use was non-commercial since the users were private people in their homes who were not selling the tapes. And second, the copyright holder suffered no financial harm because the works had already been made available to the public free of charge through television.[154]

The fact that 2 Live Crew used Roy Orbison's song "Oh Pretty Woman" to create a new rap parody song "Pretty Woman" meant that the use was a transformative use in the recent Supreme Court case of *Campbell v. Acuff–Rose Music, Inc.*[155] That transformative use helped to swing the balance in favor of a finding of fair use despite the commercial nature of the band and the fact that 2 Live Crew derived their profit directly from their use of Roy Orbison's song.

In 1985 the AAP filed a class action suit against Texaco even though Texaco had earlier agreed to pay license fees for copying through the CCC. The AAP claimed that Texaco made only token payments and copied far more than was permissible under the copyright law or covered by the fees Texaco paid to the CCC. Texaco lost the case at the District Court and Court of Appeals levels. The commercial nature of Texaco as a whole was an important factor to the judge at the District Court level. Although the Court of Appeals decided that the District Court put too much emphasis on Texaco's commercial status, it still found that copying by a scientist from journals that Texaco subscribed to was not a fair use because the scientist filed the copies

---

154. 464 U.S. 417 (1984).
155. 510 U.S. 569 (1994).

in his personal files and had apparently not used the articles directly in any of his research. Although many experts disagree with the analysis in both opinions, both courts in *Texaco* found that the use by research scientists was nonproductive because it did not lead to the creation of new copyrightable works. It could, however, lead to the creation of new patentable inventions, an argument that neither court seems to have considered. Although *Texaco* is the only corporate research case that has gone to trial so far, several similar cases have been settled when the corporations have agreed to enter into licensing plans with the CCC.

8.2 Nature of the Copyrighted Work

The scope of fair use is greater when factual/informational types of works are used than when fictional or entertainment types of works are used.[156] Thus, uses of factual articles are more likely to be fair than uses of fictional short stories. Uses of news broadcasts are more likely to be fair than uses of feature motion pictures. Uses of factual compilations are more likely to be fair than uses of creative works.[157]

The scope of fair use is also greater when published works are used than when material from unpublished works is used. The Senate Report states:

> The applicability of the fair use doctrine to unpublished works is narrowly limited since, although the work is unavailable, this is the result of a deliberate choice of the copyright owner. Under ordinary circumstances, the copyright owner's "right of first publication" would outweigh any needs of reproduction for classroom purposes.[158]

Several cases in the 1980s focused on the unpublished nature of the work, and nearly all eventually found that the uses involved in the cases were not fair.

In *Harper & Row Publishers v. Nation Enterprises*,[159] former President Ford had an agreement with Harper & Row to publish his memoirs. That agreement gave Harper & Row the right to license prepublication use of the manuscript. Harper & Row sold *Time* an exclusive license to use parts of the manuscript prior to publication. Before *Time* published its article, an unknown person secretly provided the editor of *The Nation* with a copy of the manuscript. The editor of *The Nation* knew that his possession of the manuscript was unauthorized, but he nevertheless wrote and published a news story

---

156. *Marcus v. Rowley*, 695 F.2d at 1176; *Stewart v. Abend*, 495 U.S. 207, 237–238 (1990).
157. *Feist*, 499 U.S. at 348–351.
158. S. Rep. No. 94-473 at 64.
159. 471 U.S. 539 (1985).

8.2 continued   composed of quotes, paraphrases and facts from the unpublished manuscript. He used no other sources. The court found
that the 13 percent of the article that was direct quotation from the manuscript
exceeded fair use. The Court noted that under common law copyright which
protected unpublished works prior to the 1976 Act, there was no such thing
as fair use of unpublished works. But "[i]n a given case, factors such as implied
consent through *de facto* publication or performance or dissemination of a
work may tip the balance of equities in favor of prepublication use. ... Publication of an author's expression before he has authorized its dissemination
seriously infringes the author's right to decide when and whether it will be
made public." The Court concluded that the unpublished nature of a work is
a key though not necessarily determinative factor tending to negate a defense
of fair use.

It should be noted, however, that the unpublished nature of the work was
not the only factor that weighed against a finding of fair use in *Harper & Row
v. Nation Enterprises. The Nation*'s use was not only commercial, but it was the
intended purpose of *The Nation* to "scoop" the *Time* article and the book and
to supplant some of the market for the copied work.

In *Salinger v. Random House*,[160] an author decided to write a biography of
J. D. Salinger. He tried to get Salinger's cooperation but Salinger refused. The
writer nevertheless proceeded with the biography using several unpublished
letters that Salinger wrote between 1939 and 1961. The author found the letters in the archives of several major academic libraries. When the galleys were
sent to Salinger, he learned that the people to whom he had written the letters had donated them to the libraries. He then registered his letters and filed
suit for copyright infringement against the publisher of the biography. In
response, the publisher removed most of the direct quotes from the letters and
substituted paraphrasing instead. After the editing, the book still contained
more than 200 words of quotations and close paraphrasing in 59 places. The
court treated the close paraphrasing as taking the expression and thus infringing the copyright as much as the quotation.

The *Salinger* court like the *Harper & Row* court recognized that under
the 1976 Act, the author's right of first publication is subject to the defense of
fair use. Unpublished letters normally enjoy insulation from fair use copying.
The court found that the balance of the factors weighed in favor of finding
that the biographer's use was not fair. The unpublished nature of the letters
and the amount of the book which relied on the letters weighed heavily in favor
of finding no fair use. There was also a slight possibility that the biography
would supplant some of the market for future publication of Salinger's letters.
The court found that only the historical reporting and scholarly purpose of

---

160. 811 F.2d 90 (2d Cir. 1987).

the book weighed in favor of finding a fair use and it was not enough to out-weigh the other factors.

However, the fact that a work is unpublished does not automatically mean that any use of the work is unfair. After *Harper & Row* and *Salinger* seemed to imply that no use of an unpublished work could be a fair use, §107 was amended in 1992. The amendment added a sentence which states that "The fact that a work is unpublished shall not itself bar a finding of fair use if such finding is made upon consideration of all the above factors."

While Congress was considering the bill that added this sentence to §107, the Second Circuit decided *Wright v. Warner Books, Inc.*[161] In *Wright*, the famous author Richard Wright had written letters to a biographer who later used the letters in writing a biography of Wright. Wright's widow sued alleging copy-right infringement. The court found that all of the factors except the nature of the work weighed in favor of a finding of fair use. The court refused to rule out fair use based solely on the unpublished nature of the letters. In discussing the case, the House Report on the amendment to §107 states

> the *Wright* opinion did not reach the outer limits of what might be regarded as fair use. ... Certainly uses beyond those permitted in *Wright* may also be fair use, depending upon the facts of a particular case. For example, in some circumstances it would be a fair use to copy an author's unpublished expression where necessary to report fairly and accurately a fact set forth in the author's writings. Additionally, as Judge Leval has written: "Often, it is the words used by [a] public figure (or the particular manner of expres-sion) that are the facts calling for comment."[162]

One of the circumstances in which the unpublished nature of a work might not weigh very heavily against a finding of fair use would be where a work was widely distributed although it might not meet the definition of pub-lished. For example, when an online database is made available to the public only through remote access directly from the copyright holder, it has not been published under the Copyright Act. (See page 49 for a discussion of what constitutes publication under the Copyright Act.) Nevertheless, the copyright holder has had the opportunity to decide when and under what conditions the work will first be distributed to the public. The copyright holder has also had the opportunity to commercially exploit first availability to the public. Since the reasons that unpublished works are given greater protection than pub-lished works under fair use is to protect the copyright holder's right to deter-mine the conditions of first release to the public and to commercially exploit

---

161. 953 F.2d 731 (2d Cir. 1991).
162. H.R. Rep. No. 102-836 at 8 quoting *New Era Publications International v. Henry Holt & Co.*, 695 F. Supp. 1493, 1502 (S.D.N.Y. 1989).

| 8.2 continued | that release, it makes no sense to continue that greater pro-
tection after the copyright holder has already exploited first
release to the public.

8.3 Amount and Substantiality of the Part Used

If the material used is covered by more than one copyright, the first step is to decide which copyright should be looked at in analyzing the amount and substantiality of the portion used. When articles published in journals or other selections from collective works are used, the work used may be covered both by a copyright in the individual contributed works and by a compilation or collective copyright in a larger work. If all the material used comes from a single contribution, then the individual smaller work is the proper work to focus on. If material is used from more than one contribution, then you may need to go through the analysis twice—once for the individual copyright and once for the compilation copyright.

Both the quantity and quality of the portion used must be analyzed under this factor.[163] If the quantity and quality of the portion used are reasonable in relation to the purpose of the use, this factor will weigh in favor of a finding of fair use.[164]

Use of a short piece which is "the heart of" a work may not be fair use in circumstances where use of a longer piece which is peripheral in nature may be fair use.[165] But at times, the use of even the most central parts of a work may be fair. For example, in parody, it is often necessary to use the "heart" of a work to conjure up the original in the audience's mind, even though it might not be reasonable to use the "heart" of a work in a prepublication review. If a work copies verbatim and does little to transform the use into a new and different work, then it is less likely that taking the "heart" of the work will be considered reasonable. If the new work transforms the work into a new and different work without verbatim copying, then it is more likely that taking the "heart" of the work will be considered reasonable.[166]

"There are no absolute rules as to how much of a copyrighted work may be copied and still be considered a fair use."[167] But use of the whole work generally precludes a finding that the third factor weighs in favor of fair use.[168]

---

163. *Marcus v. Rowley*, 695 F.2d 1171.
164. *Campbell v. Acuff-Rose Music*, Inc, 510 U.S. 569, 114 S.Ct. 1164, 1175 (1994).
165. *Harper & Row v. Nation Enterprises*, 471 U.S. 539, 564–565 (1985).
166. 114 S.Ct. at 1175–76.
167. *Maxtone-Graham v. Burtchaell*, 803 F.2d 1253 (2d Cir.), cert. denied, 481 U.S. 1059 (1987).
168. *Marcus v. Rowley*, 695 F.2d 1171; *Benny v. Loew's*, Inc., 239 F.2d 532 (9th Cir. 1956).

And the fact that the work in question is a short work which is only a small part of a larger collective work does not change the fact that an entire work has been used.

In *Wihtol v. Crow*,[169] a teacher and church choir director did a new arrangement of an entire hymn. He made 48 copies of his new arrangement. The arrangement was performed once by the school choir and once by the church choir. The court said that "[w]hatever may be the breadth of the doctrine of 'fair use,' it is not conceivable to us that copying of all, or substantially all, of a copyrighted song can be held to be a 'fair use' merely because the infringer had no intent to infringe."[170]

Although use of the whole work weighs against a finding of fair use, it does not necessarily prevent a finding of fair use. If all of the other factors weigh in favor of a finding of fair use, as they did in *Sony*, use of the whole work may still be allowed. The legislative history gives two other examples in which complete copying may be both necessary and reasonable: nonprofit conversion of single copies of works to formats useable by the handicapped and the making of duplicate copies of old films for archival preservation. A similar situation in which use of the entire work might be allowed under fair use would be nonprofit archival conversion of obsolete formats of works which cannot be used without the aid of machines when newer formats are not commercially available. Note that in each of these examples, all of the factors other than the amount and substantiality of the part of the work used weigh in favor of finding fair use.

Usually, however, use of the entire work will not be considered reasonable. In general, the smaller and less significant the portion used, the more likely that the third factor will weigh in favor of a finding of fair use. The larger and more significant the portion used, the more likely that this factor will weigh against a finding of fair use.

In *Marcus v. Rowley*, copying 50 percent of the plaintiff's book which included most of the substance of the book was considered too much copying for fair use. In *Salinger v. Random House*, the court found that taking more than one-third of 17 letters and more than 10 percent of 42 letters was so much copying that it weighed against a finding of fair use.

In *Kinko's*, the court considered use of 5–24 percent of 12 works by a commercial copy firm for educational anthologies to be substantial enough to weigh against finding fair use. The language of the Kinko's decision seems to indicate that copying of an entire chapter is enough to weigh against a finding of fair use, at least when the copying is for profit.

In *New Era Pubs. Int'l. v. Carol Publishing Group*,[171] the court considered

---

169. 309 F.2d 777 (8th Cir. 1962).
170. 309 F.2d at 780.
171. 904 F.2d 152 (2d Cir. 1990).

8.3 continued

5–6 percent of 12 works and 8 percent or more of 11 works for a critical biography to be small enough to weigh in favor of a finding of fair use. On the other hand, the same court considered use of 8 percent of a film by a commercial television network in a news report to be sufficiently substantial to weigh against a finding of fair use.[172]

Some courts have found that use of longer portions of out-of-print materials are more likely to be considered fair than of in print material.[173] Other courts have pointed out that when works are out-of-print, there may be a greater market for permission fees.[174] When the copyright holder is actively licensing the use of an out-of-print work, the fact that the work is out-of-print may not indicate that a longer portion can be used without permission.

8.4 Market Effect

Many commentators and cases state that the effect upon the market is the most important of the four fair use factors. When a use has a significant negative effect upon the current or potential market for the copyrighted work, that fact will usually weigh against a finding of fair use.

In order for the market factor to weigh against a finding of fair use, the copyright holder must show either that the particular use is presently harmful or that if the type of use should become widespread, it would adversely affect the potential market for the copyrighted work. The copyright holder does not need to show actual present harm under this standard. Nor is it necessary to show with certainty that future harm will occur. What is necessary is a showing by the preponderance of the evidence that there is some meaningful likelihood of future harm. If the use is a nontransformative one and the intended purpose is for commercial gain, the likelihood of future harm may be presumed. If the intended purpose is noncommercial, the likelihood of future harm must be demonstrated. If the use is transformative, there is no presumption concerning the effect on the market.

In considering the potential for future harm, the analysis must consider not only the potential for harm to the market for the original work but also the harm to potential markets for derivative works.[175] Analysis of the potential market for derivative works is particularly important when the alleged infringing use is a transformative one.

The reason that a new transformative work negatively affects the market

---

172. *Iowa State University Research Foundation v. ABC*, 621 F.2d 57 at 61–62 (2d Cir. 1980).

173. *Wright v. Warner Books, Inc.*, 748 F. Supp. 105, 112 (S.D.N.Y. 1990).

174. 758 F. Supp. at 1533.

175. *Harper & Row*, 471 U.S. at 568; 114 S. Ct. at 1177.

for the original work is also important. If it has a negative effect because it replaces the potential market for the original work or derivative works, then this factor weighs against a finding of fair use. If it has a negative effect because it criticizes the value of the original work, and by inference the value of derivative works, then the negative market effect should not be considered in the fair use analysis.

The fact that the alleged infringing work competes in the same market as the original work suggests a greater likelihood of impact on the market value of the work than if the two works are aimed at different audiences and marketed to different groups.[176] One congressional report concerning an early version of bills to modify the 1909 Act said that "Textbooks and other material prepared primarily for the school market would be less susceptible to [fair use] reproduction for classroom use than material prepared for general public distribution."[177]

One of the most controversial issues in fair use analysis is the extent to which the effect on the potential market for licenses should be considered. The Supreme Court has said that the market for license fees is relevant when the market for the particular type of license has been traditionally developed and considered reasonable. Markets for licenses that the copyright holders are not likely to develop or cannot reasonably be expected to develop in the future, however, are not relevant to fair use analysis. There is little guidance, however, on what license markets are traditional and reasonable. Some people argue that if any copyright holders have done anything to try to collect fees for a particular type of use, then the potential loss of those fees should be considered. However, the other argument is if potential licensing fees are considered relevant in fair use analysis for uses where licensing schemes were not already widely developed and generally accepted in the past, copyright holders will have the power to eliminate all fair use by setting up or demanding licenses for all uses.

The Supreme Court cases suggest that at least in some areas where it is unlikely that copyright holders would ever market licenses, the loss of potential license fees does not weigh against a finding of fair use. For example, copyright holders are unlikely to ever willingly license reproduction for purposes of negative criticism or unflattering parody. Thus the loss of license fees for parodies is not relevant to fair use analysis. However, other Supreme Court cases indicate that the market for license fees is relevant where a use destroys the value of licensing serials to print excerpts before publication.

Between these two examples from the Supreme Court is a large area of

---

176. *Marcus v. Rowley*, 695 F.2d 1171; *Haberman v. Hustler Magazine, Inc.*, 626 F. Supp. 201, 211 (D. Mass. 1986); *Jartech, Inc. v. Clancy*, 666 F.2d 403 (1982); *Iowa State Univ. Research Foundation v. ABC*, 621 F.2d 57.

177. H.R. Rep. No. 83, 90th Cong., 1st Sess. (1967).

| 8.4 continued | uncertainty. In the *Texaco* case, the Second Circuit Court of Appeals split two to one on the issue of whether the potential market for license fees for reproduction of journal articles by for profit companies is relevant in fair use analysis. The majority decided that where publishers have chosen to exploit the market by making licenses available through the CCC, the potential loss of licensing income is important and does weigh against a finding of fair use. The third judge disagreed with that conclusion because he did not find the CCC licensing scheme to be either a traditional or a reasonable market which ought to be considered in fair use analysis. Since the *Texaco* decision was a split decision and the majority carefully confined its decision to the exact facts in the case, no one knows whether other courts will follow the reasoning of the majority decision. It is also unclear whether the Second Circuit would apply the same reasoning to CCC licenses in a nonprofit library environment.

If there is no negative effect on any current or potential market that is relevant to fair use analysis, the market effect factor will weigh in favor of a finding of fair use. Since the market effect factor is so important, the lack of any negative market effect may be enough to swing the balance in favor of a finding of fair use even where other factors such as the amount and substantiality of the use weigh against a finding of fair use. The lack of any negative effect on a relevant market was a major factor in the Supreme Court's decision that time shifting copying of entire free television programs was a fair use in *Sony v. Universal City Studios*.

In *Sony* the plaintiffs owned the copyrights for movies broadcast on television. Members of the public used their VCRs to tape the movies during the broadcasts. Sony sued the maker of the VCRs claiming that they contributed to and encouraged massive copyright infringement by selling machines to the public that were capable of making infringing copies. The Court found that most people used the machines to tape free broadcast programs for later viewing after which they reused the tapes. According to the Court, time shifting copying of programs available for free viewing to the public did not have a negative impact on the value of the copyrighted work, and thus the effect on the market weighed in favor of finding a fair use. It is important to note that the *Sony* decision does not find that videotaping television programs and keeping the copies for repeated viewing is a fair use. Keeping the programs for repeated viewing might have an impact on the market for the sale of home videos. The fact that the programs copied in *Sony* were widely distributed to the public free of charge was very important in reaching the conclusion that the use in *Sony* did not have a negative market impact and therefore was a fair use.

8.5 Balancing the Factors and Using Guidelines

The *Guidelines for Classroom Copying in Not-for-Profit Educational Institutions* (see Appendix B), *Guidelines for Educational Uses of Music* (see Appendix C), and the *Guidelines for Off-Air Recording of Broadcast Programming for Educational Purposes* (see Appendix D) give bright line guides for certain areas in which the interested parties have agreed that specific examples qualify as fair uses. These guidelines are minimum standards. The guidelines were intended to sketch out safe harbors. They were not intended to describe all uses that could be fair uses in a nonprofit educational institution. In some situations, use that exceeds these guidelines will be fair use. If a situation or use is not covered by these guidelines or exceeds the amounts determined to be fair under these guidelines, the situation requires an independent analysis of all the fair use factors.

The *Classroom and Reserve Use Guidelines (ACRL/ALA)* (see Appendix E) also offer guidance to help users decide whether particular common uses are likely to be considered fair use. These guidelines, however, are more likely to discuss general principles and less likely to set out bright line safe harbors. Since they are less specific and less conservative than the guidelines described in the previous paragraph, fewer groups of copyright holders have formally agreed to them. They are, however, generally accepted among groups in librarianship and higher education.

9. Permissions and Licenses

9.1 Has Permission Been Given Already?

Anything in which the copyright holder grants permission to use any of the copyright rights is a license. The license can take the form of a formal legal document, a letter, a statement on a publication, or even words spoken in a telephone call or other conversation. Although written evidence of the license is not required by law, vendors and duplication departments may require written evidence of permission before they will reproduce the material you need. Schools, universities and other organizations may also require written evidence of permission before allowing their facilities and equipment to be used for public displays and performances.

The most common places where permission statements can be found are
1. attached to the copyright notice on a work,
2. in the first few footnotes of articles or contributions to collective works,
3. in the prefatory pages to works such as inside the cover, on the title page or on the back of the title page of journals,
4. in formal license agreements, and
5. on bills, invoices and order forms.

If you cannot find the permission you need in one of these places, you may have to make a special request for permission directly to the copyright holder.

HOW TO READ A PERMISSION STATEMENT

Permission statements or licenses are documents which alter the law as it applies to particular works. The principles of copyright law described in the Introduction and chapters 1 to 8 continue to apply to any work covered by a permission statement except for those specific situations in which the permission statement modifies the law. Thus if an action involves one of the copyright holder's exclusive rights and the action is not authorized by a limitation in the law, you must start with the presumption that you do not have permission to engage in that action. Read the permission statement very carefully. The permission statement authorizes a particular action only if it contains language authorizing the action in question. You cannot assume from the lack of certain terms that the copyright holder has granted permission to use any of the rights that the law reserves to the copyright holder.

For example, you cannot assume that networking a CD-ROM product is authorized by a license merely because the license does not prohibit networking. Many of the copyright holder's rights, such as reproduction, public performance and public display, are often involved in the process of using a CD-ROM product on a network. Although a few of the reproductions, performances and displays might occasionally be authorized by some of the limitations in the law, the limitations do not give users sufficient authorization to cover the day to day use of a CD-ROM product on a network. Since the law does not authorize these activities, a user cannot assume that a permission statement or license authorizes networking unless there is some language in the permission statement that specifically relates to networking. Silence on the subject of networking means that the license does *not* authorize networking.

Permission statements in journals frequently authorize reproduction and distribution of multiple copies for classroom use in excess of what might otherwise be permitted by fair use. But the conditions under which the permission is granted vary from journal to journal and even from article to article within the same journal. Compare the two statements in Figure 3 and Figure 4. The statement in Figure 3 is limited to classroom use while the statement in Figure 4 permits reproduction for scholarly and instructional purposes. The statement in Figure 4 also requires that a notice be attached to each copy and that copies must be distributed at or below cost.

| The author of each article in this issue has granted permission for copies of that article to be made for not-for-profit classroom use. | All articles copyright 1994 by [the organization], except where otherwise expressly indicated. Except as otherwise expressly provided, the author of each article in this issue has granted permission for copies of that article to be made for classroom use, provided that (1) copies are distributed at or below cost, (2) author and [journal] are identified, and (3) proper notice of copyright is affixed to each copy. For articles in which it holds copyright, [organization] grants permission for copies to be made for classroom use under the same conditions. |

Figure 3 (above): Permission Statement B; figure 4 (right): Permission Statement A.

Some journals include a permission statement allowing educational use but require the user to notify the author or the journal of each use.

Chart 9: Permission

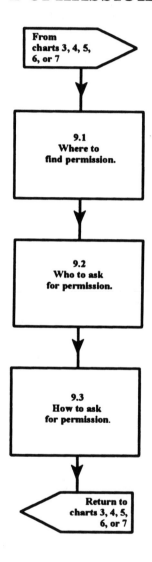

From
charts 3, 4, 5,
6, or 7

9.1
Where to
find permission.

9.2
Who to ask
for permission.

9.3
How to ask
for permission.

Return to
charts 3, 4, 5,
6, or 7

Occasionally authors use permission statements that seem to allow a variety of uses that would ordinarily infringe copyright. Shareware and Freeware notices, such as figures 5 and 6, are examples of this type of permission statement. Such notices do not place the works in the public domain unless they give anyone the right to exercise all the copyright holder's rights without restriction. Both of the notices in figures 5 and 6 are only partial grants of the copyright holder's rights, and both place restrictions on those grants.

> Permission is granted to make and distribute verbatim copies of this guide provided the copyright notice and this permission notice are preserved on all copies. Permission is granted to copy and distribute modified versions of this booklet under the conditions for verbatim copying, provided that the entire resulting derived work is distributed under the terms of a permission notice identical to this one. Permission is granted to copy and distribute translations of this booklet into another language, under the above conditions for modified versions, except that this permission notice may be stated in a translation approved by the author.

Figure 5: Permission statement C.

> You are free to use, copy and distribute [program] for NON-COMMERCIAL use if:
>   No fee is charged for use, copying or distribution.
>   It is not modified in any way.
> Clubs and user groups may charge a nominal fee not to exceed $10 for expenses and handling while distributing [program].

Figure 6: Permission statement D.

The statement in Figure 5 places no limits on how much you can charge for reproducing copies of the work, but it requires you to use a notice that would allow someone who purchased a copy from you to make more copies without paying any fee. The statement in Figure 6 places limits on how much you can charge for reproducing copies. Figure 5 authorizes some reproduction, public distribution and the creation of some derivative works. But it does not authorize any public displays or performances. Figure 6 authorizes some reproduction and public distribution. The word *use* in the statement may also authorize some public performances and displays. However, it does not authorize any creation of derivative works. The prohibition against modifying the work effectively eliminates any authority to create a derivative work.

9.2 Who Can Grant Permission

Only the copyright holder, or someone to whom the copyright holder has delegated the authority, can grant permission to use any of the copyright rights. A grant of permission by someone who erroneously thinks they own the copyright or by someone who erroneously thinks they have the right to grant permission is not a valid grant of permission. In fact, granting permission to use any of the copyright holder's rights without the authority to grant such permission is itself an act of copyright infringement. Thus, determining who is the copyright holder is an essential step in the permission process.

The initial copyright holder is nearly always the author of the work.[178] The author remains the copyright holder until the copyright is validly assigned to someone else. Section 204 of the Copyright Act requires all assignments of copyright to be in writing and signed by the copyright holder. Despite the apparent beliefs of some publishers, copyrights are not automatically assigned to publishers when authors submit manuscripts or when manuscripts are accepted for publication.

Assignment of specific rights such as the exclusive right to exploit print versions of a work is not the equivalent of an assignment of the entire copyright. For example, if an author sells the print rights to a novel, he has not necessarily sold either the electronic or the film rights to the novel. If an author of an article sells first North American print rights to a journal, she has not necessarily sold the right to grant permission to reprint nor the right to produce or license electronic copies of the article.

The blanket statements that some publishers use which state that by submitting a manuscript authors agree that the copyright in their articles or works are transferred to the publisher when a manuscript is accepted for publication have no effect on the ownership of the copyright. The use of such erroneous statements by publishers can create traps for unwary users of copyrighted works because these publishers usually use copyright notices which indicate that the publisher is the copyright holder. The copyright is not transferred to the publishers unless and until the author signs a written assignment to the publishers. Some of these same publishers have entered into agreements with collective licensing agencies such as the CCC for all of their publications even though they may not have the right to authorize reproduction of the work.

Although a collective rights organization or document supplier may not have the right to grant permission to use such works, a user who pays the collective rights organization or document supplier still obtains some protection

---

178. In a few situations such as where the work qualifies as a work made for hire or where contracts concerning ownership of copyrights have been entered into before the creation of a work, the initial copyright holder may be an organization or someone other than the person who actually created the work.

from being sued for infringement. Obtaining permission from someone who appears to have the authority to grant permission to use a work is probably sufficient evidence to allow users to prove that they are innocent infringers. The law limits statutory damages against innocent infringers to $200. This limit makes it too expensive for a copyright holder to sue someone who has obtained permission from an organization that appears to, but does not actually, have the authority to grant permission for a use. The innocent infringer defense, however, applies only to suits for statutory damages. If the actual copyright holder can prove that the unauthorized use resulted in a lot of actual financial damage, a suit may still be economically feasible.

Unfortunately, it is extremely difficult to determine whether many copyrights have been transferred from the initial author to someone else. Although registration of copyrights and transfers is a prerequisite to a suit for infringement by American copyright holders, neither the initial copyright nor any transfers are required to be registered. Even if most transfers were registered, the cost of searching the registrations for every use would often be prohibitive. (See Appendix G on pages 188 to 204 for information in searching copyright records.) So where a notice or something else indicates that someone other than the author is the copyright holder, it is often wise to seek permission both from the organization listed as the copyright holder and from the author.

Some copyright holders register their works with collective rights organizations which serve as clearinghouses for permission requests. The largest clearinghouse for print works is the Copyright Clearance Center which publishes a triennial catalog listing fees for member publishers.

Copyright Clearance Center
27 Congress Street
Salem, MA 01970
(508) 744-3350
fax (508) 741-2318

The two largest collective rights organizations for music are

American Society of Composers, Authors and Publishers
(ASCAP)
One Lincoln Plaza
New York, NY 10023
(212) 595-3050

Broadcast Music Inc. (BMI)
320 W 57th Street
New York, NY 10019
(800) 669-4264 (212) 586-2000
fax (212) 582-5972

9.3 How to Ask for Permission

Although permission does not have to be in writing, written permission can save a lot of headaches. Copyshops, including photocopy services run by universities, are often reluctant to take your word that you have oral permission to copy. The same is true of media centers and broadcast and distance education studios. If time is of the essence, try faxing your request, giving your fax number and requesting an answer by fax. Addressing your request directly to the permissions department of a publisher may speed up the handling of your request if you are writing to a publisher. Remember, however, that authors frequently do not assign their copyrights and individuals often respond to permission requests faster than publishers do. Calling the publisher or copyright holder first to find out exactly how to address your letter may also result in a faster response to your request. Even if you use all these methods, response time may vary from a few days to several months. So allow yourself as much lead time as possible.

After you have determined that you need to ask permission and who has the power to grant the permission you need, you have to figure out exactly what to ask for. First, you need to clearly identify the work that you are asking permission to use. At a minimum you should list the author or editor, title, and edition and date of the work. Other identifying information such as the ISBN or LC-Card number may help to identify the work and speed processing of your request.

Second, tell the author or copyright holder exactly what you want to do with a work. Clearly identify the part of the work you want to use if you do not intend to use the whole work. Specify chapters and page numbers, stanzas and verses, numbered figures or other segment identification if possible. Specify the number of copies you want to make or the number of times you want to display or perform a work, and describe the size and nature of the expected audience. If other information gives a better idea of the distribution that will result from the use, give that information as well.

For example, if you want to edit a work to make it searchable by WAIS, say so. If you want to create an ASCII version of the work or mark it up with SGML or HTML or if you want to post it for anonymous FTP access, put that information in the request. If you are willing to limit access in some manner, specify the manner in which access will be limited. Do not tell the copyright holder that only a set number of copies will be made unless you have a reliable means to control the number of copies. In short, make sure that any permission you get allows you to do what you intend to do. Make sure that the person requesting permission and the person giving permission have the same understanding of what will be done with the work.

Be prepared to accept a negative answer from the copyright holder or a response that requires the payment of a fee higher than you are able or willing to pay. Copyright holders are under no obligation to grant permission at a rate that you consider reasonable. If you cannot get permission to use a particular work under conditions that you can accept, look for another work to use instead. Or consider modifying your project so that you use only the information or ideas from the work instead of the copyrighted elements. (See pages 57 to 59.)

Finally, if you expect a continuing need to use the work, ask for continuing permission in your request. Do not assume that a permission given for one use applies to another use. If you later decide to use a work in a manner not covered by the first request, send another request.

SAMPLE REQUEST LETTER FOR CLASS USE COPIES

> August 1, 1994
> John Doe
> Permissions Department
> Popular Books Co.
> 1221 Volume St.
> Books, DE 00001
>
> Dear Mr. Doe:
>
> I would like to reproduce the following material for use in my Copyright class this semester and in following semesters.
>> Title: *Copyright Confusion*, 3rd edition 1991
>> Author: Prof. Elizabeth Swift
>> ISBN: 99-99999-X
>> Material to be reproduced: Chapter 1: "The Origins of Copyright"
>> Distribution: The material will be included in an electronic course packet of supplementary readings that will be sold on disk to students at cost.
>> Expected Class Size: This class is taught every semester with ordinary enrollment of 20-30 students.
>
> If you are not the copyright holder or do not have authority to grant this request, I would appreciate any information you can provide concerning the current copyright holder.
>
> I have enclosed a stamped self-addressed envelope for your convenience in replying to this request. Or you may respond via fax to (999) 999-9999 or via E-mail to jjohn@copyrite.class.edu.
>
> Sincerely,
> Prof. James John
>
> encl.

9.3 *continued* SAMPLE REQUEST LETTER FOR
ELECTRONIC RESERVE USE

August 1, 1994

John Doe
Permissions Department
Popular Books Co.
1221 Volume St.
Books, DE 00001

Dear Mr. Doe:

I would like to include the following material in our library's electronic reserve system for this semester and following semesters.

> Title: *Copyright Confusion*, 3rd edition 1991
> Author: Prof. Elizabeth Swift
> ISBN: 99-99999-X
> Material to be reproduced: Chapter 1: "The Origins of Copyright"
> Distribution: The material will be scanned into our electronic reserve system and made available to students through our campus wide network.
> Expected Class Size: This class is taught every semester with ordinary enrollment of 20-30 students.

If you are not the copyright holder or do not have authority to grant this request, I would appreciate any information you can provide concerning the current copyright holder.

I have enclosed a stamped self-addressed envelope for your convenience in replying to this request. Or you may respond via fax to (111) 111-1111 or via E-mail to aolsen@ip.univ.edu.

Sincerely,
Anne Olsen
Librarian
encl.

SAMPLE REQUEST LETTER FOR PERFORMANCE OF A FILM IN A LIBRARY

August 1, 1994

Jane Smith
Permissions Department
Historic Films, Inc.
1221 Volume St.
Cinema, CA 00009

Dear Ms. Smith:

In connection with National Library Week, our library would like to present a free showing of *The Library at Alexandria* for the public. This film was produced by Historic Films, Inc. in 1990. The film would be shown in our community room on a large screen television attached to a VCR. The room seats approximately 200 people. The film would be shown once at 7 p.m. Friday, April 7, 1995. No admission would be charged.

If you are not the copyright holder or do not have authority to grant this request, I would appreciate any information you can provide concerning the current copyright holder.

I have enclosed a stamped self-addressed envelope for your convenience in replying to this request. Or you may respond via fax to (111) 111-1111 or via E-mail to aolsen@library.alex.org.

Sincerely,
Anne Olsen
Librarian
encl.

Part III.
Practice Projects

10. Using the System for a Variety of Projects

This chapter contains three additional practice projects. These projects are based on questions raised repeatedly in workshops that I have conducted. Working through these projects may be useful in reaching a better understanding of the various areas of copyright law and the system presented in this book.

Replacement of Damaged Out-of-Print Works

The Justinian Law School Library owned three copies of the *West Virginia Code of 1932*. This work is an annotated edition of the laws of West Virginia as they existed in 1932. It was published by the Michie Company in Charlottesville, Virginia, in 1932. The back of the title page contains a notice that reads as follows: *Copyright 1932 by the Michie Company*. Last winter, a pipe in the ceiling of the reserve room broke and water severely damaged the two copies that were in the reserve room. They are not repairable. The third copy, housed in the Rare Book Room, was not damaged. The two copies were in the Reserve Room because Professor Simpkin assigns a special project requiring the legal history class to use the 1932 Code every fall. This fall Professor Simpkin has asked the librarian to make two complete photocopies of the remaining copy to put on reserve for the class project. The librarian has already attempted to buy replacement copies of the code and has discovered that they are out-of-print. The librarian also contacted several used book dealers, but none could locate any additional copies of the 1932 code. Will the library encounter any copyright problems if the librarian makes two copies of the code to replace the two damaged copies?

Most works are copyrighted, so I started with the assumption that the 1932 Code is probably copyrighted. (See page 44.) The Code does not fit into any of the exceptions to the general rule that most works are copyrighted. The *West Virginia Code of 1932* is clearly not a work of the United States government.

146

At first glance, it might appear to be a government work because employees of the State of West Virginia might have written it. The government works exception, however, does not apply to works of state governments. (See page 45.)

The *West Virginia Code of 1932* does contain the laws of West Virginia. Thus, the text of the actual statutes in this volume is not copyrightable. But any annotations or additional material added by a private compiler is copyrightable. (See page 47.) This edition is an annotated edition which is the reason that Michie was able to register a copyright in this work in 1932.

Using the timeline on page 49, I found that works originally copyrighted in 1932 may be protected for a maximum of 75 years. Since the *West Virginia Code of 1932* was first published in 1932, its original term of copyright was 28 years. That term would have expired in 1960. Thus the copyright should have been renewed sometime in 1959 or 1960. To find out whether the renewal application was properly filed, I would have to search the Copyright Office records for 1959, 1960 and 1961. (See page 51.) Since searching Copyright Office records for renewals can be very expensive and time consuming, I decided to assume that the copyright had been properly renewed for purposes of this project. That means that the copyright in the *West Virginia Code of 1932* might not expire until the end of 2007.

Next I checked to see if the copyright had been forfeited for failure to comply with the notice requirements. The *1932 Code* was published when the 1909 Act governed notice. The notice in the *1932 Code* meets the notice requirements of the 1909 Act, so its copyright was not forfeited for failure to use proper notice. (See page 53.)

There is no mention in the facts of any action that would dedicate the *1932 Code* to the public domain. (See page 55.)

The *1932 Code of West Virginia* did not fit into any of the exceptions, so I concluded that it is currently protected by copyright. Professor Simpkin has clearly indicated that copies of the entire annotated code need to be placed on reserve. So I could tell without going through the analysis that the project could not be limited to uncopyrightable parts of the work.

Photocopying is clearly reproduction (see page 35), so I followed Chart 3 to see if I could find a provision in the law that would authorize the reproduction without permission. I started my analysis with §108.

Only libraries or archives open to the public or which make their collections available to outside researchers can use the §108 limitation. (See page 60.) Most university libraries make their collections available to researchers and many are open to the public, so the Justinian Law School Library probably meets this criteria. A library must also show that it will obtain no direct commercial advantage from a reproduction to take advantage of the exceptions in §108. (See discussion on page 60.) Since no money is involved in this project, the library should have no problem with this condition.

The *West Virginia Code of 1932* is a literary work. So the fact that §108 does not generally cover musical works, graphic works and audiovisual works should not present a problem. (See page 61.)

Section 108 covers three major types of reproduction:
1. preservation and replacement reproduction,
2. reproductions for patrons, and
3. interlibrary loan.

The sections concerning preservation and replacement reproduction are the ones most likely to be applicable to this project.

The code 17 U.S.C. §108(c) gives a library or archives the right to reproduce a copy or a phonorecord of a published work

> duplicated in facsimile form solely for purposes of replacement of a copy or phonorecord that is damaged, deteriorating, lost, or stolen, if the library or archives has, after a reasonable effort, determined that an unused replacement cannot be obtained at a fair price. [See pages 61 to 64.]

The limitation to facsimile form should be no problem because the legislative history specifically mentions photocopying as a form of facsimile copying. (See page 63.) The library should have no problem with the other two conditions of subsection (c) either. The library owned two copies of the *Code* which have already been damaged. And the library has made a reasonable effort to find replacement copies. It has determined that unused copies are probably not available at any price since the work is out-of-print. The library has gone even further than the statute requires in finding that used copies are not even readily available. (See page 64.) Thus, 17 U.S.C. §108(c) authorizes the reproduction in this project. Since §108 authorizes the reproduction without obtaining permission from the copyright holder, I skipped the rest of Chart 3. However, I returned to the Overview Chart to see if any other copyright issues were involved in the project.

There are no public displays or performances in this project. (See page 35 for a definition of public display and page 39 for a definition of public performance.)

Lending to the public is a form of public distribution. (See page 40.) Since most libraries lend reserve materials to patrons at least for a few hours, the Justinian Law School Library will probably distribute these copies publicly. Once I determined that the project would probably involve public distribution, I consulted Chart 6 to see if I could find a section of the law that authorized the public distribution without permission from the copyright holder. The same section that authorized the reproduction of the *West Virginia Code of 1932* also authorizes the public distribution of copies made to replace the damaged copy. (See page 105.)

Finally, I checked to see if there were any derivative work or moral rights issues in the project. (Derivative works are defined on page 41. Moral rights in visual art are defined on page 41.) There are no derivative works in this project. The *Code* is not a work of visual art, so the Justinian Law School Library need not be concerned with moral rights.

I found authorization in the law for the use of all the copyright rights involved in this project. So the Justinian Library may make two complete copies of the *West Virginia Code of 1932* without permission of the copyright holder. The library may place these copies on reserve without being concerned about copyright problems.

Backup Copies of Audiocassette Tapes

The Mytown High School Library has a large collection of audiocassette tapes. About one-third of the collection is recorded books. The other two-thirds consists of musical sound recordings. Cassette tapes are easily damaged and often difficult to replace. The library has been making backup copies of the disks from its circulating computer program collection for many years. The media librarian thinks that making backup tapes would be an excellent solution to the problems that the library has been having with damaged tapes. The media librarian would like to make copies of the tapes for circulation and keep the originals in a safe location at the library. When a tape is lost or returned damaged, the librarian would then make another copy to replace the lost or damaged circulating copy. Will the library have any copyright problems if it makes backup copies of its audiotapes?

For sound recordings made after February 15, 1972, there are two copyrights which may cause problems for projects—the copyright in the works recorded and the copyright in the actual sounds of the recording. (See page 72.) Before February 15, 1972, only the works which were recorded were protected by federal copyright law. At that time, federal copyright law did not protect the actual sounds in the recording. Although cassettes did exist in the 1960s, they did not become popular until the 1970s. So for most cassettes, the analysis must include the copyrights in both the recorded work and the sounds.

As with the *Replacement of Out-of-Print Works* project, I started with the assumption that the audiotapes contain copyrighted works since most works are copyrighted. (See page 44.) I then checked the categories covered in Chart 1 to see if any of the taped works might fit into the exceptions to the general rule that most works are copyrighted.

Most of the audiotapes probably will not be works of the United States government. If some recorded books came from the Library of Congress Recording for the Blind Program, they might appear to be works of the United States Government. The government works exception, however, does not cause private copyright holders to lose their copyrights when the government republishes their works. (See page 45.) Most of the taped books produced in the

Recording for the Blind Program are tapes of privately written books recorded by the Library of Congress with the copyright holder's permission.

Although it is possible that some recorded books might contain the text of an occasional statute or case, it is unlikely that any of the taped books will consist entirely of laws or court opinions. The musical tapes are clearly not laws or court opinions.

When several works are involved in a project, each work must be examined to see if the copyright has expired. This can be time consuming and expensive (see pages 47 to 49), so the media librarian may want to assume that all the tapes are still protected by copyright. However, since it is possible that the copyright may have expired on some of the tapes, I divided the tapes into several categories to see if copyright expiration could eliminate the copyright problems for some tapes. For those tapes produced before February 15, 1972, I only needed to figure out whether the copyright in the work that was recorded had expired because there was no federal copyright protection for the recorded sounds prior to 1972. (See page 72.) All these tapes contain recordings of works covered by the 1909 Act or earlier Acts. Using the Duration Timeline on page 49, I can see that the copyright has definitely expired on any works first published more than 75 years ago. Thus, there is no copyright on any sound recording produced before February 15, 1972, of a work first published at least 75 years ago. The media librarian can clearly make backup copies of these tapes without being concerned about copyright problems.

For tapes made before February 15, 1972, of works first published less than 75 years ago, I had to either assume that the copyright in the underlying work was renewed or figure out whether an application for renewal was filed at the proper time. This process is usually time consuming and expensive for recorded literary works, so I assumed that the copyrights on these works had been renewed. (See pages 50 to 52.) However, there is a book that lists songs that have fallen into the public domain. (See page 50.) If the media librarian has access to this book, it should be relatively easy to figure out which tapes contain recordings of songs in the public domain. If the underlying songs are in the public domain and the recording was produced before 1972, there are no valid copyrights in the tapes. The media librarian can clearly make backup copies of these tapes without being concerned about copyright problems.

For tapes produced between 1972 and 1978, I had to figure out whether the copyright in the recorded work had expired and whether the copyright in the sounds had expired. Copyrights in works first published after January 1, 1964, are automatically renewed. (See page 50.) Thus the copyright in the sounds of all recordings produced between February 15, 1972, and December 31, 1977, will automatically be protected for 75 years. (See the Duration Timeline on page 49.) Even if the copyright in the recorded work has expired, none of these copyrighted sound recordings will enter the public domain until at least 2048 because of the copyright in the sounds.

Using the Duration Timeline on page 49, I found that works produced after 1977 are copyrighted for the life of the author plus 50 years. Nothing will enter the public domain under this rule until at least the end of 2028. (See page 49.) Even if the copyright in the recorded work has expired, none of these copyrighted sound recordings will enter the public domain until at least 2029 because of the copyright in the sounds. So I had to assume that the copyright in any tape produced after 1977 has not expired.

Even though the copyright in the sounds of a recording made after February 15, 1972, has not expired, the copyright in the underlying recorded work may have expired. If the copyright in a recorded work has expired, it may reduce the number of copyright problems and improve the chances that some provision in the law will authorize the backup copies. Searching the renewal records for literary works is time consuming and expensive. Since there is a book that lists songs that have fallen into the public domain, (see page 50), it may be relatively easy for the media librarian to determine which tapes contain recordings of songs in the public domain.

Some audiotapes may have been published before 1989. The media librarian may want to examine these tapes to see if they contain proper copyright notices. (The requirements for a proper notice under the 1909 Act are described on page 53. The requirements for a proper notice under the 1976 Act before March 1, 1989, are described in page 54.) If the cassettes were published before 1989, without proper notice, the lack of proper notice may invalidate the copyright in the sounds of the recording. However, the lack of a proper notice on the sound recording usually will not affect the copyright in the underlying work. Thus, even if the cassettes do not contain proper notice, the media librarian may still have to look for authorization to make backup copies because of the copyright in the underlying work. Although the media librarian may find a few cassettes that do not contain proper notice, most of the cassettes will probably contain a proper notice.

It is unlikely that the media librarian will find many audiocassettes dedicated to the public domain. However, any recorded works dedicated to the public domain may be used in this project without copyright problems. (See page 55.)

Many cassettes probably will not fit into any of the exceptions to the general rule that most works are copyrighted. I concluded that these cassettes are currently protected by copyright.

To serve the backup purpose, the media librarian must copy all of each tape. So I could tell without going through the analysis that the media librarian will be unable to limit the project to uncopyrightable parts of the work. I had to continue my analysis to determine which if any of the copyright rights might be involved in the project.

Making a copy of an audiotape is clearly reproduction. (See page 35.) Since the project involves reproduction, I needed to figure out whether the law authorizes the reproduction without permission. According to Chart 3, the sections of the law which might authorize reproductions are sections 108, 112, 113, 114, 115, 117, 118, 1008 and 107 on fair use.

Section 108 covers three major types of reproduction:

1. preservation and replacement reproduction,
2. reproductions for patrons, and
3. interlibrary loan.

The sections concerning preservation and replacement reproduction are the only ones that could to be applicable to this project.

Section 108(b) allows libraries to make facsimile reproductions of unpublished works for purposes of preservation and security. Unfortunately for the Mytown High School Library, most of its audiotapes are probably published, so this subsection is unlikely to authorize much of the reproduction in the project. (See page 63.)

Section 108(c) allows libraries to reproduce published works to replace damaged, deteriorating, lost or stolen copies. At first glance it might appear that this subsection would authorize all of the reproduction involved in the project. However, subsection (c) only permits the reproduction *after* the damage has occurred or the copy has begun to deteriorate. It does not authorize preventive backup copying which is important to the media librarian. In addition, subsection (c) authorizes the reproduction only if an unused replacement cannot be found at a fair price. The Mytown High School Library could probably repurchase many tapes through a variety of dealers for a reasonable price. Thus, subsection (c) is unlikely to authorize the reproduction involved in this project. (See page 64.)

The ephemeral recordings limitation in §112 applies only in conjunction with an authorized transmission of a performance or display of a work. (See page 69.) Since there is no transmission of a performance or display associated with this project, §112 will not authorize the reproduction in this project.

Since this project does not involve any pictorial, graphic or sculptural works, §113 will not authorize the reproductions in this project.

Section 114 limits the reproduction rights of the sound recording's copyright holder to the actual sounds in the recording. Section 114 also gives public broadcasting entities the right to reproduce sound recordings as part of the process of including the recordings in educational television or radio programs. Neither of these limitations helps in this project since the media librarian wants to reproduce the actual sounds in the sound recordings, and the project does not involve the production of educational television or radio programs. (See page 72.) Thus, §114 is unlikely to be of any help in this project.

Section 115 provides a compulsory license that allows anyone to make a new recording of a nondramatic musical work that has previously been recorded and distributed to the public. The compulsory license usually does not allow the duplication of another person's recording of a musical work. (See page 73.) The media librarian does not want to make a new recording of any of the works on the tapes. The project requires duplication of the sounds in existing recordings. Thus, §115 will not authorize the reproduction in this project.

Section 117 is limited to computer programs. Although it authorizes the making of preventive backup copies for computer programs, it does not authorize backup copies for other types of works even if they are stored on the same type of media as computer programs. (See page 73.) Since the media librarian wants to make backup copies of musical and literary works rather than computer programs, §117 will be of little assistance.

The noncommercial broadcasting exemption rarely applies to libraries because it applies only to entities which meet the definition of educational broadcasting stations under 47 U.S.C. §397. Even if a library meets that definition, §118 applies only to reproduction in the process of producing and transmitting noncommercial educational broadcast programs. So §118 will not authorize the reproduction involved in this project. (See page 75.)

The title of §1008 seems to suggest that it applies only to reproductions that occur at home. However, §1008 prohibits a copyright holder from suing *any consumer* for noncommercial digital or analog reproduction of musical recordings. (See page 75.) There is nothing in the act or legislative history that would preclude a library from being a consumer under the Act. The facts in this example do not say anything that would indicate that the reproductions in the project might be considered commercial. So it would appear that §1008 would cover the reproduction that the media librarian wants to do for the musical tapes. However, §1008 is limited to musical works. It does not cover recordings of literary works, and thus, it would not authorize preventive backup copies of the literary part of the collection.

Since I found a section that covered reproducing the musical tapes, I only needed to go through the fair use analysis for tapes of literary works. (Fair use analysis is discussed in Chapter 8 on pages 118 to 133.) In determining whether preventive backup copies of audiotapes of literary works would be a fair use, I had to consider each of the four factors listed in the statute. (See page 119.)

The purpose of the use presents little or no problem in an academic or school library. The reason for the copying is to facilitate research, scholarship, and education which are purposes that the statute specifically recognizes as weighing in favor of finding a fair use. Preservation of endangered materials is also mentioned in the legislative history as a purpose that could, in some cases, weigh in favor of finding a fair use. Thus the first factor would clearly weigh in favor of finding that fair use authorizes the reproduction in this project.

The fact that the purpose of the use is educational and weighs in favor of finding a fair use does not automatically mean that the reproduction is fair. (See page 121.) Other factors may weigh against a finding of fair use.

The second factor is the nature of the copyrighted work. (See pages 125

to 128.) The scope of copyright protection is greater for fictional or entertainment works than it is for factual works. Consequently, the nature of the
work is more likely to weigh against a finding of fair use when fictional or
entertainment works are involved than when factual works are involved. Many
of the taped books are likely to be fictional works. So this factor is likely to
weigh against a finding of fair use for those titles. It will weigh in favor of fair
use for the nonfiction titles in the tape collection.

The third factor, the amount and substantiality of the part used, is very
important. (See pages 128 to 130.) In order for this project to serve its purpose
of preventing loss of usable tapes, the media librarian needs to copy whole
tapes. The librarian has no way of determining which parts may be damaged until after the damage occurs. When whole works are reproduced, the likelihood of finding fair use decreases dramatically. This factor will weigh heavily against a finding that making backup copies of taped books is a fair use.

The fourth factor, the effect on the potential market for or value of the
work, is often considered to be the most important factor. (See pages 130 to
132.) If backup copies of taped books substitute for the purchase of additional
copies which the library might otherwise buy, then there would be detrimental effect on the market for the work. For example, with lost or damaged works,
libraries often charge the patron who loses or damages the work a fee. These
funds are usually used to purchase a new copy of the work. Even when a library
cannot collect a fee for a lost or damaged work, it still may be able to purchase
a new copy of the work. If the library replaces the lost or damaged work with
a previously made copy, it will cut into profits the copyright holder might
have earned from the purchase of replacement copies. So it appears that making preventive replacement copies of recorded works would negatively affect
the potential market for additional copies of the taped books. Thus, this factor weighs against a finding of fair use.

Three of the four factors, including market effect—the most important
factor, weigh against a finding of fair use in this example. The only factor that
weighs in favor of a finding of fair use is the first factor, the purpose and character of the use. As many of the cases discussed on page 121 indicate, when
educational purpose is the only factor that weighs in favor of fair use, courts
frequently find no fair use. Therefore, I would not recommend that the
Mytown High School Library rely on fair use to authorize reproduction of the
taped books.

Reproduction is only one of the rights reserved to the copyright holder.
I also needed to figure out whether any of the other copyright rights are
involved in this project.

There are no public displays, public performances, or derivative works in
this project. (See pages 35, 39 and 41 for definitions of public display, public
performance and derivative works.) Audiotapes are not works of visual art (see
page 41), so the media librarian need not be concerned with moral rights.

The Mytown High School Library lends the tapes to students for use at home. Lending to the public is a form of public distribution, (see page 40) so I looked for authorization to lend backup copies to patrons. Chart 6 lists sections 108, 109, 112, 113, 115, 117 and 107 on fair use as the sections which might authorize public distributions. I have already determined that sections 108, 112, 113, 115, and 117 do not cover this project.

Section 109(a) authorizes the owner of any copy or phonorecord lawfully made under the Copyright Act to transfer possession of that particular copy. This provision authorizes a library to lend any copy that it has purchased or is authorized to make under any other section of the law or under a license. (See page 108.) Thus, §109(a) should cover the lending of copies of musical tapes made under §1008. Once the library acquires lawfully made backup copies of the taped books, §109 would also authorize the library to lend those copies.

I found sections in the law which cover the reproduction and distribution involved in this project for the musical tapes. So the media librarian at the Mytown High School Library may make and lend preventive backup copies of the musical tapes without the permission of the copyright holders. However, I did not find sections of the law that would authorize the reproduction of taped books. So the library should either

a. abandon the recorded books part of the project,
b. buy additional copies of recorded books to serve the backup purpose, or
c. obtain permission to make the backup copies from the copyright holders in both the sound recordings and the underlying books recorded on tape.

Dial-a-Story

The Anytown Public Library has had a successful children's story hour program for the last five years. Recently, a tornado destroyed the children's wing of the library, so facilities no longer exist where children can gather to hear librarians read stories. Instead of abandoning story hour, the children's librarian suggested that an automatic phone system could be set up so that children could call the library and listen to recordings of stories read by a librarian. Librarians would select books from those not destroyed by the tornado and those collected in recent book drives. The librarian would then take the books to a local recording studio that has volunteered to record for the library. The librarian would read the books aloud, and the studio would record the readings on tape. The tapes would be kept in the administrative offices at the library. Children would call the library and talk to the children's librarian. The librarian would select a tape, load it into a tape player attached to the phone and start the tape playing. The phone will hang up automatically when the tape ends. Will the library encounter any copyright problems in this project?

As with the *Replacement of Out-of-Print Works* project and the *Backup Audio Tapes* project, I started with the assumption that the stories were copyrighted because most works are copyrighted. (See page 44.) I then looked for groups of children's stories that might fit into the exceptions to the general rule that most works are copyrighted. Even if some of the children's stories are copyrighted, it might be possible to avoid all the copyright issues by limiting the project to uncopyrighted stories.

Most of the children's books probably will not be works of the United States government, so this exception is not likely to be of much help. The text of laws and court opinions are not generally suitable stories for children, so this exception is not likely to be of much help either.

However, there are many stories that may be old enough to have expired copyrights which are still favorites for children. Using the Duration Timeline on page 49, I could see that books originally copyrighted at least 75 years ago are in the public domain. These old books can be used in the Dial-a-Story project with no copyright problems.

Books published less than 75 years ago will be more of a problem. Some may be in the public domain because the copyright holders failed to renew the copyrights. But searching Copyright Office records to determine which copyrights were renewed would be time consuming and expensive. (See pages 50 to 52.) So the Anytown Public Library should probably assume that all copyrights were properly renewed for purposes of this project.

Some children's books owned by or donated to the library may have been published before 1989. The librarian will need to examine these books to see if they contain proper notices. (The requirements for a proper notice under the 1909 Act are described on page 53. The requirements for a proper notice under the 1976 Act prior to March 1, 1989, are described on page 54.) The library may use books published before 1989 without proper notice in the Dial-a-Story project without obtaining permission from the copyright holder. Although the librarian may find a few books that do not contain proper notice, most books will contain a proper notice.

It is unlikely that the librarian will find many children's books dedicated to the public domain. (See page 55.) However, if the librarian does find books dedicated to the public domain, the library may use these books in the project without the permission of the copyright owner.

Some projects can be limited to parts of works not protected by copyright. However, the point of this project is to read entire stories to children. Reading titles or just mentioning ideas or facts from the children's stories would not accomplish the purpose of the project. So I could see from the Decision Charts without going through the analysis that the project could not be limited to uncopyrightable parts of works.

Many children's books will not fit into any of the exceptions, so the librarian must conclude that they are currently protected by copyright. If the Anytown Public Library wants to include these books in the project, it will be necessary to go through the rest of the analysis to determine

a. which rights are involved,
b. whether any sections of the law authorize the uses of the rights involved, and
c. what permissions will be needed.

A reproduction occurs when the words of the story are recorded on the tape. The tape is an object into which the story has been transcribed and from which it can be perceived and reproduced. (See page 35.) Chart 3 lists sections 108, 112, 113, 114, 115, 117, 118, 1008 and 107 on fair use as sections which might authorize a reproduction. From the brief information given in the chart, I could quickly see that §113 on pictorial, graphic and sculptural works, §115 on compulsory licenses for nondramatic musical works, and §117 on computer programs are not likely to be of much help for this project.

Section 108 covers three major types of reproduction:

1. preservation and replacement reproduction;
2. reproductions for patrons; and
3. interlibrary loan.

This project obviously does not involve interlibrary loan, but the reproduction might be characterized as replacement reproduction or reproduction for patrons.

Unfortunately, §108(c) on replacement copying, is limited to reproduction in facsimile form. Since the stories were originally in book form, reproducing them by reading them aloud onto tape would not be reproduction in facsimile form. Therefore, §108(c) will not authorize the reproduction involved in this project. (See pages 63.)

Subsections (d) and (e) cover reproduction for patrons. Copies made under subsections (d) and (e) must be made at the request of a patron and must become the property of the requesting patron. (See page 64.) The tapes made in this project are not made specifically upon the request of a patron and do not become the property of a particular patron, so neither subsection (d) nor (e) will authorize the reproduction.

The exception for ephemeral recordings, §112, applies only to reproductions made in connection with a transmission of a performance. The library must have a right to transmit the performance under either a license or another section of the law. (See page 70.) If the library has a license from the copyright holder to transmit performances of a book, then §112(a) would give the library the right to make a copy to facilitate that transmission. However, §112(a) applies only if the library has acquired a license to transmit a public performance. Section 112(a) also limits the time that the library can keep and use the copy for additional transmissions to six months. At the end of the six month period, the library would have to find some other authorization to retain and continue to use the copy.

The other subsections of §112 are not applicable to this project. Subsection (b) only authorizes the making of copies when a library has a right to transmit a public performance under §110(2). The Anytown Public Library probably does not have a right to transmit a public performance under §110(2). (See page 92.) Subsection (c) is limited to religious musical works. Subsection (d) applies only to transmissions of public performances directed primarily to the handicapped.

Section 114 applies to the scope of copyright in works that already exist in the form of sound recordings. (See pages 72 to 73.) The rights of the copyright holder in the underlying work (the copyright holder in the children's book) are separate from the rights of the copyright holder in the sound recording and are not affected by §114. Thus, §114 is not applicable to the reproduction involved in converting a printed literary work to a sound recording of a literary work.

Section 118 will not authorize any of the reproduction involved in the Dial-a-Story project. First, only organizations which meet the definition of public broadcasting entities contained in 47 U.S.C. §397 may take advantage of §118. Very few libraries meet this definition. Second, §118 applies only to published nondramatic musical, pictorial, graphic and sculptural works. It does not apply to literary works such as the children's books involved in this project. (See page 75.)

The Audio Home Recording Act applies only to reproductions of recorded music, so it will not authorize any of the reproductions involved in this project. (See page 76.)

In determining whether recording books for Dial-a-Story would be fair use, I had to consider each of the four factors listed in the statute. (See page 119.) The basic framework of the analysis is the same as it was for the *Replacement of Out-of-Print Works* problem and the *Backup Audio Tapes* problem. But even minor differences in the facts of the problems can change the outcome on any particular factor or the whole analysis.

The first factor is the purpose and character of the use. The purpose of the reproduction is to create tapes to substitute for children's story hour after the destruction of much of the public library in a tornado. While that purpose may seem to be obviously fair to many librarians, it is important not to base the answers to legal questions on a personal innate sense of fairness or what seems right. The statute, legislative history and case law determine what purposes will be considered fair. The statute lists six purposes which are likely to weigh in favor of a finding of fair use. They are criticism, comment, news reporting, teaching, scholarship, and research. Dial-a-Story's purposes do not fit within any of these categories. They come closest to fitting within the teaching category, since children can learn a variety of things from the stories including life skills and a respect for books and the information they contain. But learning is not the only, and perhaps not even the primary, reason that children listen to stories or that libraries offer story hours. Entertainment and giving children a safe way to spend time are other purposes for story hours. While these are excellent reasons for encouraging programs like Dial-a-Story, they weaken the argument that the purpose of the project fits squarely within the statutorily favored purposes. The courts appear to be construing the scope of the favored purposes narrowly. (See the discussion of the *Kinko's* and *Texaco* cases on pages 123 and 124.) So I could not conclude that the first factor clearly weighs in favor of finding that the reproduction involved in Dial-a-Story is a fair use. I might conclude that the first factor leans slightly in favor of finding a fair use or that it leans slightly against a finding of fair use. (See pages 119 to 125.)

The second factor is the nature of the copyrighted work. (See pages 125 to 128.) When fictional or entertainment works are involved, the nature of the work often weighs against a finding of fair use because the scope of copyright protection is greater for these types of works than it is for factual works. Most of the books that librarians are likely to select for the Dial-a-Story project will probably be either fiction or entertainment works. So this factor is likely to weigh against a finding of fair use.

The third factor, the amount and substantiality of the part used, is very important. (See pages 128 to 130.) It is unlikely that librarians will want to record, or children will want to listen to, short incomplete parts of stories. The project is likely to involve the recording of entire children's books. As the cases make clear, when an entire work is reproduced, the third factor weighs against a finding of fair use even when the work is short. (See page 128.) When whole works are reproduced, the likelihood of finding no fair use rises dramatically. This factor will weigh heavily against a finding that taping books for the Dial-a-Story project is a fair use.

The effect on the potential market for or value of the work, the fourth factor, is often considered the most important factor. (See pages 130 to 132.) If the recording of children's books substitutes for the purchase of additional copies which the library might otherwise buy, then there is a detrimental effect on the market for the work. In recent years, the recorded book industry has grown substantially. Recorded children's stories are readily available in catalogs, bookstores, toy stores and even supermarkets. While the selection of stories available in retail stores may be limited, the selection of taped books marketed to libraries and schools is considerably larger. If the Anytown Public Library had the funds and decided for any reason that it wanted to develop a collection of children's books on audiotape, it could easily buy authorized commercially produced tapes. If libraries make their own tapes instead of purchasing the ones authorized by the copyright holder, the copyright holder may receive less income. Thus the fourth factor weighs against a finding that the reproduction involved in the Dial-a-Story project would be a fair use.

Three of the four factors, including the important effect on the market factor, weigh against a finding that the reproduction in this example is a fair use. The only factor that might weigh in favor of a finding of fair use is the first factor, the purpose and character of the use. Even the purpose and character of the use factor does not clearly weigh in favor of finding a fair use in this example. When the only factor that weighs in favor of fair use is the educational purpose of the copier, courts frequently find no fair use. (See page 121.) Therefore, I would not advise the Anytown Public Library to rely on fair use to authorize taping readings of children's books for the Dial-a-Story project.

None of the sections in the copyright law authorizes the reproduction involved in the Dial-a-Story project. The Anytown Public Library will either need the permission of each copyright holder to tape the stories or will have to restructure the project to avoid the reproduction issues. The project would not involve any reproduction issues if the library purchased commercially recorded tapes of children's books instead of making the tapes themselves. But before deciding to purchase tapes for the Dial-a-Story project, the analysis should be completed to see if any other copyright issues might raise other obstacles to the project.

There are no public displays in this project. (See page 35 for a definition of public displays.) This project does not involve public distribution, because the library does not deliver copies or phonorecords of the stories to patrons. Patrons are only allowed to listen to the stories. (See page 40.) Audiotapes are not works of visual art, so I do not need to be concerned with moral rights. (See page 41.)

A public performance occurs every time a tape is played. When a tape is played, the story on it is recited. The performance includes not only the original playing of the tape but also the process by which that performance is transmitted over the telephone to a child. (See page 55.) The performances are public because they are transmitted to members of the public. (See page 37.) Chart 5 suggests sections 109, 110, 111, 114, 116, 118 and 107 on fair use as sections which might authorize public performances. I was able to tell from the brief information given in the chart that §109 and §116 are not likely to be applicable to this project.

Section 110 is divided into ten subsections. Each subsection is a separate exception with different elements that must be analyzed separately. (See page 89.)

Section 110(1) permits performances during face-to-face teaching activities in a classroom or similar place of instruction. (See page 91.) The Dial-a-Story project does not meet either the face-to-face part of the requirements or the requirement that the teaching activity be a part of systematic instruction. So §110(1) will not authorize the performances in this project.

Unlike §110(1), §110(2) is not limited to face-to-face activities. It allows performances of nondramatic literary works during systematic instructional activities conducted by nonprofit educational institutions or government bodies. Most of the children's books are likely to be nondramatic literary works, so the type of work does not present a problem. The Anytown Public Library is not an educational institution, but it probably is a governmental body. However, the requirement that the transmitted performance must be a part of systematic instructional activities is still a problem. Section 110(2) does not authorize transmitted performances for purposes of entertainment or recreation. (See page 93.)

Subsection 3 of §110 does not apply to libraries unless religious services are being conducted in the library. (See page 94.)

Section 110 (4), which applies to nonprofit performances of nondramatic literary and musical works, will not authorize the performances involved in the Dial-a-Story project either. It does not authorize any performances transmitted to members of the public. (See page 94.)

The home receiving device exception contained in §110 (5) might appear to apply at first glance because a telephone is a machine commonly found in the home. However, §110(5) only authorizes the reception of a performance using a home receiving device. It does not authorize any transmissions, and the Anytown Public Library needs to find a limitation that will authorize it to transmit public performances. (See page 95.)

Neither §110(6), §110(7) nor §110(10) are usually applicable to libraries. §110(6) applies to some performances at agricultural and horticultural fairs. (See page 97.) Section 110(7) concerns performances related to the selling of phonorecords and sheet music. (See page 98.) Section 110(10) concerns certain performances conducted by veterans' or fraternal organizations. (See page 99.)

Subsections (8) and (9) cover certain transmitted performances targeted at handicapped audiences. (See page 98.) They do not apply to the Dial-a-Story facts. None of the subsections of §110 will authorize the public performances that occur in the Dial-a-Story project.

The Dial-a-Story project does not involve any secondary transmissions, so §111 will not be of any assistance. (See page 99.)

If the Anytown Public Library purchases recorded books for the project, it must consider two copyrights: the copyright that covers the recorded sound on the tape and the copyright that covers the written book that was recorded. The two copyrights are separate and must be analyzed separately. Section 114 makes it clear that the owner of the copyright in a sound recording does not usually have the right to prohibit the library from publicly performing the recorded books. (See page 100.) This is not the same thing as giving the library the right to publicly perform the recorded books. Section 114 does not affect the owners of the copyrights in the written versions of the books. They usually have a separate right to prohibit public performances of other works that include their works. This means that they can prohibit the public playing of the sound recordings of their works even though the copyright holder in the sound recording cannot. Thus, while §114 may reduce the number of copyright holders who have a right to object to the public performances in the Dial-a-Story project, it does not actually authorize any of the performances.

The exception to the general rule of no performance rights in sound recordings is that the copyright holder of a digital sound recording has the exclusive right to perform the recording by means of a digital transmission. The digital performance right might be of importance if the library acquires recorded books on CD and transmits them over digital phone lines. But the library could easily avoid the digital performance right by purchasing the books on analog cassette tapes. (See page 100.)

Section 118 applies only to published nondramatic musical, pictorial, graphic and sculptural works. It does not apply to literary works such as the children's books involved in this project.

Most of the reasoning used to decide whether the reproductions involved in Dial-a-Story are a fair use also apply to determining whether the public performances in the project could be considered a fair use. The first three factors, the purpose and character of the use, the nature of the works, and the amount and substantiality of the portion of the works used, are the same. (See discussion on pages 158 to 159.)

However, the analysis of the fourth factor, the effect on the market is different for public performance issues than it is for reproduction issues. Public performance rights are generally marketed separately from reproduction rights. So I had to focus specifically on the market for performance rights instead of the general market for the children's books.

Although the Anytown Public Library could probably purchase copies of recorded books fairly easily, it would probably be much harder to acquire public performance licenses for recorded books. Most recorded books have been created with the expectation that they will be listened to by individuals in situations that do not involve public performances. So the copyright holders have not created an easy market for acquiring public performance licenses for recorded books. When a copyright holder has done nothing to market a particular type of license, those license fees are not part of the usual income for the work and do not have much impact on the market effect factor in fair use analysis. (See pages 131 to 132.)

There are also several other factors which tend to suggest that any impact that this project might have on the market for public performance rights would be very small. Only one child at a time is likely to listen to a story on the phone. The Anytown Public Library does not intend to collect any fees for the service. And the project could be limited to a short time if it is only used as a substitute for story hour until the library can be repaired and a basic collection rebuilt.

The need for a quick response to the tornado destruction also decreases the likelihood that the library would have time to track down all the copyright holders and negotiate public performance licenses. A spontaneous decision to use a work for a short time is generally seen as a factor that limits the negative effect on the market.

On balance, it appears that the fourth factor would weigh in favor of finding that the public performances involved in Dial-a-Story are a fair use. However, this factor might change if the project were a permanent project instead of a quick temporary replacement for story hour in an emergency setting. (See pages 130 to 132.)

Since the effect on the market is often considered the single most important factor in fair use analysis, it might be enough to tip the balance in favor of finding a fair use. But this result is not certain, since at least two of the other factors still weigh against a finding of fair use and the purpose and character of the use does not fit squarely within any of the favored purposes.

Because there is a substantial creative element involved in performing a story by reading it aloud, creating a recording of that performance could be the creation of a derivative work. According to Chart 7, sections 114, 117, and 107 on fair use are the sections which might authorize the creation of a derivative work.

Section 114 limits the copyright holder's right to prepare derivative works based on the sound recording to the right to rearrange, remix or otherwise alter the actual sounds on the recording. This means, for example, that the copyright holder in a sound recording can prohibit the making of bootleg copies of her own recording but cannot prohibit other people from imitating her recording. Of course, the owner of the copyright in the underlying work (the children's book) may have the right to prohibit such imitations, because the imitations are still reproductions of the underlying work. This limitation is not likely to apply to the creation of the derivative works involved in the Dial-a-Story project since the librarians will be creating their own sound recordings rather than imitating the sounds in an existing recording.

Section 117 is applicable only to computer programs. This project involves the creation of derivative works based on children's books rather than computer programs, so §117 will not authorize any of the derivative works involved in this project. (See page 115.)

Most of the reasoning applicable to determining whether the reproductions and public performances involved in Dial-a-Story could be considered a fair use also applies to determining whether the derivative works involved in the project could be considered a fair use. The first three factors, the purpose and character of the use, the nature of the works, and the amount and substantiality of the portion of the works used, are the same. (See discussion on pages 158 to 159.)

As with the public performance analysis, the fourth factor, the effect on the market, is the only factor in which derivative works fair use analysis may differ from fair use analysis for reproduction issues. Like performance rights, derivative work rights are generally marketed separately from other reproduction rights. Most derivative work rights are fairly unique and are usually individually negotiated. There usually are no standard terms or prices for derivative work licenses. These factors make the transaction costs of licensing derivative work rights very high. When transaction costs are high, it is not worth the copyright holder's time and effort to exploit the rights for small projects. The fact that transaction costs are high enough to discourage copyright holders from seriously marketing rights is generally considered evidence that the effect of the use on the market for the work is not sufficient to weigh against a finding of fair use. (See pages 130 to 132.)

Since the effect on the market is often considered the most important factor in fair use analysis, it might be enough to tip the balance in favor of finding a fair use. However this result is no more certain than it was for the public performance issues since at least two of the other factors still weigh against a finding of fair use and the purpose and character of the use does not fit squarely within any of the favored purposes.

Again, fair use is the only exception that might authorize the derivative works involved in Dial-a-Story. And the fair use argument is as weak on the derivative works issues as it is for the public performance issues. (See pages 162 to 163.) However, there are at least two ways to avoid the derivative works problems in the Dial-a-Story project. First, if the library purchases recorded books instead of making the recordings itself, then it will not be making any derivative works. If the library cannot purchase the recorded books quickly enough, it could still reduce the derivative works problems by obtaining permission for the project from a single large publisher and limiting the project to children's books from that publisher.

The Dial-a-Story project involves reproduction of, public performances of and the creation of derivative works based on copyrighted works. No specific section or combination of sections in the copyright law clearly authorizes the reproductions, the public performances or the derivative works involved in the project. Since fair use is the only section that might authorize some of the rights used in this project and the outcome of the fair use analysis is uncertain, the Anytown Public Library may want to consider limiting the project to books in the public domain or obtaining permission and paying license fees. The library will still have to tackle the problem of getting permission with a reasonable amount of effort. But it may be possible to tailor the project to reduce that effort and still achieve the library's goals. At the start of the project, the library might limit the project to books which are not protected by copyright. Later, the library might locate the largest publisher of recorded children's books. It could then purchase tapes from and negotiate a public performance license with that publisher. As the librarians gain more experience in negotiating licenses, they may add books from additional publishers as they work out the permission problems.

Part IV.
Appendices

A. Interlibrary Loan Guidelines (CONTU)

Photocopying—Interlibrary Arrangements

INTRODUCTION

Subsection 108(g)(2) of the bill deals, among other things, with limits on interlibrary arrangements for photocopying. It prohibits systematic photocopying of copyrighted materials but permits interlibrary arrangements "that do not have, as their purpose or effect, that the library or archives receiving such copies or phonorecords for distribution does so in such aggregate quantities as to substitute for a subscription to or purchase of such work."

The National Commission on New Technological Uses of Copyrighted Works offered its good offices to the House and Senate subcommittees in bringing the interested parties together to see if agreement could be reached on what a realistic definition would be of "such aggregate quantities." The Commission consulted with the parties and suggested the interpretation which follows, on which there has been substantial agreement by the principal library, publisher, and author organizations. The Commission considers the guidelines which follow to be a workable and fair interpretation of the intent of the proviso portion of subsection 108(g)(2).

These guidelines are intended to provide guidance in the application of §108 to the most frequently encountered interlibrary case: a library's obtaining from another library, in lieu of interlibrary loan, copies of articles from relatively recent issues of periodicals—those published within five years prior to the date of the request. The guidelines do not specify what aggregate quantity of copies of an article or articles published in a periodical, the issue date of which is more than five years prior to the date when the request for the copy thereof is made, constitutes a substitute for a subscription to such periodical. The meaning of the proviso to subsection 108(g)(2) in such case is left to future interpretation.

The point has been made that the present practice on interlibrary loans and use of photocopies in lieu of loans may be supplemented or even largely replaced by a system in which one or more agencies or institutions, public or private, exist for the specific purpose of providing a central source for photocopies. Of course, these guidelines would not apply to such a situation.

Guidelines for the Proviso of Subsection 108(g)(2)

1. As used in the proviso of subsection 108(g)(2), the words "... such aggregate quantities as to substitute for a subscription to or purchase of such work" shall mean:
   (a) with respect to any given periodical (as opposed to any given issue of a periodical), filled requests of a library or archives (a "requesting entity") within any calendar year for a total of six or more copies of an article or articles published in such periodical within five years prior to the date of the request. These guidelines specifically shall not apply, directly or indirectly, to any request of a requesting entity for a copy or copies of an article or articles published in any issue of a periodical, the publication date of which is more than five years prior to the date when the request is made. These guidelines do not define the meaning, with respect to such a request, of "... such aggregate quantities as to substitute for a subscription to [such periodical]."
   (b) With respect to any other material described in subsection 108(d), (including fiction and poetry), filled requests of a requesting entity within any calendar year for a total of six or more copies or phonorecords of or from any given work (including a collective work) during the entire period when such material shall be protected by copyright.
2. In the event that a requesting entity—
   (a) shall have in force or shall have entered an order for a subscription to a periodical, or
   (b) has within its collection, or shall have entered an order for, a copy or phonorecord of any other copyrighted work,
   material from either category of which it desires to obtain by copy from another library or archives (the "supplying entity"), because the material to be copied is not reasonably available for use by the requesting entity itself, then the fulfillment of such request shall be treated as though the requesting entity made such copy from its own collection. A library or archives may request a copy or phonorecord from a supplying entity only under those circumstances where the requesting entity would have been able, under the other provisions of §108, to supply such copy from materials in its own collection.

3. No request for a copy or phonorecord of any material to which these guidelines apply may be fulfilled by the supplying entity unless such request is accompanied by a representation by the requesting entity that the request was made in conformity with these guidelines.

4. The requesting entity shall maintain records of all requests made by it for copies or phonorecords of any materials to which these guidelines apply and shall maintain records of the fulfillment of such requests, which records shall be retained until the end of the third complete calendar year after the end of the calendar year in which the respective request shall have been made.

5. As part of the review provided for in subsection 108(i), these guidelines shall be reviewed not later than five years from the effective date of this bill [Jan. 1, 1978].

B. Educational Photocopying Guidelines

Agreement on Guidelines for Classroom Copying
in Not-for-Profit Educational Institutions
with Respect to Books and Periodicals

The purpose of the following guidelines is to state the minimum and not the maximum standards of educational fair use under §107 of H.R. 2223. The parties agree that the conditions determining the extent of permissible copying for educational purposes may change in the future; that certain types of copying permitted under these guidelines may not be permissible in the future; and conversely that in the future other types of copying not permitted under these guidelines may be permissible under revised guidelines.

Moreover, the following statement of guidelines is not intended to limit the types of copying permitted under the standards of fair use under judicial decision and which are stated in §107 of the Copyright Revision Bill. There may be instances in which copying which does not fall within the guidelines stated below may nonetheless be permitted under the criteria of fair use.

Guidelines

I. Single Copying for Teachers

A single copy may be made of any of the following by or for a teacher at his or her individual request for his or her scholarly research or use in teaching or preparation to teach a class:

    A.   A chapter from a book;

    B.   An article from a periodical or newspaper;

    C.   A short story, short essay or short poem, whether or not from a collective work;

    D.   A chart, graph, diagram, drawing, cartoon or picture from a book, periodical, or newspaper;

II. Multiple Copies for Classroom Use

Multiple copies (not to exceed in any event more than one copy per pupil in a course) may be made by or for the teacher giving the course for classroom use or discussion; provided that:

A. The copying meets the tests of brevity and spontaneity as defined below; and,

B. Meets the cumulative effect test as defined below; and,

C. Each copy includes a notice of copyright.

DEFINITIONS

Brevity

    (i) Poetry:

        (a) A complete poem if less than 250 words and if printed on not more than two pages or,

        (b) from a longer poem, an excerpt of not more than 250 words.

    (ii) Prose:

        (a) Either a complete article, story or essay of less than 2,500 words, or

        (b) an excerpt from any prose work of not more than 1,000 words or 10 percent of the work, whichever is less, but in any event a minimum of 500 words.

[Each of the numerical limits stated in "i" and "ii" above may be expanded to permit the completion of an unfinished line of a poem or of an unfinished prose paragraph.]

    (iii) Illustration:

One chart, graph, diagram, drawing, cartoon or picture per book or per periodical issue.

    (iv) "Special" works:

Certain works in poetry, prose or in "poetic prose" which often combine language with illustrations and which are intended sometimes for children and at other times for a more general audience fall short of 2,500 words in their entirety. Paragraph "ii" above notwithstanding such "special works" may not be reproduced in their entirety; however, an excerpt comprising not more than two of the published pages of such special work and containing not more than 10 percent of the words found in the text thereof, may be reproduced.

Spontaneity

    (i) The copying is at the instance and inspiration of the individual teacher, and

    (ii) The inspiration and decision to use the work and the moment of its use for maximum teaching effectiveness are so close in time that it would be unreasonable to expect a timely reply to a request for permission.

Cumulative Effect

(i) The copying of the material is for only one course in the school in which the copies are made.

(ii) Not more than one short poem, article, story, essay or two excerpts may be copied from the same author, nor more than three from the same collective work or periodical volume during one class term.

(iii) There shall not be more than nine instances of such multiple copying for one course during one class term.

[The limitations stated in "ii" and "iii" above shall not apply to current news periodicals and newspapers and current news sections of other periodicals.]

III. Prohibitions as to I and II Above

Notwithstanding any of the above, the following shall be prohibited:

A. Copying shall not be used to create or to replace or substitute for anthologies, compilations or collective works. Such replacement or substitution may occur whether copies of various works or excerpts therefrom are accumulated or reproduced and used separately.

B. There shall be no copying of or from works intended to be "consumable" in the course of study or of teaching. These include workbooks, exercises, standardized tests and test booklets and answer sheets and like consumable material.

C. Copying shall not:

(a) substitute for the purchase of books, publishers' reprints or periodicals;

(b) be directed by higher authority;

(c) be repeated with respect to the same item by the sameteacher from term to term.

D. No charge shall be made to the student beyond the actual costof the photocopying.

Agreed March 19, 1976.

Ad Hoc Committee on Copyright Law Revision:
BY SHELDON ELLIOTT STEINBACH.

Author-Publisher Group:
Authors League of America:
BY IRWIN KARP, Counsel.

Association of American Publishers, Inc.:
BY ALEXANDER C. HOFFMAN,
Chairman, Copyright Committee.

C. Educational Music Guidelines

Guidelines for Educational Uses of Music

The purpose of the following guidelines is to state the minimum and not the maximum standards of educational fair use under §107 of H.R. 2223. The parties agree that the conditions determining the extent of permissible copying for educational purposes may change in the future; that certain types of copying permitted under these guidelines may not be permissible in the future, and conversely that in the future other types of copying not permitted under these guidelines may be permissible under revised guidelines.

Moreover, the following statement of guidelines is not intended to limit the types of copying permitted under the standards of fair use under judicial decision and which are stated in §107 of the Copyright Revision Bill. There may be instances in which copying which does not fall within the guidelines stated below may nonetheless be permitted under the criteria of fair use.

A. Permissible Uses
1. Emergency copying to replace purchased copies which for any reason are not available for an imminent performance provided purchased replacement copies shall be substituted in due course.
2. (a) For academic purposes other than performance, single or multiple copies of excerpts of works may be made, provided that the excerpts do not comprise a part of the whole which would constitute a performable unit such as a section, movement or aria, but in no case more than 10 percent of the whole work. The number of copies shall not exceed one copy per pupil.
   (b) For academic purposes other than performance, a single copy of an entire performable unit (section, movement, aria, etc.) that is,
   (1) confirmed by the copyright proprietor to be out-of-print or
   (2) unavailable except in a larger work, may be made by or for a

teacher solely for the purpose of his or her scholarly research or in preparation to teach a class.

3. Printed copies which have been purchased may be edited or simplified provided that the fundamental character of the work is not distorted or the lyrics, if any, altered or lyrics added if none exist.

4. A single copy of recordings of performances by students may be made for evaluation or rehearsal purposes and may be retained by the educational institution or individual teacher.

5. A single copy of a sound recording (such as a tape, disc or cassette) of copyrighted music may be made from sound recordings owned by an educational institution or an individual teacher for the purpose of constructing aural exercises or examinations and may be retained by the educational institution or individual teacher. (This pertains only to the copyright of the music itself and not to any copyright which may exist in the sound recording.)

B. Prohibitions

1. Copying to create or replace or substitute for anthologies, compilations or collective works.

2. Copying of or from works intended to be "consumable" in the course of study or of teaching such as workbooks, exercises, standardized tests and answer sheets and like material.

3. Copying for the purpose of performance, except as in A(1) above.

4. Copying for the purpose of substituting for the purchase of music, except as in A(1) and A(2) above.

5. Copying without inclusion of the copyright notice which appears on the printed copy.

D. Off-Air Taping Guidelines

Guidelines for Off-Air Recording of Broadcast
Programming for Educational Purposes

The following guidelines reflect the Negotiating Committee's consensus as to the application of "fair use" to the recording, retention and use of television broadcast programs for educational purposes. They specify periods of retention and use of such off-air recordings in classrooms and similar places devoted to instruction and for homebound instruction. The purpose of establishing these guidelines is to provide standards for both owners and users of copyrighted television programs.

1. The guidelines were developed to apply only to off-air recording by nonprofit educational institutions.

2. A broadcast program may be recorded off-air simultaneously with broadcast transmission (including simultaneous cable retransmission) and retained by a nonprofit educational institution for a period not to exceed the first forty-five (45) consecutive calendar days after date of recording. Upon conclusion of such retention period, all off-air recordings must be erased or destroyed immediately. "Broadcast programs" are television programs transmitted by television stations for reception by the general public without charge.

3. Off-air recordings may be used once by individual teachers in the course of relevant teaching activities, and repeated once only when instructional reinforcement is necessary, in classrooms and similar places devoted to instruction within a single building, cluster or campus, as well as in the home of students receiving formalized home instruction during the first ten (10) consecutive school days in the forty-five (45) day calendar day retention period. "School days" are school session days—not counting weekends, holidays, vacations, examination periods, or other scheduled interruptions—within the forty-five (45) calendar day retention period.

4. Off-air recordings may be made only at the request of and used by individual teachers, and may not be regularly recorded in anticipation of requests. No broadcast program may be recorded off-air more than once at the request of the same teacher, regardless of the number of times the program may be broadcast.

5. A limited number of copies may be reproduced from each off-air recording to meet the legitimate needs of teachers under these guidelines. Each such additional copy shall be subject to all provisions governing the original recording.

6. After the first ten (10) consecutive school days, off-air recordings may be used up to the end of the forty-five (45) calendar day retention period only for teacher evaluation purposes, i.e., to determine whether or not to include the broadcast program in the teaching curriculum, and may not be used in the recording institution for student exhibition or any other non-evaluation purpose without authorization.

7. Off-air recordings need not be used in their entirety, but the recorded programs may not be altered from their original content. Off-air recordings may not be physically or electronically combined or merged to constitute teaching anthologies or compilations.

8. All copies of off-air recordings must include the copyright notice on the broadcast program as recorded.

9. Educational institutions are expected to establish appropriate control procedures to maintain the integrity of these guidelines.

E. Classroom and Reserve Use Guidelines (ACRL/ALA)

Model Policy Concerning College and University Photocopying for Classroom, Research and Library Reserve Use

I. The Copyright Act and Photocopying

From time to time, the faculty and staff of this University [College] may use photocopied materials to supplement research and teaching. In many cases, photocopying can facilitate the University's [College's] mission; that is, the development and transmission of information. However, the photocopying of copyrighted materials is a right granted under the copyright law's doctrine of "fair use" which must not be abused. This report will explain the University's [College's] policy concerning the photocopying of copyrighted materials by faculty and library staff. Please note that this policy does not address other library photocopying which may be permitted under other sections of the copyright law, e.g. 17 U.S.C. §108.

Copyright is a constitutionally conceived property right which is designed to promote the progress of science and the useful arts by securing for an author the benefits of his or her original work of authorship for a limited time. U.S. Constitution, Art. I, Sec. 8. The Copyright statute, 17 U.S.C. §101 *et seq.*, implements this policy by balancing the author's interest against the public interest in the dissemination of information affecting areas of universal concern, such as art, science, history and business. The grand design of this delicate balance is to foster the creation and dissemination of intellectual works for the general public.

The Copyright Act defines the rights of a copyright holder and how they may be enforced against an infringer. Included within the Copyright Act is the "fair use" doctrine which allows, under certain conditions, the copying of copyrighted material. While the Act lists general factors under the heading of "fair use" it provides little in the way of specific directions for what constitutes fair use. The law states:

17 U.S.C. §107. Limitations of exclusive rights: Fair use.

Notwithstanding the provisions of section 106, *the fair use of a copyrighted work, including such use by reproduction in copies or phonorecords or by any other means specified by that section for purposes such as criticism, comment, news reporting, teaching (including multiple copies for classroom use), scholarship, or research, is not an infringement of copyright.* In determining whether the use made of a work in any particular case is a fair use the factors to be considered shall include—

(1) The purpose and character of the use, including whether such use is of a commercial nature or is for nonprofit educational purposes;

(2) the nature of the copyrighted work;

(3) the amount of substantiality of the portion used in relation to the copyrighted work as a whole; and

(4) the effect of the use upon the potential market for or value of the copyrighted work. (*Emphasis added.*) [Text of §107 as it read in 1976; see page 218 for text as amended in 1992.]

The purpose of this report is to provide you, the faculty and staff of this University [College], with an explanation of when the photocopying of copyrighted material in our opinion is permitted under the fair use doctrine. Where possible, common examples of research, classroom, and library reserve photocopying have been included to illustrate what we believe to be the reach and limits of fair use.

Please note that the copyright law applies to all forms of photocopying, whether it is undertaken at a commercial copying center, at the University's [College's] central or departmental copying facilities or at a self-service machine. While you are free to use the services of a commercial establishment, you should be prepared to provide documentation of permission from the publisher (if such permission is necessary under this policy), since many commercial copiers will require such proof.

We hope this report will give you an appreciation of the factors which weigh in favor of fair use and those factors which weigh against fair use, but faculty members must determine for themselves which works will be photocopied. This University [College] does not condone a policy of photocopying instead of purchasing copyrighted works where such photocopying would constitute an infringement under the Copyright law, but it does encourage faculty members to exercise good judgement in serving the best interests of students in an efficient manner. This University [College] and its faculty and staff will make a conscientious effort to comply with these guidelines.

Instructions for securing permission to photocopy copyrighted works when such copying is beyond the limits of fair use appear at the end of this report. It is the policy of this University that the user (faculty, staff or librarian) secure such permission whenever it is legally necessary.

II. Unrestricted Photocopying

A. UNCOPYRIGHTED PUBLISHED WORKS

Writings published before January 1, 1978, which have never been copyrighted may be photocopied without restriction. Copies of works protected by copyright must bear a copyright notice, which consists of the letter "c" in a circle, or the word "Copyright," or the abbreviation "Copr.," plus the year of first publication, plus the name of the copyright owner. 17 U.S.C. §401. As to works published before January 1, 1978, in the case of a book, the notice must be placed on the title page or the reverse side of the title page. In the case of a periodical the notice must be placed either on the title page, the first page of text, or in the masthead. A pre-1978 failure to comply with the notice requirements resulted in the work being injected into the public domain, i.e., unprotected. Copyright notice requirements have been relaxed since 1978, so that the absence of notice on copies of a work published after January 1, 1978, does not necessarily mean the work is in the public domain. 17 U.S.C. §405(a) and (c). However, you will not be liable for damages for copyright infringement of works published after that date, if, after normal inspection, you photocopy a work on which you cannot find a copyright symbol and you have not received actual notice of the fact the work is copyrighted. 17 U.S.C. §405(b). [Note this exemption from liability applies only to works published before March 1, 1989.] However, a copyright owner who found out about your photocopying would have the right to prevent further distribution of the copies if in fact the work were copyrighted and the copies are infringing. 17 U.S.C. §405(b).

B. PUBLISHED WORKS WITH EXPIRED COPYRIGHTS

Writings with expired copyrights may be photocopied without restriction. All copyrights prior to 1906 have expired. 17 U.S.C. §304(b). Copyrights granted after 1906 may have been renewed; however the writing will probably not contain notice of the renewal. Therefore, it should be assumed all writings dated 1906 or later are covered by a valid copyright, unless information to the contrary is obtained from the owner or the U.S. Copyright Office (see Copyright Office Circular 15t). [Note: As of the date of publication of this book, the copyright in all works published before 1921 has expired.]

Copyright Office Circular R22 [see Appendix G] explains how to investigate the copyright status of a work. One way is to use the *Catalog of Copyright Entries* published by the Copyright Office and available in [the University Library] many libraries. Alternatively you may request the Copyright Office to conduct a search of its registration and or assignment records. The Office charges an hourly fee for this service. You will need to submit as much information as you have concerning the work in which you are interested, such as the title, author, approximate date of publication, the type of work or any available copyright data. The Copyright Office does caution that its searches are not conclusive; for instance, if a work obtained copyright less than 28 years ago, it may be fully protected although there has been no registration or deposit.

C. UNPUBLISHED WORKS

Unpublished works, such as theses and dissertations, may be protected by copyright. If such a work was created before January 1, 1978, and has not been copyrighted or published without copyright notice, the work is protected under the new Act for the life of the author plus fifty years. 17 U.S.C. §303, but in no case earlier than December 31, 2002. If such a work is published on or before that date, the copyright will not expire before December 31, 2027. Works created after January 1, 1978, and not published enjoy copyright protection for the life of the author plus fifty years. 17 U.S.C §302.

D. U.S. GOVERNMENT PUBLICATIONS

All U.S. Government publications with the possible exceptions of some National Technical Information Service publications less than five years old may be photocopied without restrictions, except to the extent they contain copyrighted materials from other sources. 17 U.S.C. §105. U.S. Government publications are documents prepared by an official or employee of the government in an official capacity. 17 U.S.C. §101. Government publications include the opinions of courts in legal cases, Congressional Reports on proposed bills, testimony offered at Congressional hearings and the works of government employees in their official capacities. Works prepared by outside authors on contract to the government may or may not be protected by copyright, depending on the specifics of the contract. In the absence of copyright notice on such works, it would be reasonable to assume they are government works in the public domain. It should be noted that state government works may be protected by copyright, *see*, 17 U.S.C. §105. However, the opinions for state courts are not protected.

III. Permissible Photocopying of Copyrighted Works

The Copyright Act allows anyone to photocopy copyrighted works without securing permission from the copyright owner when the photocopying amounts to a "fair use" of the material. 17 U.S.C. §107. The guidelines in this report discuss the boundaries for fair use of photocopied material used in research or the classroom or in a library reserve operation. Fair use cannot always be expressed in numbers—either the number of pages copied or the number of copies distributed. Therefore, you should weigh the various factors listed in the Act and judge whether the intended use of photocopied, copyrighted material is within the spirit of the fair use doctrine. Any serious questions concerning whether a particular photocopying constitutes fair use should be directed to University [College] counsel.

A. RESEARCH USES

At the very least, instructors may make a single copy of any of the following for scholarly research or use in teaching or preparing to teach a class:
1. a chapter from a book;
2. an article from a periodical or newspaper;
3. a short story, short essay, or short poem, whether or not from a collective work;
4. a chart, diagram, graph, drawing, cartoon or picture from a book, periodical, or newspaper.

These examples reflect the most conservative guidelines for fair use. They do not represent inviolate ceilings for the amount of copyrighted material which can be photocopied within the boundaries of fair use. When exceeding these minimum levels, however, you again should consider the four factors listed in Section 107 of the Copyright Act to make sure that any additional photocopying is justified. The following demonstrate situations where increased levels of photocopying would continue to remain within the ambit of fair use:
1. the inability to obtain another copy of the work because it is not available from another library or source or cannot be obtained within your time constraints;
2. the intention to photocopy the material only once and not to distribute the material to others;
3. the ability to keep the amount of material photocopied within a reasonable proportion to the entire work (the larger the work, the greater amount for material which may be photocopied).

Most single-copy photocopying for your personal use in research—even when it involves a substantial portion of a work—may well constitute fair use.

B. CLASSROOM USES

Primary and secondary school educators have, with publishers, developed the following guidelines, which allow a teacher to distribute photocopied material to students in a class without the publisher's prior permission, under the following conditions:

1. the distribution of the same photocopied material does not occur every semester;
2. only one copy is distributed for each student which copy must become the student's property;
3. the material includes a copyright notice on the first page of the portion of material photocopied;
4. the students are not assessed any fee beyond the actual cost of the photocopying.

In addition, the educators agreed that the amount of material distributed should not exceed certain brevity standards. Under those guidelines, a prose work may be reproduced in its entirety if it is less than 2,500 words in length. If the work exceeds such length, the excerpt reproduced may not exceed 1,000 words, or 10 percent of the work, whichever is less. In the case of poetry, 250 words is the maximum permitted.

These minimum standards normally would not be realistic in the University setting. Faculty members needing to exceed these limits for college education should not feel hampered by these guidelines, although they should attempt a "selective and sparing" use of photocopied, copyrighted material.

The photocopying practices of an instructor should not have a significant detrimental impact on the market for the copyrighted work. 17 U.S.C. §107(4). To guard against this effect, you usually should restrict use of an item of photocopied material to one course and you should not repeatedly photocopy excerpts from one periodical or author without the permission of the copyright owner.

C. LIBRARY RESERVE USES

At the request of a faculty member, a library may photocopy and place on reserve excerpts from copyrighted works in its collection in accordance with guidelines similar to those governing formal classroom distribution for face-to-face teaching discussed above. This University [College] believes that these guidelines apply to the library reserve shelf to the extent it functions as an extension of classroom readings or reflects an individual student's right to photocopy for his personal scholastic use under the doctrine of fair use. In general, librarians may photocopy materials for reserve room use for the convenience of students both in preparing class assignments and in pursuing informal educational activities which higher education require, such as advanced independent study and research.

If the request calls for only *one* copy to be placed on reserve, the library may photocopy an entire article, or an entire chapter from a book or an entire poem. Requests for *multiple* copies on reserve should meet the following guidelines:

1. the amount of material should be reasonable in relation to the total amount of material assigned for one term of a course taking into account the nature of the course, its subject matter and level, 17 U.S.C. §107(1) and (3);

2. the number of copies should be reasonable in light of the number of students enrolled, the difficulty and timing of assignments, and the number of other courses which may assign the same material, 17 U.S.C. §107(1) and (3);

3. the material should contain a notice of copyright, *see*, 17 U.S.C. §401;

4. the effect of photocopying the material should not be detrimental to the market for the work. (In general, the library should own at least one copy of the work.) 17 U.S.C. §107(4).

For example, a professor may place on reserve as a supplement to the course textbook a reasonable number of copies of articles from academic journals or chapters from trade books. A reasonable number of copies will in most instances be less than six, but factors such as the length or difficulty of the assignment, the number of enrolled students and the length of time allowed for completion of the assignment may permit more in unusual circumstances.

In addition, a faculty member may also request that multiple copies of photocopied, copyrighted material be placed on the reserve shelf if there is insufficient time to obtain permission from the copyright owner. For example, a professor may place on reserve several photocopies of an entire article from a recent issue of *Time* magazine or the *New York Times* in lieu of distributing a copy to each member of the class. If you are in doubt as to whether a particular instance of photocopying is fair use in the reserve reading room, you should seek the publisher's permission. Most publishers will be cooperative and will waive any fee for such a use.

D. USES OF PHOTOCOPIED MATERIAL REQUIRING PERMISSION

1. *Repetitive copying:* The classroom or reserve use of photocopied materials in multiple courses or successive years will normally require advance permission from the owner of the copyright, 17 U.S.C. §107(3).

2. *Copying for profit:* Faculty should not charge students more than the actual cost of photocopying the material, 17 U.S.C. §107(1).

3. *Consumable works:* The duplication of works that are consumed in the classroom, such as standardized tests, exercises, and workbooks, normally requires permission from the copyright owner, 17 U.S.C. §107(4).

4. *Creation of anthologies as basic text material for a course:* Creation of a collective work or anthology by photocopying a number of copyrighted articles and excerpts to be purchased and used together as the basic text for a course will in most instances require the permission of the copyright owners. Such photocopying is more likely to be considered as a substitute for purchase of a book and thus less likely to be deemed fair use, 17 U.S.C. §107(4).

E. HOW TO OBTAIN PERMISSION

When a use of photocopied material requires that you request permission, you should communicate complete and accurate information to the copyright owner. The American Association of Publishers suggests that the following information be included in a permission request letter in order to expedite the process:
1. Title, author and or editor, and edition of materials to be duplicated.
2. Exact material to be used, giving amount, page numbers, chapters and, if possible, a photocopy of the material.
3. Number of copies to be made.
4. Use to be made of duplicated materials.
5. Form of distribution (classroom, newsletter, etc.).
6. Whether or not the material is to be sold.
7. Type of reprint (ditto, photography, offset, typeset).

The request should be sent, together with a self-addressed return envelope, to the permissions department of the publisher in question. If the address of the publisher does not appear at the front of the material, it may be readily obtained in a publication entitled *The Literary Marketplace*, published by the R.R. Bowker Company and available in all libraries.

The process of granting permission requires time for the publisher to check the status of the copyright and to evaluate the nature of the request. It is advisable, therefore, to allow enough lead time to obtain permission before the materials are needed. In some instances, the publisher may assess a fee for the permission. It is not inappropriate to pass this fee on to the students who receive copies of the photocopied material.

The Copyright Clearance Center also has the right to grant permission and collect fees for photocopying rights for certain publications. Libraries may copy from any journal which is registered with the CCC and report the copying beyond fair use to CCC and pay the set fee. A list of publications for which the CCC handles fees and permissions is available from the CCC, 310 Madison Avenue, New York, N.Y. 10017.

SAMPLE LETTER TO COPYRIGHT OWNER (PUBLISHER)
REQUESTING PERMISSION TO COPY

March 1, 1982

Material Permissions Department
Hypothetical Book Company
500 East Avenue
Chicago, Illinois 60601

Dear Sir or Madam:

I would like permission to copy the following for continued use in my classes
in future semesters:

Title: *Learning Is Good*, Second Edition
Copyright: Hypothetical Book Co., 1965, 1971
Author: Frank Jones
Material to be duplicated: Chapters 10, 11 and 14 (photocopy enclosed).
Number of copies: 500
Distribution: The material will be distributed to students in my classes
and they will pay only the cost of the photocopying.
Type of reprint: Photocopy
Use: The chapter will be used as supplementary teaching materials.

I have enclosed a self-addressed envelope for your convenience in replying to
this request.

Sincerely,
Faculty Member

F. INFRINGEMENT

Courts and legal scholars alike have commented that the fair use provisions in the Copyright Act are among the most vague and difficult that can be found anywhere in the law. In amending the Copyright Act in 1976, Congress anticipated the problem this would pose for users of copyrighted materials who wished to stay under the umbrella of protection offered by fair use. For this reason, the Copyright Act contains specific provisions which grant additional rights to libraries and insulate employees of a nonprofit educational institution, library, or archives from statutory damages for infringement where the infringer believed or had reasonable grounds to believe the photocopying was a fair use of the material. 17 U.S.C. §504(c)(2).

Normally, an infringer is liable to the copyright owner for the actual losses sustained because of the photocopying and any additional profits of the infringer. 17 U.S.C. §504(a)(1) and (b). Where the monetary losses are nominal, the copyright owner usually will claim statutory damages instead of the actual losses. 17 U.S.C. §504(a)(2) and (c). The statutory damages may reach as high at $10,000 (or up to $50,000 if the infringement is willful). [Note: Maximum damages were raised to $20,000 to $100,000 after these guidelines were written.] In addition to suing for money damages, a copyright owner can usually prevent future infringement through a court injunction. 17 U.S.C. §502.

F. Notice Required
on Circulating Copies
of Computer Programs

37 C.F.R. §201.24 Warning of copyright for software lending by nonprofit libraries.

(a) Definition. *A Warning of Copyright for Software Rental* is a notice under paragraph (b)(2)(A) of section 109 of the Copyright Act, title 17 of the United States Code, as amended by the Computer Software Rental Amendments Act of 1990, Public Law 101-650. As required by that paragraph, the "Warning of Copyright for Software Rental" shall be affixed to the packaging that contains the computer program which is lent by a nonprofit library for nonprofit purposes.

(b) Contents. *A Warning of Copyright for Software Rental* shall consist of a verbatim reproduction of the following notice, printed in such size and form and affixed in such manner as to comply with paragraph (c) of this section.

Notice: Warning of Copyright Restrictions
The copyright law of the United States (Title 17, United States Code) governs the reproduction, distribution, adaptation, public performance, and public display of copyrighted material.

Under certain conditions specified in law, nonprofit libraries are authorized to lend, lease, or rent copies of computer programs to patrons on a nonprofit basis and for nonprofit purposes. Any person who makes an unauthorized copy or adaptation of the computer program, or redistributes the loan copy, or publicly performs or displays the computer program, except as permitted by title 17 of the United States Code, may be liable for copyright infringement.

This institution reserves the right to refuse to fulfill a loan request if, in its judgement, fulfillment of the request would lead to violation of the copyright law.

(c) Form and manner of use. *A Warning of Copyright for Software Rental* shall be affixed to the packaging that contains the copy of the computer program, which is the subject of a library loan to patrons, by means of a label cemented, gummed, or otherwise durably attached to the copies or to a box, reel, cartridge, cassette, or other container used as a permanent receptacle for the copy of the computer program. The notice shall be printed in such manner as to be clearly legible, comprehensible, and readily apparent to a casual user of the computer program.

G. Circular 22
How to Investigate
the Copyright Status
of a Work

CIRCULAR 22

**HOW TO INVESTIGATE THE
COPYRIGHT STATUS OF A WORK**

Copyright Office
Library of Congress
Washington, DC 20559-6000
June 1995

IN GENERAL

Methods of Approaching a Copyright Investigation

There are several ways to investigate whether a work is under copyright protection and, if so, the facts of the copyright. These are the main ones:

1. Examine a copy of the work for such elements as a copyright notice, place and date of publication, author and publisher. If the work is a sound recording, examine the disk, tape cartridge, or cassette in which the recorded sound is fixed, or the album cover, sleeve, or container in which the recording is sold.
2. Make a search of the Copyright Office catalogs and other records; or
3. Have the Copyright Office make a search for you.

A Few Words of Caution About Copyright Investigations

Copyright investigations often involve more than one of these methods. Even if you follow all three approaches, the results may not be conclusive. Moreover, as explained in this circular, the changes brought about under the Copyright Act of 1976, the Berne Convention Implementation Act of 1988 and the Copyright Renewal Act of 1992 must be considered when investigating the copyright status of a work.

This circular offers some practical guidance on what to look for if you are making a copyright investigation. It is important to realize, however, that this circular contains only general information and that there are a number of exceptions to the principles outlined here. In many cases it is important to consult with a copyright attorney before reaching any conclusions regarding the copyright status of a work.

HOW TO SEARCH COPYRIGHT OFFICE
CATALOGS AND RECORDS

Catalog of Copyright Entries

The Copyright Office published the *Catalog of Copyright Entries* (CCE) in printed format from 1891 through 1978. From 1979 through 1982 the CCE was issued in microfiche format. The catalog was divided into parts according to the classes of works registered. Each CCE segment covers all registrations made during a particular period of time. Renewal registrations made from 1979 through 1982 are found in Section 8 of the catalog. Renewals prior to that time were generally listed at the end of the volume containing the class of work to which they pertained.

A number of libraries throughout the United States maintain copies of the *Catalog*, and this may provide a good starting point if you wish to make a search yourself. There are some cases, however, in which a search of the *Catalog* alone will not be sufficient to provide the needed information. For example:

- Since the *Catalog* does not include entries for assignments or other recorded documents, it cannot be used for searches involving the ownership of rights.
- The *Catalog* entry contains the essential facts concerning a registration, but it is not a verbatim transcript of the registration record. It does not contain the address of the copyright claimant.

Effective with registrations made since 1982, the only method of searching outside the Library of Congress is by using the Internet to access the automated catalog. The automated catalog contains entries from 1978 forward. See page 190 for accessing the catalog via the Internet.

Individual Searches of Copyright Records

The Copyright Office is located in the Library of Congress James Madison Memorial Building, 101 Independence Ave., S.E., Washington, D.C. 20559-6000.

Most records of the Copyright Office are open to public inspection and searching from 8:30 a.m. to 5 p.m., Eastern Time, Monday–Friday except Federal holidays. The various records freely available to the public include an extensive card catalog, an automated catalog containing records from 1978 forward, record books, and microfilm records of assignments and related documents. Other records, including correspondence files and deposit copies, are not open to the public for searching. However, they may be inspected upon request and payment of a $20-per-hour search fee.

If you wish to do your own searching in the Copyright Office files open to the public, you will be given assistance in locating the records you need and in learning procedures for searching. If the Copyright Office staff actually makes the search for you, a search fee must be charged. The search will not be done while you wait.

In addition, the following files dating from 1978 forward are now available over the Internet: COHM, which includes all material except serials and documents; COHD, which includes documents; and COHS, which includes serials.

The Internet site addresses for the Copyright Office files are:
World Wide Web URL: **http://lcweb.loc.gov/copyright**
Gopher: **marvel.loc.gov**
Telnet: **locis.loc.gov**
The Copyright Office does **not** offer search assistance to users on the Internet.

SEARCHING BY THE COPYRIGHT OFFICE

In General

Upon request, the Copyright Office staff will search its records at the statutory rate of $20 for each hour or fraction of an hour consumed. Based on the information you furnish, we will provide an estimate of the total search fee. If you decide to have the Office staff conduct the search, you should send the estimated amount with your request. The Office will then proceed with the search and send you a typewritten report or, if you prefer, an oral report by telephone. If you request an oral report, please provide a telephone number where you can be reached during normal business hours 8:30 a.m.–5 p.m. Eastern time.

Search reports can be certified on request for an extra fee of $20. Certified searches are most frequently requested to meet the evidentiary requirements of litigation.

Your request and any other correspondence, should be addressed to:

Reference and Bibliography Section, LM-451
Copyright Office
Library of Congress
Washington, D.C. 20559-6000
Tel: (202) 707-6850
Fax: (202) 707-6859
TTY: (202) 707-6737

What the Fee Does Not Cover

The search fee does **not** include the cost of additional certificates, photocopies of deposits, or copies of other Office records. For information concerning these services, request Circular 6, "Obtaining Access to and Copies of Copyright Office Records and Deposits."

Information Needed

The more detailed information you can furnish with your request, the less time-consuming and expensive the search will be. Please provide as much of the following information as possible:

- The title of the work, with any possible variants;
- The names of the authors, including possible pseudonyms;
- The name of the probable copyright owner, which may be the publisher or producer;
- The approximate year when the work was published or registered;
- The type of work involved (book, play, musical composition, sound recording, photograph, etc.);
- For a work originally published as a part of a periodical or collection, the title of that publication and any other information, such as the volume or issue number, to help identify it;
- Motion pictures are often based on other works such as books or serialized contributions to periodicals or other composite works. **If you desire a search for an underlying work or for music from a motion picture, you must specifically request such a search. You must also identify the underlying works and music and furnish the specific titles, authors, and approximate dates of these works;** and
- The registration number or any other copyright data.

*Searches Involving Assignments and Other Documents
Affecting Copyright Ownership*

The Copyright Office staff will also, for the standard hourly search fee, search its indexes covering the records of assignments and other recorded documents concerning ownership of copyrights. The reports of searches in these cases will state the facts shown in the Office's indexes of the recorded documents but will offer no interpretation of the content of the documents or their legal effect.

LIMITATIONS ON SEARCHES

In determining whether or not to have a search made, you should keep the following points in mind:

No Special Lists: The Copyright Office does not maintain any listings of works by subject or any lists of works that are in the public domain.

Contributions Not Listed Separately in Copyright Office Records: Individual works such as stories, poems, articles, or musical compositions that were published as contributions to a copyrighted periodical or collection are usually not listed separately by title in our records.

No Comparisons: The Copyright Office does not search or compare copies of works to determine questions of possible infringement or to determine how much two or more versions of a work have in common.

Titles and Names Not Copyrightable: Copyright does not protect names and titles, and our records list many different works identified by the same or similar titles. Some brand names, trade names, slogans, and phrases may be entitled to protection under the general rules of law relating to unfair competition. They may also be entitled to registration under the provisions of the trademark laws. Questions about the trademark laws should be addressed to the Commissioner of Patents and Trademarks, Washington, D.C. 20231. Possible protection of names and titles under common law principles of unfair competition is a question of state law.

No Legal Advice: The Copyright Office cannot express any opinion as to the legal significance or effect of the facts included in a search report.

SOME WORDS OF CAUTION

Searches Not Always Conclusive

Searches of the Copyright Office catalogs and records are useful in helping to determine the copyright status of a work, but they cannot be regarded as conclusive in all cases. The complete absence of any information about a work in the Office records does not mean that the work is unprotected. The following are examples of cases in which information about a particular work may be incomplete or lacking entirely in the Copyright Office:

- Before 1978, unpublished works were entitled to protection under common law without the need of registration.
- Works published with notice prior to 1978 may be registered at **any** time within the first 28-year term.
- Works copyrighted between January 1, 1964, and December 31, 1977, are affected by the Copyright Renewal Act of 1992 which automatically extends the copyright term and makes renewal registrations optional.
- For works under copyright protection on or after January 1, 1978, registration may be made at any time during the term of protection. Although registration is not required as a condition of copyright protection, there are certain definite advantages to registration. For further information, request Circular 1, "Copyright Basics."
- Since searches are ordinarily limited to registrations that have already been cataloged, a search report may not cover recent registrations for which catalog records are not yet available.
- The information in the search request may not have been complete or specific enough to identify the work.
- The work may have been registered under a different title or as part of a larger work.

Protection in Foreign Countries

Even if you conclude that a work is in the public domain in the United States, this does not necessarily mean that you are free to use it in other countries. Every nation has its own laws governing the length and scope of copyright protection, and these are applicable to uses of the work within that nation's borders. Thus, the expiration or loss of copyright protection in the United States may still leave the work fully protected against unauthorized use in other countries.

OTHER CIRCULARS

For further information, request Circular 6, "Obtaining Access to and Copies of Copyright Office Records and Deposits"; Circular 15, "Renewal of Copyright"; Circular 15a. "Duration of Copyright"; and Circular 15t, "Extension of Copyright Terms," from:

Publications Section, LM-455
Copyright Office
Library of Congress
Washington, D.C. 20559-6000

You may call (202) 707-9100 at any time, day or night, to leave a request for forms or circulars as a recorded message on the Forms HOTLINE. Requests made on the HOTLINE number are filled and mailed promptly.

IMPACT OF COPYRIGHT ACT ON COPYRIGHT INVESTIGATIONS

On October 19, 1976, the President signed into law a complete revision of the copyright law of the United States (Title 17 of the United States Code). Most provisions of this statute came into force on January 1, 1978, superseding the copyright act of 1909. The provisions made significant changes in the copyright law. Further important changes resulted from the Berne Convention Implementation Act of 1988, which took effect March 1, 1989, and the Copyright Renewal Act of 1992 (PL 102-307) enacted June 26, 1992, which amended the renewal provisions of the copyright law. If you need more information about the provisions of either the 1909 or the 1976 law, write or call the Copyright Office. For information about the Berne Convention Implementation Act, request Circular 93, "Highlights of U.S. Adherence to the Berne Convention." For information about renewals, request Circular 15, "Renewal of Copyright." For single copies of the law only, request Circular 92, "Copyright Law of the United States of America," from:

Publications Section, LM-455
Copyright Office
Library of Congress
Washington, D.C. 20559-6000

For multiple copies of the law, request "Copyright Law, Circular 92" $4.75 each, stock number 030-002-00182-9 from:

New Orders
Superintendent of Documents
P.O. Box 371954
Pittsburgh, PA 15250-7954
Tel: (202) 783-3238
Fax: (202) 512-2250

For copyright investigations, the following points about the impact of the Copyright Act of 1976, the Berne Convention Implementation Act of 1988, and the Copyright Renewal Act of 1992 should be considered:

A Changed System of Copyright Formalities

Some of the most sweeping changes under the 1976 Act involve copyright formalities, that is, the procedural requirements for securing and maintaining full copyright protection. The old system of formalities involved copyright notice, deposit and registration, recordation of transfers and licenses of copyright ownership, and United States manufacture, among other things. In general, while retaining formalities, the 1976 law reduced the chances of mistakes, softened the consequences of errors and omissions, and allowed for the correction of errors.

The Berne Convention Implementation Act of 1988 reduced formalities, most notably making the addition of the previously mandatory copyright notice optional. It should be noted that the amended notice requirements are not retroactive.

The Copyright Renewal Act of 1992, enacted June 26, 1992, automatically extends the term of copyrights secured between January 1, 1964, and December 31, 1977, making renewal registration optional. Consult Circular 15, "Renewal of Copyright," for details. For additional information, you may contact the Renewals Section.

Tel: (202) 707-8180
Fax: (202) 707-3849

Automatic Copyright

Under the present copyright law, copyright exists in original works of authorship created and fixed in any tangible medium of expression, now known or later developed, from which they can be perceived, reproduced, or otherwise communicated, either directly, or indirectly with the aid of a machine or device. In other words, copyright is an incident of creative authorship not dependent on statutory formalities. Thus, registration with the Copyright Office generally is not required, but there are certain advantages that arise from a timely registration. For further information on the advantages of registration, write or call the Copyright Office and request Circular 1, "Copyright Basics."

Copyright Notice

The 1909 Copyright Act and, as originally enacted, the 1976 Copyright Act required a notice of copyright on published works. For most works, a copyright notice consists of the symbol ©, the word "Copyright," or the abbreviation "Copr.," together with the name of the owner of copyright and the year of first publication. For example: "© Joan Crane 1994" or "Copyright 1994 by Abraham Adams."

For sound recordings published on or after February 15, 1972, a copyright notice might read "℗1994 XYZ Records, Inc." See below for more information about sound recordings.

For mask works, a copyright notice might read "Ⓜ SDR Industries." Request Circular 100, "Federal Statutory Protection for Mask Works," for more information.

As originally enacted, the 1976 law prescribed that all visually perceptible published copies of a work, or published phonorecords of a sound recording, should bear a proper copyright notice. This applies to such works published before March 1, 1989. After March 1, 1989, notice of copyright on these works is optional. Adding the notice, however, is strongly encouraged and, if litigation involving the copyright occurs, certain advantages exist for adding the notice.

Prior to March 1, 1989, the requirement for the notice applied equally whether the work was published in the United States or elsewhere by authority of the copyright owner. Compliance with the statutory notice requirements was the responsibility of the copyright owner. Unauthorized publication without the copyright notice, or with a defective notice, does not affect the validity of the copyright in the work.

Advance permission from, or registration with, the Copyright Office is not required before placing a copyright notice on copies of the work or on phonorecords of a sound recording. Moreover, for works first published on or after January 1, 1978, through February 28, 1989, omission of the required notice, or use of a defective notice, did not result in forfeiture or outright loss of copyright protection. Certain omissions of, or defects in, the notice of copyright, however, could have lead to loss of copyright protection if steps were not taken to correct or cure the omissions or defects. The Copyright Office has issued a final regulation (37 CFR 201.20) which suggests various acceptable positions for the notice of copyright. For further information, write to the Copyright Office and request Circular 3, "Copyright Notice" and Circular 96, Section 201.20, "Methods of Affixation and Positions of the Copyright Notice on Various Types of Works."

Works Already in the Public Domain

Neither the 1976 Act, the Berne Convention Implementation Act of 1988, nor the Copyright Renewal Act of 1992 will restore protection to works that fell into the public domain before the passage of the laws. However, the North American Free Trade Agreement Implementation Act (NAFTA) and the Uruguay Round Agreements Act (URAA) may restore copyright in certain works of foreign origin that were in the public domain in the United States. Under the copyright law in effect prior to January 1, 1978, copyright could be lost in several situations. The most common were publication without the required copyright notice, expiration of the first 28-year copyright term without renewal, or final expiration of the second copyright term. The Copyright

Renewal Act of 1992 automatically renews first term copyrights secured between January 1, 1964, and December 31, 1977.

Scope of Exclusive Rights Under Copyright

The present law has changed and enlarged in some cases the scope of the copyright owner's rights. The new rights apply to all uses of a work subject to protection by copyright after January 1, 1978, regardless of when the work was created.

DURATION OF COPYRIGHT PROTECTION

Works Originally Copyrighted on or After January 1, 1978

A work that is created and fixed in tangible form for the first time on or after January 1, 1978, is automatically protected from the moment of its creation and is ordinarily given a term enduring for the author's life plus an additional 50 years after the author's death. In the case of "a joint work prepared by two or more authors who did not work for hire," the term lasts for 50 years after the last surviving author's death. For works made for hire and for anonymous and pseudonymous works (unless the author's identity is revealed in the Copyright Office records), the duration of copyright will be 75 years from publication or 100 years from creation, whichever is less.

Works created before the 1976 law came into effect but neither published nor registered for copyright before January 1, 1978, have been automatically brought under the statute and are now given Federal copyright protection. The duration of copyright in these works will generally be computed in the same way as for new works: the life-plus-50 or 75/100-year terms will apply. However, all works in this category are guaranteed at least 25 years of statutory protection.

Works Copyrighted Before January 1, 1978

Under the law in effect before 1978, copyright was secured either on the date a work was published with notice of copyright or on the date of registration if the work was registered in unpublished form. In either case, copyright endured for a first term of 28 years from the date on which it was secured. During the last (28th) year of the first term, the copyright was eligible for renewal. The 1976 copyright law extended the renewal term from 28 to 47 years for copyrights in existence on January 1, 1978.

However, for works copyrighted prior to January 1, 1964, the copyright still must have been renewed in the 28th calendar year to receive the 47-year period of added protection. The amending legislation enacted June 26, 1992, automatically extends this second term for works first copyrighted between January 1, 1964, and December 31, 1977. For more detailed information on the copyright term, write or call the Copyright Office and request Circular 15a, "Duration of Copyright," and Circular 15t, "Extension of Copyright Terms."

WORKS FIRST PUBLISHED BEFORE 1978: THE COPYRIGHT NOTICE

General Information About the Copyright Notice

In investigating the copyright status of works first published before January 1, 1978, the most important thing to look for is the notice of copyright. As a general rule under the previous law, copyright protection was lost permanently if the notice was omitted from the first authorized published edition of a work or if it appeared in the wrong form or position. The form and position of the copyright notice for various types of works were specified in the copyright statute. Some courts were liberal in overlooking relatively minor departures from the statutory requirements, but a basic failure to comply with the notice provisions forfeited copyright protection and put the work into the public domain in this country.

Absence of Copyright Notice

For works first published before 1978, the complete absence of a copyright notice from a published copy generally indicates that the work is not protected by copyright. For works first published before March 1, 1989, the copyright notice is mandatory, but omission could have been cured by registration before or within five years of publication and by adding the notice to copies published in the United States after discovery of the omission. Some works may contain a notice, others may not. The absence of a notice in works published on or after March 1, 1989, does not necessarily indicate that the work is in the public domain.

Unpublished Works. No notice of copyright was required on the copies of any unpublished work. The concept of "publication" is very technical, and it was possible for a number of copies lacking a copyright notice to be reproduced and distributed without affecting copyright protection.

Foreign Editions. In the case of works seeking *ad interim* copyright,179 copies of a copyrighted work were exempted from the notice requirements if they were first published outside the United States. Some copies of these foreign editions could find their way into the United States without impairing the copyright.

Accidental Omission. The 1909 statute preserved copyright protection if the notice was omitted by accident or mistake from a "particular copy or copies."

Unauthorized Publication. A valid copyright was not secured if someone deleted the notice and or published the work without authorization from the copyright owner.

Sound Recordings. Reproductions of sound recordings usually contain two different types of creative works: the underlying musical, dramatic, or literary work that is being performed or read, and the fixation of the actual sounds embodying the performance or reading. For protection of the underlying musical or literary work embodied in a recording, it is not necessary that a copyright notice covering this material appear on the phonograph records or tapes on which the recording is reproduced. As noted above, a special notice is required for protection of the recording of a series of musical, spoken, or other sounds which were fixed on or after February 15, 1972. Sound recordings fixed before February 15, 1972, are not eligible for Federal copyright protection. The Sound Recording Act of 1971, the present copyright law, and the Berne Convention Implementation Act of 1988 cannot be applied or be construed to provide any retroactive protection for sound recordings fixed before February 15, 1972. Such works, however, may be protected by various state laws or doctrines of common law.

The Date in the Copyright Notice

If you find a copyright notice, the date it contains may be important in determining the copyright status of the work. In general, the notice on works published before 1978 must include the year in which copyright was secured by publication or, if the work was first registered for copyright in unpublished form, the year in which registration was made. There are two main exceptions to this rule.

1. For pictorial, graphic, or sculptural works (Classes F through K under the 1909 law), the law permitted omission of the year date in the notice.
2. For "new versions" of previously published or copyrighted works, the notice was not usually required to include more than the year of first

---

179. "*Ad interim* copyright" refers to a special short term of copyright available to certain pre–1978 books and periodicals. For further information on *ad interim* copyright see page 203.

publication of the new version itself. This is explained further under "Derivative Works" below.

The year in the notice usually (though not always) indicated when the copyright began. It is therefore significant in determining whether a copyright is still in effect; or, if the copyright has not yet run its course, the year date will help in deciding when the copyright is scheduled to expire. For further information about the duration of copyright, request Circular 15a, "Duration of Copyright."

In evaluating the meaning of the date in a notice, you should keep the following points in mind:

WORKS PUBLISHED AND COPYRIGHTED BEFORE JANUARY 1, 1978: A work published before January 1, 1978, and copyrighted within the past 75 years may still be protected by copyright in the United States if a valid renewal registration was made during the 28th year of the first term of the copyright. If renewed by registration or under the Copyright Renewal Act of 1992 and if still valid under the other provisions of the law, the copyright will expire 75 years from the end of the year in which it was first secured.

Therefore, the United States copyright in any work published or copyrighted more than 75 years ago (75 years from January 1st in the present year) has expired by operation of law, and the work has permanently fallen into the public domain in the United States. For example, on January 1, 1995, copyright in works first published or copyrighted before January 1, 1920, will have expired; on January 1, 1996, copyright in works first published or copyrighted before January 1, 1921, will have expired.

WORKS FIRST PUBLISHED OR COPYRIGHTED BETWEEN JANUARY 1, 1920, AND DECEMBER 31, 1949, BUT NOT RENEWED: If a work was first published or copyrighted between January 1, 1920, and December 31, 1949, it is important to determine whether the copyright was renewed during the last (28th) year of the first term of the copyright. This can be done by searching the Copyright Office records or catalogs as explained above. If no renewal registration was made, copyright protection expired permanently at the end of the 28th year of the year date it was first secured.

WORKS FIRST PUBLISHED OR COPYRIGHTED BETWEEN JANUARY 1, 1920, AND DECEMBER 31, 1949, AND REGISTERED FOR RENEWAL: When a valid renewal registration was made and copyright in the work was in its second term on December 31, 1977, the renewal copyright term was extended under the present act to 47 years. In these cases, copyright will last for a total of 75 years from the end of the year in which copyright was originally secured. Example: Copyright in a work first published in 1920, and renewed in 1948, will expire on December 31, 1995.

WORKS FIRST PUBLISHED OR COPYRIGHTED BETWEEN JANUARY 1, 1950, AND DECEMBER 31, 1963: If a work was in its first 28-year term of copyright protection on January 1, 1978, it must have been renewed in a timely fashion to secure the maximum term of copyright protection. If renewal registration was made during the 28th calendar year of its first term, copyright would endure for 75 years from the end of the year copyright was originally secured. If not renewed, the copyright expired at the end of its 28th calendar year.

WORKS FIRST PUBLISHED OR COPYRIGHTED BETWEEN JANUARY 1, 1964, AND DECEMBER 31, 1977: If a work was in its first 28-year term of copyright protection on June 26, 1992, renewal registration is now optional. The term of copyright for works published or copyrighted during this time period has been extended to 75 years by the Copyright Renewal Act of 1992. There is no need to make the renewal filing in order to extend the original 28-year copyright term to the full 75 years.

However, there are several advantages to making a renewal registration during the 28th year of the original term of copyright. If renewal registration is made during the 28th year of the original term of copyright, the renewal copyright vests in the name of the renewal claimant on the effective date of the renewal registration; the renewal certificate constitutes *prima facie* evidence as to the validity of the copyright during the renewed and extended term and of the facts stated in the certificate; and, the right to use the derivative work in the extended term may be affected. Request Circular 15, "Renewal of Copyright," for further information.

UNPUBLISHED, UNREGISTERED WORKS: Before 1978, if a work had been neither "published" in the legal sense nor registered in the Copyright Office, it was subject to perpetual protection under the common law. On January 1, 1978, all works of this kind, subject to protection by copyright, were automatically brought under the Federal copyright statute. The duration of copyright for these works will vary, but none of them will expire before December 31, 2002.

Derivative Works

In examining a copy (or a record, disk, or tape) for copyright information, it is important to determine whether that particular version of the work is an original edition of the work or a "new version." New versions include musical arrangements, adaptations, revised or newly edited editions, translations, dramatizations, abridgments, compilations, and works republished with new matter added. The law provides that derivative works, published or unpublished, are independently copyrightable and that the copyright in such a work does not affect or extend the protection, if any, in the underlying work. Under the 1909 law, courts have also held that the notice of copyright on a derivative work ordinarily need not include the dates or other information pertaining to the earlier works incorporated in it. This principle is specifically preserved in the present copyright law. Thus, if the copy (or the record, disk, or tape) constitutes a derivative version of the work, these points should be kept in mind:

- The date in the copyright notice is not necessarily an indication of when copyright in all of the material in the work will expire. Some of the material may already be in the public domain, and some parts of the work may expire sooner than others.
- Even if some of the material in the derivative work is in the public domain and free for use, this does not mean that the "new" material added to it can be used without permission from the owner of copyright in the derivative work. It may be necessary to compare editions to determine what is free to use and what is not.
- Ownership of rights in the material included in a derivative work and in the preexisting work upon which it may be based may differ, and permission obtained from the owners of certain parts of the work may not authorize the use of other parts.

The Name in the Copyright Notice

Under the copyright statute in effect before 1978, the notice was required to include "the name of the copyright proprietor." The present act requires that the notice include "the name of the owner of copyright in the work, or an abbreviation by which the name can be recognized, or a generally known alternative designation of the owner." The name in the notice (sometimes in combination with the other statements on the copy, record, disk, tape, container, or label) often gives persons wishing to use the work the information needed to identify the owner from whom licenses or permission can be sought. In other cases, the name provides a starting point for a search in the Copyright Office records or catalogs, as explained at the beginning in this circular.

In the case of works published before 1978, copyright registration is made in the name of the individual person or the entity identified as the copyright owner in the notice. For works published on or after January 1, 1978, registration is made in the name of the person or entity owning all the rights on the date the registration is made. This may or may not be the name appearing in the notice. In addition to its records of copyright registration, the Copyright Office maintains extensive records of assignments, exclusive licenses, and other documents dealing with copyright ownership.

Ad Interim

Ad interim copyright was a special short-term copyright that applied to certain books and periodicals in the English language that were first manufactured and published outside the United States. It was a partial exception to the manufacturing requirements of the previous United States copyright law. Its purpose was to secure temporary United States protection for a work, pending the manufacture of an edition in the United States. The *ad interim* requirements changed several times over the years and were subject to a number of exceptions and qualifications.

The manufacturing provisions of the copyright act expired on July 1, 1986, and are no longer a part of the copyright law. The transitional and supplementary provisions of the act provide that for any work in which *ad interim* copyright was subsisting or capable of being secured on December 31, 1977, copyright protection would be extended for a term compatible with the other works in which copyright was subsisting on the effective date of the new act. Consequently, if the work was first published on or after July 1, 1977, and was eligible for *ad interim* copyright protection, the provisions of the present copyright act will be applicable to the protection of these works. Anyone investigating the copyright status of an English-language book or periodical first published outside the United States before July 1, 1977, should check carefully to determine:

- Whether the manufacturing requirements were applicable to the work and
- If so, whether the *ad interim* requirements were met.

search request form Copyright Office
Library of Congress
Washington, D.C.
20559-6000

Reference & Bibliography
Section
(202) 707-6850
8:30 a.m.-5 p.m. Monday-Friday
Eastern Time

Type of work:

☐ Book ☐ Music ☐ Motion Picture ☐ Drama ☐ Sound Recording ☐ Computer Program
☐ Photograph/Artwork ☐ Map ☐ Periodical ☐ Contribution ☐ Architectural Work ☐ Mask Work

Search information you require:

☐ Registration ☐ Renewal ☐ Assignment ☐ Address

Specifics of work to be searched:

TITLE: _____

AUTHOR: _____

COPYRIGHT CLAIMANT: _____
(name in © notice)

APPROXIMATE YEAR DATE OF PUBLICATION/CREATION: _____

REGISTRATION NUMBER (if known): _____

OTHER IDENTIFYING INFORMATION: _____

If you need more space please attach additional pages.

*Estimates are based on the Copyright Office fee of $20.00 an hour or fraction of an hour consumed. The more informa-
tion you furnish as a basis for the search the better service we can provide. The time between the date of receipt of your
fee for the search and your receiving a report will vary from 8 to 12 weeks depending on workload.*

Names, titles, and short phrases are not copyrightable.

Please read Circular 22 for more information on copyright searches.

YOUR NAME: _____ DATE: _____

ADDRESS: _____

DAYTIME TELEPHONE NO. (——) _____

Convey results of estimate/search by telephone
☐ yes ☐ no

Fee enclosed? ☐ yes Amount $ _____
☐ no

June 1995

H. Title 17
United States Code
(Selected Sections)

17 U.S.C. §101 Definitions

Except as otherwise provided in this title, as used in this title, the following terms and their variant forms mean the following:

An "anonymous work" is a work on the copies or phonorecords of which no natural person is identified as author.

An "architectural work" is the design of a building as embodied in any tangible medium of expression, including a building, architectural plans, or drawings. The work includes the overall form as well as the arrangement and composition of spaces and elements in the design, but does not include individual standard features.

"Audiovisual works" are works that consist of a series of related images which are intrinsically intended to be shown by the use of machines or devices such as projectors, viewers, or electronic equipment, together with accompanying sounds, if any, regardless of the nature of the material objects, such as films or tapes, in which the works are embodied.

The "Berne Convention" is the Convention for the Protection of Literary and Artistic Works, signed at Berne, Switzerland, on September 9, 1886, and all acts, protocols, and revisions thereto.

A work is a "Berne Convention work" if—

(1) in the case of an unpublished work, one or more of the authors is a national of a nation adhering to the Berne Convention, or in the case of a published work, one or more of the authors is a national of a nation adhering to the Berne Convention on the date of first publication;

(2) the work was first published in a nation adhering to the Berne Convention, or was simultaneously first published in a nation adhering to the Berne Convention and in a foreign nation that does not adhere to the Berne Convention;

(3) in the case of an audiovisual work—

205

§101 continued   (A) if one or more of the authors is a legal entity, that author has its headquarters in a nation adhering to the Berne Convention; or

(B) if one or more of the authors is an individual, that author is domiciled, or has his or her habitual residence in, a nation adhering to the Berne Convention;

(4) in the case of a pictorial, graphic, or sculptural work that is incorporated in a building or other structure, the building or structure is located in a nation adhering to the Berne Convention; or

(5) in the case of an architectural work embodied in a building, such building is erected in a country adhering to the Berne Convention.

For purposes of paragraph (1), an author who is domiciled in or has his or her habitual residence in, a nation adhering to the Berne Convention is considered to be a national of that nation. For purposes of paragraph (2), a work is considered to have been simultaneously published in two or more nations if its dates of publication are within 30 days of one another.

The "best edition" of a work is the edition, published in the United States at any time before the date of deposit, that the Library of Congress determines to be most suitable for its purposes.

A person's "children" are that person's immediate offspring, whether legitimate or not, and any children legally adopted by that person.

A "collective work" is a work, such as a periodical issue, anthology, or encyclopedia, in which a number of contributions, constituting separate and independent works in themselves, are assembled into a collective whole.

A "compilation" is a work formed by the collection and assembling of preexisting materials or of data that are selected, coordinated, or arranged in such a way that the resulting work as a whole constitutes an original work of authorship. The term "compilation" includes collective works.

"Copies" are material objects, other than phonorecords, in which a work is fixed by any method now known or later developed, and from which the work can be perceived, reproduced, or otherwise communicated, either directly or with the aid of a machine or device. The term "copies" includes the material object, other than a phonorecord, in which the work is first fixed.

"Copyright owner," with respect to any one of the exclusive rights comprised in a copyright, refers to the owner of that particular right.

The "country of origin" of a Berne Convention work, for purposes of section 411, is the United States if—

(1) in the case of a published work, the work is first published—

(A) in the United States;

(B) simultaneously in the United States and another nation or nations adhering to the Berne Convention, whose law grants a term of copyright protection that is the same as or longer than the term provided in the United States;

(C) simultaneously in the United States and a foreign nation that does not adhere to the Berne Convention; or

(D) in a foreign nation that does not adhere to the Berne Convention, and all of the authors of the work are nationals, domiciliaries, or habitual residents of, or in the case of an audiovisual work legal entities with headquarters in, the United States;

(2) in the case of an unpublished work, all the authors of the work are nationals, domiciliaries, or habitual residents of the United States, or, in the case of an unpublished audiovisual work, all the authors are legal entities with headquarters in the United States; or

(3) in the case of a pictorial, graphic, or sculptural work incorporated in a building or structure, the building or structure is located in the United States.

For the purposes of section 411, the "country of origin" of any other Berne Convention work is not the United States.

A work is "created" when it is fixed in a copy or phonorecord for the first time; where a work is prepared over a period of time, the portion of it that has been fixed at any particular time constitutes the work as of that time, and where the work has been prepared in different versions, each version constitutes a separate work.

A "derivative work" is a work based upon one or more preexisting works, such as a translation, musical arrangement, dramatization, fictionalization, motion picture version, sound recording, art reproduction, abridgment, condensation, or any other form in which a work may be recast, transformed, or adapted. A work consisting of editorial revisions, annotations, elaborations, or other modifications which, as a whole, represent an original work of authorship, is a "derivative work."

A "device," "machine," or "process" is one now known or later developed.

A "digital transmission" is a transmission in whole or in part in a digital or other non-analog format.

To "display" a work means to show a copy of it, either directly or by means of a film, slide, television image, or any other device or process or, in the case of a motion picture or other audiovisual work, to show individual images nonsequentially.

A work is "fixed" in a tangible medium of expression when its embodiment in a copy or phonorecord, by or under the authority of the author, is sufficiently permanent or stable to permit it to be perceived, reproduced, or otherwise communicated for a period of more than transitory duration. A work consisting of sounds, images, or both, that are being transmitted, is "fixed" for purposes of this title if a fixation of the work is being made simultaneously with its transmission.

The terms "including" and "such as" are illustrative and not limitative.

A "joint work" is a work prepared by two or more authors with the intention

§101 continued   that their contributions be merged into inseparable or inter-
dependent parts of a unitary whole.

"Literary works" are works, other than audiovisual works, expressed in
words, numbers, or other verbal or numerical symbols or indicia, regardless
of the nature of the material objects, such as books, periodicals, manuscripts, phonorecords, film, tapes, disks, or cards, in which they are embodied.

"Motion pictures" are audiovisual works consisting of a series of related
images which, when shown in succession, impart an impression of motion,
together with accompanying sounds, if any.

To "perform" a work means to recite, render, play, dance, or act it, either
directly or by means of any device or process or, in the case of a motion picture or other audiovisual work, to show its images in any sequence or to make
the sounds accompanying it audible.

"Phonorecords" are material objects in which sounds, other than those
accompanying a motion picture or other audiovisual work, are fixed by any
method now known or later developed, and from which the sounds can be
perceived, reproduced, or otherwise communicated, either directly or with
the aid of a machine or device. The term "phonorecords" includes the material object in which the sounds are first fixed.

"Pictorial, graphic, and sculptural works" include two-dimensional and
three-dimensional works of fine, graphic, and applied art, photographs,
prints and art reproductions, maps, globes, charts, diagrams, models, and
technical drawings, including architectural plans. Such works shall include
works of artistic craftsmanship insofar as their form but not their mechan-
ical or utilitarian aspects are concerned; the design of a useful article, as
defined in this section, shall be considered a pictorial, graphic, or sculptural work only if, and only to the extent that, such design incorporates pictorial, graphic, or sculptural features that can be identified separately from,
and are capable of existing independently of, the utilitarian aspects of the
article.

A "pseudonymous work" is a work on the copies or phonorecords of which
the author is identified under a fictitious name.

"Publication" is the distribution of copies or phonorecords of a work to
the public by sale or other transfer of ownership, or by rental, lease, or lending. The offering to distribute copies or phonorecords to a group of persons
for purposes of further distribution, public performance, or public display,
constitutes publication. A public performance or display of a work does not
of itself constitute publication.

"Registration," for purposes of sections 205(c)(2), 405, 406, 410(d), 411,
412, and 506(e), means a registration of a claim in the original or the renewed
and extended term of copyright.

To perform or display a work "publicly" means—

(1) to perform or display it at a place open to the public or at any place where a substantial number of persons outside of a normal circle of a family and its social acquaintances is gathered; or

(2) to transmit or otherwise communicate a performance or display of the work to a place specified by clause (1) or to the public, by means of any device or process, whether the members of the public capable of receiving the performance or display receive it in the same place or in separate places and at the same time or at different times.

"Sound recordings" are works that result from the fixation of a series of musical, spoken, or other sounds, but not including the sounds accompanying a motion picture or other audiovisual work, regardless of the nature of the material objects, such as disks, tapes, or other phonorecords, in which they are embodied.

"State" includes the District of Columbia and the Commonwealth of Puerto Rico, and any territories to which this title is made applicable by an Act of Congress.

A "transfer of copyright ownership" is an assignment, mortgage, exclusive license, or any other conveyance, alienation, or hypothecation of a copyright or of any of the exclusive rights comprised in a copyright, whether or not it is limited in time or place of effect, but not including a nonexclusive license.

A "transmission program" is a body of material that, as an aggregate, has been produced for the sole purpose of transmission to the public in sequence and as a unit.

To "transmit" a performance or display is to communicate it by any device or process whereby images or sounds are received beyond the place from which they are sent.

The "United States," when used in a geographical sense, comprises the several States, the District of Columbia and the Commonwealth of Puerto Rico, and the organized territories under the jurisdiction of the United States Government.

A "useful article" is an article having an intrinsic utilitarian function that is not merely to portray the appearance of the article or to convey information. An article that is normally a part of a useful article is considered a "useful article."

The author's "widow" or "widower" is the author's surviving spouse under the law of the author's domicile at the time of his or her death, whether or not the spouse has later remarried.

A "work of visual art" is—

(1) a painting, drawing, print, or sculpture, existing in a single copy, in a limited edition of 200 copies or fewer that are signed and consecutively numbered by the author, or, in the case of a sculpture, in multiple cast, carved, or fabricated sculptures of 200 or fewer that are consecutively

§101 *continued*   numbered by the author and bear the signature or other identifying mark of the author; or

(2) a still photographic image produced for exhibition purposes only, existing in a single copy that is signed by the author, or in a limited edition of 200 copies or fewer that are signed and consecutively numbered by the author.

A work of visual art does not include—

(A)(i) any poster, map, globe, chart, technical drawing, diagram, model, applied art, motion picture or other audiovisual work, book, magazine, newspaper, periodical, database, electronic information service, electronic publication, or similar publication;

(ii) any merchandising item or advertising, promotional, descriptive, covering, or packaging material or container;

(iii) any portion or part of any item described in clause (i) or (ii);

(B) any work made for hire; or

(C) any work not subject to copyright protection under this title.

A "work of the United States Government" is a work prepared by an officer or employee of the United States Government as part of that person's official duties.

A "work made for hire" is—

(1) a work prepared by an employee within the scope of his or her employment; or

(2) a work specially ordered or commissioned for use as a contribution to a collective work, as a part of a motion picture or other audiovisual work, as a translation, as a supplementary work, as a compilation, as an instructional text, as a test, as answer material for a test, or as an atlas, if the parties expressly agree in a written instrument signed by them that the work shall be considered a work made for hire. For the purpose of the foregoing sentence, a "supplementary work" is a work prepared for publication as a secondary adjunct to a work by another author for the purpose of introducing, concluding, illustrating, explaining, revising, commenting upon, or assisting in the use of the other work, such as forewords, afterwards, pictorial illustrations, maps, charts, tables, editorial notes, musical arrangements, answer material for tests, bibliographies, appendixes, and indexes, and an "instructional text" is a literary, pictorial, or graphic work prepared for publication and with the purpose of use in systematic instructional activities.

A "computer program" is a set of statements or instructions to be used directly or indirectly in a computer in order to bring about a certain result. (PL 94-553, Title I, §101, Oct. 19, 1976, 90 Stat. 2541; PL 96-517, §10[a], Dec. 12, 1980, 94 Stat. 3028; PL 100-568, §4[a][1], Oct. 31, 1988, 102 Stat. 2854; PL 101-650, Title VI, §602, Title VII, §702, Dec. 1, 1990, 104 Stat. 5128, 5133; PL 102-307, Title I, §102[b][2], June 26, 1992, 106 Stat. 266;

PL 102-563, §3[b], Oct. 28, 1992, 106 Stat. 4248; PL 104-39, §5[a], Nov. 1, 1995, 109 Stat. 348.)

17 U.S.C. §102 Subject matter of copyright: In general

(a) Copyright protection subsists, in accordance with this title, in original works of authorship fixed in any tangible medium of expression, now known or later developed, from which they can be perceived, reproduced, or otherwise communicated, either directly or with the aid of a machine or device. Works of authorship include the following categories:

(1) literary works;
(2) musical works, including any accompanying words;
(3) dramatic works, including any accompanying music;
(4) pantomimes and choreographic works;
(5) pictorial, graphic, and sculptural works;
(6) motion pictures and other audiovisual works;
(7) sound recordings; and
(8) architectural works.

(b) In no case does copyright protection for an original work of authorship extend to any idea, procedure, process, system, method of operation, concept, principle, or discovery, regardless of the form in which it is described, explained, illustrated, or embodied in such work. (PL 94-553, Title I, §101, Oct. 19, 1976, 90 Stat. 2544 amended by PL 101-650, Title VII, §703, Dec. 1, 1990, 104 Stat. 5133.)

17 U.S.C. §103 Subject matter of copyright: Compilations and derivative works

(a) The subject matter of copyright as specified by section 102 includes compilations and derivative works, but protection for a work employing pre-existing material in which copyright subsists does not extend to any part of the work in which such material has been used unlawfully.

(b) The copyright in a compilation or derivative work extends only to the material contributed by the author of such work, as distinguished from the pre-existing material employed in the work, and does not imply any exclusive right in the preexisting material. The copyright in such work is independent of, and does not affect or enlarge the scope, duration, ownership, or subsistence of, any copyright protection in the preexisting material. (PL 94-553, Title I, §101, Oct. 19, 1976, 90 Stat. 2545.)

§104A. Copyright in restored works

(a) Automatic protection and term.—
(1) Term.—
(A) Copyright subsists, in accordance with this section, in restored works, and vests automatically on the date of restoration.
(B) Any work in which copyright is restored under this section shall

§104A continued   subsist for the remainder of the term of copyright that the
work would have otherwise been granted in the United States
if the work never entered the public domain in the United States.

(2) Exception.—Any work in which the copyright was ever owned or administered by the Alien Property Custodian and in which the restored copyright would be owned by a government or instrumentality thereof, is not a restored work.

(b) Ownership of restored copyright.—A restored work vests initially in the author or initial rightholder of the work as determined by the law of the source country of the work.

(c) Filing of notice of intent to enforce restored copyright against reliance parties.—On or after the date of restoration, any person who owns a copyright in a restored work or an exclusive right therein may file with the Copyright Office a notice of intent to enforce that person's copyright or exclusive right or may serve such a notice directly on a reliance party. Acceptance of a notice by the Copyright Office is effective as to any reliance parties but shall not create a presumption of the validity of any of the facts stated therein. Service on a reliance party is effective as to that reliance party and any other reliance parties with actual knowledge of such service and of the contents of that notice.

(d) Remedies for infringement of restored copyrights.—

(1) Enforcement of copyright in restored works in the absence of a reliance party.—As against any party who is not a reliance party, the remedies provided in chapter 5 of this title shall be available on or after the date of restoration of a restored copyright with respect to an act of infringement of the restored copyright that is commenced on or after the date of restoration.

(2) Enforcement of copyright in restored works as against reliance parties.—As against a reliance party, except to the extent provided in paragraphs (3) and (4), the remedies provided in chapter 5 of this title shall be available, with respect to an act of infringement of a restored copyright, on or after the date of restoration of the restored copyright if the requirements of either of the following subparagraphs are met:

(A)(i) The owner of the restored copyright (or such owner's agent) or the owner of an exclusive right therein (or such owner's agent) files with the Copyright Office, during the 24-month period beginning on the date of restoration, a notice of intent to enforce the restored copyright; and

(ii)(I) the act of infringement commenced after the end of the 12-month period beginning on the date of publication of the notice in the Federal Register; (II) the act of infringement commenced before the end of the 12-month period described in subclause (I) and continued after the end of that 12-month period, in which case remedies shall be available only for infringement occurring after the end of that 12-month period; or (III) copies or phonorecords of a work in which copyright has been restored under this section are made after publication of the notice of intent in the Federal Register.

(B)(i) The owner of the restored copyright (or such owner's agent) or the owner of an exclusive right therein (or such owner's agent) serves upon a reliance party a notice of intent to enforce a restored copyright; and

(ii)(I) the act of infringement commenced after the end of the 12-month period beginning on the date the notice of intent is received; (II) the act of infringement commenced before the end of the 12-month period described in subclause (I) and continued after the end of that 12-month period, in which case remedies shall be available only for the infringement occurring after the end of that 12-month period; or (III) copies or phonorecords of a work in which copyright has been restored under this section are made after receipt of the notice of intent.

In the event that notice is provided under both subparagraphs (A) and (B), the 12-month period referred to in such subparagraphs shall run from the earlier of publication or service of notice.

(3) Existing derivative works.—

(A) In the case of a derivative work that is based upon a restored work and is created—

(i) before the date of the enactment of the Uruguay Round Agreements Act, if the source country of the derivative work is an eligible country on such date, or

(ii) before the date of adherence or proclamation, if the source country of the derivative work is not an eligible country on such date of enactment,

a reliance party may continue to exploit that work for the duration of the restored copyright if the reliance party pays to the owner of the restored copyright reasonable compensation for conduct which would be subject to a remedy for infringement but for the provisions of this paragraph.

(B) In the absence of an agreement between the parties, the amount of such compensation shall be determined by an action in United States district court, and shall reflect any harm to the actual or potential market for or value of the restored work from the reliance party's continued exploitation of the work, as well as compensation for the relative contributions of expression of the author of the restored work and the reliance party to the derivative work.

(4) Commencement of infringement for reliance parties.—For purposes of section 412, in the case of reliance parties, infringement shall be deemed to have commenced before registration when acts which would have constituted infringement had the restored work been subject to copyright were commenced before the date of restoration.

§104A continued   (e) Notices of intent to enforce a restored copyright.—

(1) Notices of intent filed with the copyright office.—

(A)(i) A notice of intent filed with the Copyright Office to enforce a restored copyright shall be signed by the owner of the restored copyright or the owner of an exclusive right therein, who files the notice under subsection (d)(2)(A)(i) (hereafter in this paragraph referred to as the "owner"), or by the owner's agent, shall identify the title of the restored work, and shall include an English translation of the title and any other alternative titles known to the owner by which the restored work may be identified, and an address and telephone number at which the owner may be contacted. If the notice is signed by an agent, the agency relationship must have been constituted in a writing signed by the owner before the filing of the notice. The Copyright Office may specifically require in regulations other information to be included in the notice, but failure to provide such other information shall not invalidate the notice or be a basis for refusal to list the restored work in the Federal Register.

(ii) If a work in which copyright is restored has no formal title, it shall be described in the notice of intent in detail sufficient to identify it.

(iii) Minor errors or omissions may be corrected by further notice at any time after the notice of intent is filed. Notices of corrections for such minor errors or omissions shall be accepted after the period established in subsection (d)(2)(A)(i). Notices shall be published in the Federal Register pursuant to subparagraph (B).

(B)(i) The Register of Copyrights shall publish in the Federal Register, commencing not later than 4 months after the date of restoration for a particular nation and every 4 months thereafter for a period of 2 years, lists identifying restored works and the ownership thereof if a notice of intent to enforce a restored copyright has been filed.

(ii) Not less than 1 list containing all notices of intent to enforce shall be maintained in the Public Information Office of the Copyright Office and shall be available for public inspection and copying during regular business hours pursuant to sections 705 and 708. Such list shall also be published in the Federal Register on an annual basis for the first 2 years after the applicable date of restoration.

(C) The Register of Copyrights is authorized to fix reasonable fees based on the costs of receipt, processing, recording, and publication of notices of intent to enforce a restored copyright and corrections thereto.

(D)(i) Not later than 90 days before the date the Agreement on Trade-Related Aspects of Intellectual Property referred to in section 101(d)(15) of the Uruguay Round Agreements Act enters into force with respect to the United States, the Copyright Office shall issue and publish in the Federal Register regulations governing the filing under this subsection of notices of intent to enforce a restored copyright.

(ii) Such regulations shall permit owners of restored copyrights to file simultaneously for registration of the restored copyright.

(2) Notices of intent served on a reliance party.—

(A) Notices of intent to enforce a restored copyright may be served on a reliance party at any time after the date of restoration of the restored copyright.

(B) Notices of intent to enforce a restored copyright served on a reliance party shall be signed by the owner or the owner's agent, shall identify the restored work and the work in which the restored work is used, if any, in detail sufficient to identify them, and shall include an English translation of the title, any other alternative titles known to the owner by which the work may be identified, the use or uses to which the owner objects, and an address and telephone number at which the reliance party may contact the owner. If the notice is signed by an agent, the agency relationship must have been constituted in writing and signed by the owner before service of the notice.

(3) Effect of material false statements.—Any material false statement knowingly made with respect to any restored copyright identified in any notice of intent shall make void all claims and assertions made with respect to such restored copyright.

(f) Immunity from warranty and related liability.—

(1) In general.—Any person who warrants, promises, or guarantees that a work does not violate an exclusive right granted in section 106 shall not be liable for legal, equitable, arbitral, or administrative relief if the warranty, promise, or guarantee is breached by virtue of the restoration of copyright under this section, if such warranty, promise, or guarantee is made before January 1, 1995.

(2) Performances.—No person shall be required to perform any act if such performance is made infringing by virtue of the restoration of copyright under the provisions of this section, if the obligation to perform was undertaken before January 1, 1995.

(g) Proclamation of copyright restoration.—Whenever the President finds that a particular foreign nation extends, to works by authors who are nationals or domiciliaries of the United States, restored copyright protection on substantially the same basis as provided under this section, the President may by proclamation extend restored protection provided under this section to any work—

(1) of which one or more of the authors is, on the date of first publication, a national, domiciliary, or sovereign authority of that nation; or

(2) which was first published in that nation.

The President may revise, suspend, or revoke any such proclamation or impose any conditions or limitations on protection under such a proclamation.

§104A continued   (h) Definitions.—For purposes of this section and section 109(a):

(1) The term "date of adherence or proclamation" means the earlier of the date on which a foreign nation which, as of the date the WTO Agreement enters into force with respect to the United States, is not a nation adhering to the Berne Convention or a WTO member country, becomes—

(A) a nation adhering to the Berne Convention or a WTO member country; or

(B) subject to a Presidential proclamation under subsection (g).

(2) The "date of restoration" of a restored copyright is the later of—

(A) the date on which the Agreement on Trade-Related Aspects of Intellectual Property referred to in section 101(d)(15) of the Uruguay Round Agreements Act enters into force with respect to the United States, if the source country of the restored work is a nation adhering to the Berne Convention or a WTO member country on such date; or

(B) the date of adherence or proclamation, in the case of any other source country of the restored work.

(3) The term "eligible country" means a nation, other than the United States, that is a WTO member country, adheres to the Berne Convention, or is subject to a proclamation under section 104(A)(g).

(4) The term "reliance party" means any person who—

(A) with respect to a particular work, engages in acts, before the source country of that work becomes an eligible country, which would have violated section 106 if the restored work had been subject to copyright protection, and who, after the source country becomes an eligible country, continues to engage in such acts;

(B) before the source country of a particular work becomes an eligible country, makes or acquires 1 or more copies or phonorecords of that work; or

(C) as the result of the sale or other disposition of a derivative work covered under subsection (d)(3), or significant assets of a person described in subparagraph (A) or (B), is a successor, assignee, or licensee of that person.

(5) The term "restored copyright" means copyright in a restored work under this section.

(6) The term "restored work" means an original work of authorship that—

(A) is protected under subsection (a);

(B) is not in the public domain in its source country through expiration of term of protection;

(C) is in the public domain in the United States due to—

(i) noncompliance with formalities imposed at any time by United States copyright law, including failure of renewal, lack of proper notice, or failure to comply with any manufacturing requirements;

(ii) lack of subject matter protection in the case of sound recordings fixed before February 15, 1972; or

(iii) lack of national eligibility; and

(D) has at least one author or rightholder who was, at the time the work was created, a national or domiciliary of an eligible country, and if published, was first published in an eligible country and not published in the United States during the 30-day period following publication in such eligible country.

(7) The term "rightholder" means the person—

(A) who, with respect to a sound recording, first fixes a sound recording with authorization, or

(B) who has acquired rights from the person described in subparagraph (A) by means of any conveyance or by operation of law.

(8) The "source country" of a restored work is—

(A) a nation other than the United States;

(B) in the case of an unpublished work—

(i) the eligible country in which the author or rightholder is a national or domiciliary, or, if a restored work has more than 1 author or rightholder, the majority of foreign authors or rightholders are nationals or domiciliaries of eligible countries; or

(ii) if the majority of authors or rightholders are not foreign, the nation other than the United States which has the most significant contacts with the work; and

(C) in the case of a published work—

(i) the eligible country in which the work is first published, or

(ii) if the restored work is published on the same day in 2 or more eligible countries, the eligible country which has the most significant contacts with the work.

(9) The terms "WTO Agreement" and "WTO member country" have the meanings given those terms in paragraphs (9) and (10), respectively, of section 2 of the Uruguay Round Agreements Act. (PL 103-182, Title III, §334(a), Dec. 8, 1993, 107 Stat. 2115, amended PL 103-465, Title V, §514(a), Dec. 8, 1994, 108 Stat. 4976.)

17 U.S.C. §105 Subject matter of copyright: United States Government works

Copyright protection under this title is not available for any work of the United States Government, but the United States Government is not precluded from receiving and holding copyrights transferred to it by assignment, bequest, or otherwise. (PL 94-553, Title I, §101, Oct. 19, 1976, 90 Stat. 2546.)

17 U.S.C. §106 Exclusive rights in copyrighted works

Subject to sections 107 through 120, the owner of copyright under this title has the exclusive rights to do and to authorize any of the following:

§106 continued   (1) to reproduce the copyrighted work in copies or phonorecords;

(2) to prepare derivative works based upon the copyrighted work;

(3) to distribute copies or phonorecords of the copyrighted work to the public by sale or other transfer of ownership, or by rental, lease, or lending;

(4) in the case of literary, musical, dramatic, and choreographic works, pantomimes, and motion pictures and other audiovisual works, to perform the copyrighted work publicly;

(5) in the case of literary, musical, dramatic, and choreographic works, pantomimes, and pictorial, graphic, or sculptural works, including the individual images of a motion picture or other audiovisual work, to display the copyrighted work publicly; and

(6) in the case of sound recordings, to perform the copyrighted work publicly by means of a digital audio transmission. (PL 94-553, Title I, §101, Oct. 19, 1976, 90 Stat. 2546; PL 101-318, §3[d], July 3, 1990, 104 Stat. 288; PL 101-650, Title VII, §704[b][2], Dec. 1, 1990, 104 Stat. 5134; PL 104-39, §2, Nov. 1, 1995, 109 Stat. 336.)

17 U.S.C. §107 Limitations on exclusive rights: Fair use

Notwithstanding the provisions of sections 106 and 106A, the fair use of a copyrighted work, including such use by reproduction in copies or phonorecords or by any other means specified by that section, for purposes such as criticism, comment, news reporting, teaching (including multiple copies for classroom use), scholarship, or research, is not an infringement of copyright. In determining whether the use made of a work in any particular case is a fair use the factors to be considered shall include—

(1) the purpose and character of the use, including whether such use is of a commercial nature or is for nonprofit educational purposes;

(2) the nature of the copyrighted work;

(3) the amount and substantiality of the portion used in relation to the copyrighted work as a whole; and

(4) the effect of the use upon the potential market for or value of the copyrighted work.

The fact that a work is unpublished shall not itself bar a finding of fair use if such finding is made upon consideration of all the above factors. (PL 94-553, Title I, §101, Oct. 19, 1976, 90 Stat. 2546; PL 101-650, Title VI, §607, Dec. 1, 1990, 104 Stat. 5132; PL 102-492, Oct. 24, 1992, 106 Stat. 3145.)

17 U.S.C. §108 Limitations on exclusive rights: Reproduction by libraries and archives

(a) Notwithstanding the provisions of section 106, it is not an infringement of copyright for a library or archives, or any of its employees acting within the scope of their employment, to reproduce no more than one copy or phonorecord of a work, or to distribute such copy or phonorecord, under the conditions specified by this section, if—

(1) the reproduction or distribution is made without any purpose of direct or indirect commercial advantage;

(2) the collections of the library or archives are (i) open to the public, or (ii) available not only to researchers affiliated with the library or archives or with the institution of which it is a part, but also to other persons doing research in a specialized field; and

(3) the reproduction or distribution of the work includes a notice of copyright.

(b) The rights of reproduction and distribution under this section apply to a copy or phonorecord of an unpublished work duplicated in facsimile form solely for purposes of preservation and security or for deposit for research use in another library or archives of the type described by clause (2) of subsection (a), if the copy or phonorecord reproduced is currently in the collections of the library or archives.

(c) The right of reproduction under this section applies to a copy or phonorecord of a published work duplicated in facsimile form solely for the purpose of replacement of a copy or phonorecord that is damaged, deteriorating, lost, or stolen, if the library or archives has, after a reasonable effort, determined that an unused replacement cannot be obtained at a fair price.

(d) The rights of reproduction and distribution under this section apply to a copy, made from the collection of a library or archives where the user makes his or her request or from that of another library or archives, of no more than one article or other contribution to a copyrighted collection or periodical issue, or to a copy or phonorecord of a small part of any other copyrighted work, if—

(1) the copy or phonorecord becomes the property of the user, and the library or archives has had no notice that the copy or phonorecord would be used for any purpose other than private study, scholarship, or research; and

(2) the library or archives displays prominently, at the place where orders are accepted, and includes on its order form, a warning of copyright in accordance with requirements that the Register of Copyrights shall prescribe by regulation.

(e) The rights of reproduction and distribution under this section apply to the entire work, or to a substantial part of it, made from the collection of a library or archives where the user makes his or her request or from that of another library or archives, if the library or archives has first determined, on the basis of a reasonable investigation, that a copy or phonorecord of the copyrighted work cannot be obtained at a pair [sic] price, if—

(1) the copy or phonorecord becomes the property of the user, and the library or archives has had no notice that the copy or phonorecord would be used for any purpose other than private study, scholarship, or research; and

§108 continued   (2) the library or archives displays prominently, at the place where orders are accepted, and includes on its order form, a warning of copyright in accordance with requirements that the Register of Copyrights shall prescribe by regulation.

(f) Nothing in this section—

(1) shall be construed to impose liability for copyright infringement upon a library or archives or its employees for the unsupervised use of reproducing equipment located on its premises: Provided, That such equipment displays a notice that the making of a copy may be subject to the copyright law;

(2) excuses a person who uses such reproducing equipment or who requests a copy or phonorecord under subsection (d) from liability for copyright infringement for any such act, or for any later use of such copy or phonorecord, if it exceeds fair use as provided by section 107;

(3) shall be construed to limit the reproduction and distribution by lending of a limited number of copies and excerpts by a library or archives of an audiovisual news program, subject to clauses (1), (2), and (3) of subsection (a); or

(4) in any way affects the right of fair use as provided by section 107, or any contractual obligations assumed at any time by the library or archives when it obtained a copy or phonorecord of a work in its collections.

(g) The rights of reproduction and distribution under this section extend to the isolated and unrelated reproduction or distribution of a single copy or phonorecord of the same material on separate occasions, but do not extend to cases where the library or archives, or its employee—

(1) is aware or has substantial reason to believe that it is engaging in the related or concerted reproduction or distribution of multiple copies or phonorecords of the same material, whether made on one occasion or over a period of time, and whether intended for aggregate use by one or more individuals or for separate use by the individual members of a group; or

(2) engages in the systematic reproduction or distribution of single or multiple copies or phonorecords of material described in subsection (d): Provided, That nothing in this clause prevents a library or archives from participating in interlibrary arrangements that do not have, as their purpose or effect, that the library or archives receiving such copies or phonorecords for distribution does so in such aggregate quantities as to substitute for a subscription to or purchase of such work.

(h) The rights of reproduction and distribution under this section do not apply to a musical work, a pictorial, graphic or sculptural work, or a motion picture or other audiovisual work other than an audiovisual work dealing with news, except that no such limitation shall apply with respect to rights granted by subsections (b) and (c), or with respect to pictorial or graphic works published as illustrations, diagrams, or similar adjuncts to works of which copies are reproduced or distributed in accordance with subsections (d) and (e). (PL

94-553, Title I, §101, Oct. 19, 1976, 90 Stat. 2546; PL 102-307, Title III, §301, June 26, 1992, 106 Stat. 272.)

17 U.S.C. §109 Limitations on exclusive rights: Effect of transfer of particular copy or phonorecord

(a) Notwithstanding the provisions of section 106(3), the owner of a particular copy or phonorecord lawfully made under this title, or any person authorized by such owner, is entitled, without the authority of the copyright owner, to sell or otherwise dispose of the possession of that copy or phonorecord. Notwithstanding the preceding sentence, copies or phonorecords of works subject to restored copyright under section 104(A) that are manufactured before the date of restoration of copyright or, with respect to reliance parties, before publication or service of notice under section 104(A)(e), may be sold or otherwise disposed of without the authorization of the owner of the restored copyright for purposes of direct or indirect commercial advantage only during the 12-month period beginning on—

(1) the date of the publication in the Federal Register of the notice of intent filed with the Copyright Office under section 104(A)(d)(2)(A), or

(2) the date of the receipt of actual notice served under section 104(A)(d)(2)(B), whichever occurs first.

(b)(1)(A) Notwithstanding the provisions of subsection (a), unless authorized by the owners of copyright in the sound recording or the owner of copyright in a computer program (including any tape, disk, or other medium embodying such program), and in the case of a sound recording in the musical works embodied therein, neither the owner of a particular phonorecord nor any person in possession of a particular copy of a computer program (including any tape, disk, or other medium embodying such program), may, for the purposes of direct or indirect commercial advantage, dispose of, or authorize the disposal of, the possession of that phonorecord or computer program (including any tape, disk, or other medium embodying such program) by rental, lease, or lending, or by any other act or practice in the nature of rental, lease, or lending. Nothing in the preceding sentence shall apply to the rental, lease, or lending of a phonorecord for nonprofit purposes by a nonprofit library or nonprofit educational institution. The transfer of possession of a lawfully made copy of a computer program by a nonprofit educational institution to another nonprofit educational institution or to faculty, staff, and students does not constitute rental, lease, or lending for direct or indirect commercial purposes under this subsection.

(B) This subsection does not apply to—

(i) a computer program which is embodied in a machine or product and which cannot be copied during the ordinary operation or use of the machine or product; or

(ii) a computer program embodied in or used in conjunction with a

§109 *continued*   limited purpose computer that is designed for playing video games and may be designed for other purposes.

(C) Nothing in this subsection affects any provision of chapter 9 of this title.

(2)(A) Nothing in this subsection shall apply to the lending of a computer program for nonprofit purposes by a nonprofit library, if each copy of a computer program which is lent by such library has affixed to the packaging containing the program a warning of copyright in accordance with requirements that the Register of Copyrights shall prescribe by regulation.

(B) Not later than three years after the date of the enactment of the Computer Software Rental Amendments Act of 1990, and at such times thereafter as the Register of Copyrights considers appropriate, the Register of Copyrights, after consultation with representatives of copyright owners and librarians, shall submit to the Congress a report stating whether this paragraph has achieved its intended purpose of maintaining the integrity of the copyright system while providing nonprofit libraries the capability to fulfill their function. Such report shall advise the Congress as to any information or recommendations that the Register of Copyrights considers necessary to carry out the purposes of this subsection.

(3) Nothing in this subsection shall affect any provision of the antitrust laws. For purposes of the preceding sentence, "antitrust laws" has the meaning given that term in the first section of the Clayton Act and includes section 5 of the Federal Trade Commission Act to the extent that section relates to unfair methods of competition.

(4) Any person who distributes a phonorecord or a copy of a computer program (including any tape, disk, or other medium embodying such program) in violation of paragraph (1) is an infringer of copyright under section 501 of this title and is subject to the remedies set forth in sections 502, 503, 504, 505, and 509. Such violation shall not be a criminal offense under section 506 or cause such person to be subject to the criminal penalties set forth in section 2319 of title 18.

(c) Notwithstanding the provisions of section 106(5), the owner of a particular copy lawfully made under this title, or any person authorized by such owner, is entitled, without the authority of the copyright owner, to display that copy publicly, either directly or by the projection of no more than one image at a time, to viewers present at the place where the copy is located.

(d) The privileges prescribed by subsections (a) and (c) do not, unless authorized by the copyright owner, extend to any person who has acquired possession of the copy or phonorecord from the copyright owner, by rental, lease, loan, or otherwise, without acquiring ownership of it.

(e) Notwithstanding the provisions of sections 106(4) and 106(5), in the case of an electronic audiovisual game intended for use in coin-operated equipment, the owner of a particular copy of such a game lawfully made under this title, is entitled, without the authority of the copyright owner of the game, to publicly perform or display that game in coin-operated equipment, except that this subsection shall not apply to any work of authorship embodied in the audiovisual game if the copyright owner of the electronic audiovisual game is not also the copyright owner of the work of authorship. (PL 94-553, Title I, §101, Oct. 19, 1976, 90 Stat. 2548; PL 98-450, §2, Oct. 4, 1984, 98 Stat. 1727; PL 100-617, §2, Nov. 5, 1988, 102 Stat. 3194; PL 101-650, Title VIII, §§802, 803, Dec. 1, 1990, 104 Stat. 5134, 5135; PL 103-465, Title V, §514(b), Dec. 8, 1994, 108 Stat. 4981.)

17 U.S.C. §110 Limitations on exclusive rights: Exemption of certain performances and displays

Notwithstanding the provisions of section 106, the following are not infringements of copyright:

(1) performance or display of a work by instructors or pupils in the course of face-to-face teaching activities of a nonprofit educational institution, in a classroom or similar place devoted to instruction, unless, in the case of a motion picture or other audiovisual work, the performance, or the display of individual images, is given by means of a copy that was not lawfully made under this title, and that the person responsible for the performance knew or had reason to believe was not lawfully made;

(2) performance of a nondramatic literary or musical work or display of a work, by or in the course of a transmission, if—

(A) the performance or display is a regular part of the systematic instructional activities of a governmental body or a nonprofit educational institution; and

(B) the performance or display is directly related and of material assistance to the teaching content of the transmission; and

(C) the transmission is made primarily for—

(i) reception in classrooms or similar places normally devoted to instruction, or

(ii) reception by persons to whom the transmission is directed because their disabilities or other special circumstances prevent their attendance in classrooms or similar places normally devoted to instruction, or

(iii) reception by officers or employees of governmental bodies as a part of their official duties or employment;

(3) performance of a nondramatic literary or musical work or of a dramatico-musical work of a religious nature, or display of a work, in the course of services at a place of worship or other religious assembly;

(4) performance of a nondramatic literary or musical work otherwise than in a transmission to the public, without any purpose of direct or indirect

§110 *continued*   commercial advantage and without payment of any fee or
                       other compensation for the performance to any of its per-
formers, promoters, or organizers, if—

  (A) there is no direct or indirect admission charge; or

  (B) the proceeds, after deducting the reasonable costs of producing the
performance, are used exclusively for educational, religious, or charitable
purposes and not for private financial gain, except where the copyright
owner has served notice of objection to the performance under the following conditions;

    (i) the notice shall be in writing and signed by the copyright owner
  or such owner's duly authorized agent; and

    (ii) the notice shall be served on the person responsible for the per-
  formance at least seven days before the date of the performance, and
  shall state the reasons for the objection; and

    (iii) the notice shall comply, in form, content, and manner of ser-
  vice, with requirements that the Register of Copyrights shall prescribe
  by regulation;

  (5) communication of a transmission embodying a performance or display of a work by the public reception of the transmission on a single receiving apparatus of a kind commonly used in private homes, unless—

  (A) a direct charge is made to see or hear the transmission; or

  (B) the transmission thus received is further transmitted to the public,

  (6) performance of a nondramatic musical work by a governmental body
or a nonprofit agricultural or horticultural organization, in the course of an
annual agricultural or horticultural fair or exhibition conducted by such
body or organization; the exemption provided by this clause shall extend to
any liability for copyright infringement that would otherwise be imposed
on such body or organization, under doctrines of vicarious liability or related
infringement, for a performance by a concessionaire, business establishment,
or other person at such fair or exhibition, but shall not excuse any such person from liability for the performance;

  (7) performance of a nondramatic musical work by a vending establishment open to the public at large without any direct or indirect admission
charge, where the sole purpose of the performance is to promote the retail
sale of copies or phonorecords of the work, and the performance is not
transmitted beyond the place where the establishment is located and is
within the immediate area where the sale is occurring;

  (8) performance of a nondramatic literary work, by or in the course of a
transmission specifically designed for and primarily directed to blind or
other handicapped persons who are unable to read normal printed material
as a result of their handicap, or deaf or other handicapped persons who are
unable to hear the aural signals accompanying a transmission of visual signals, if the performance is made without any purpose of direct or indirect

commercial advantage and its transmission is made through the facilities of: (i) a governmental body; or (ii) a noncommercial educational broadcast station (as defined in section 397 of title 47); or (iii) a radio subcarrier authorization (as defined in 47 CFR 73.293-73.295 and 73.593-73.595); or (iv) a cable system (as defined in section 111[f]).

(9) performance on a single occasion of a dramatic literary work published at least ten years before the date of the performance, by or in the course of a transmission specifically designed for and primarily directed to blind or other handicapped persons who are unable to read normal printed material as a result of their handicap, if the performance is made without any purpose of direct or indirect commercial advantage and its transmission is made through the facilities of a radio subcarrier authorization referred to in clause (8)(iii), Provided, That the provisions of this clause shall not be applicable to more than one performance of the same work by the same performers or under the auspices of the same organization.

(10) notwithstanding paragraph 4 above, the following is not an infringement of copyright: performance of a nondramatic literary or musical work in the course of a social function which is organized and promoted by a nonprofit veterans' organization or a nonprofit fraternal organization to which the general public is not invited, but not including the invitees of the organizations, if the proceeds from the performance, after deducting the reasonable costs of producing the performance, are used exclusively for charitable purposes and not for financial gain. For purposes of this section the social functions of any college or university fraternity or sorority shall not be included unless the social function is held solely to raise funds for a specific charitable purpose. (PL 94-553, Title I, §101, Oct. 19, 1976, 90 Stat. 2549 amended by PL 97-366, §3, Oct. 25, 1982, 96 Stat. 1759.)

17 U.S.C. §111 Limitations on exclusive rights: Secondary transmissions

(a) Certain Secondary Transmissions Exempted.—The secondary transmission of a primary transmission embodying a performance or display of a work is not an infringement of copyright if—

(1) the secondary transmission is not made by a cable system, and consists entirely of the relaying, by the management of a hotel, apartment house, or similar establishment, of signals transmitted by a broadcast station licensed by the Federal Communications Commission, within the local service area of such station, to the private lodgings of guests or residents of such establishment, and no direct charge is made to see or hear the secondary transmission; or

(2) the secondary transmission is made solely for the purpose and under the conditions specified by clause (2) of section 110; or

(3) the secondary transmission is made by any carrier who has no direct or indirect control over the content or selection of the primary transmission

§111 continued   or over the particular recipients of the secondary transmission, and whose activities with respect to the secondary transmission consist solely of providing wires, cables, or other communications channels for the use of others: Provided, That the provisions of this clause extend only to the activities of said carrier with respect to secondary transmissions and do not exempt from liability the activities of others with respect to their own primary or secondary transmissions;

(4) the secondary transmission is made by a satellite carrier for private home viewing pursuant to a statutory license under section 119; or

(5) the secondary transmission is not made by a cable system but is made by a governmental body, or other nonprofit organization, without any purpose of direct or indirect commercial advantage, and without charge to the recipients of the secondary transmission other than assessments necessary to defray the actual and reasonable costs of maintaining and operating the secondary transmission service.

(b) Secondary Transmission of Primary Transmission to Controlled Group.—Notwithstanding the provisions of subsections (a) and (c), the secondary transmission to the public of a primary transmission embodying a performance or display of a work is actionable as an act of infringement under section 501, and is fully subject to the remedies provided by sections 502 through 506 and 509, if the primary transmission is not made for reception by the public at large but is controlled and limited to reception by particular members of the public: Provided, however, That such secondary transmission is not actionable as an act of infringement if—

(1) the primary transmission is made by a broadcast station licensed by the Federal Communications Commission; and

(2) the carriage of the signals comprising the secondary transmission is required under the rules, regulations, or authorizations of the Federal Communications Commission; and

(3) the signal of the primary transmitter is not altered or changed in any way by the secondary transmitter.

(c) Secondary Transmissions by Cable Systems.—

(1) Subject to the provisions of clauses (2), (3), and (4) of this subsection and section 114(d), secondary transmissions to the public by a cable system of a primary transmission made by a broadcast station licensed by the Federal Communications Commission or by an appropriate governmental authority of Canada or Mexico and embodying a performance or display of a work shall be subject to compulsory licensing upon compliance with the requirements of subsection (d) where the carriage of the signals comprising the secondary transmission is permissible under the rules, regulations, or authorizations of the Federal Communications Commission.

(2) Notwithstanding the provisions of clause (1) of this subsection, the willful or repeated secondary transmission to the public by a cable system

of a primary transmission made by a broadcast station licensed by the Federal Communications Commission or by an appropriate governmental authority of Canada or Mexico and embodying a performance or display of a work is actionable as an act of infringement under section 501, and is fully subject to the remedies provided by sections 502 through 506 and 509, in the following cases:

(A) where the carriage of the signals comprising the secondary transmission is not permissible under the rules, regulations, or authorizations of the Federal Communications Commission; or

(B) where the cable system has not deposited the statement of account and royalty fee required by subsection (d).

(3) Notwithstanding the provisions of clause (1) of this subsection and subject to the provisions of subsection (e) of this section, the secondary transmission to the public by a cable system of a primary transmission made by a broadcast station licensed by the Federal Communications Commission or by an appropriate governmental authority of Canada or Mexico and embodying a performance or display of a work is actionable as an act of infringement under section 501, and is fully subject to the remedies provided by sections 502 through 506 and sections 509 and 510, if the content of the particular program in which the performance or display is embodied, or any commercial advertising or station announcements transmitted by the primary transmitter during, or immediately before or after, the transmission of such program, is in any way willfully altered by the cable system through changes, deletions, or additions, except for the alteration, deletion, or substitution of commercial advertisements performed by those engaged in television commercial advertising market research: Provided, That the research company has obtained the prior consent of the advertiser who has purchased the original commercial advertisement, the television station broadcasting that commercial advertisement, and the cable system performing the secondary transmission: And provided further, That such commercial alteration, deletion, or substitution is not performed for the purpose of deriving income from the sale of that commercial time.

(4) Notwithstanding the provisions of clause (1) of this subsection, the secondary transmission to the public by a cable system of a primary transmission made by a broadcast station licensed by an appropriate governmental authority of Canada or Mexico and embodying a performance or display of a work is actionable as an act of infringement under section 501, and is fully subject to the remedies provided by sections 502 through 506 and section 509, if (A) with respect to Canadian signals, the community of the cable system is located more than 150 miles from the United States–Canadian border and is also located south of the forty-second parallel of latitude, or (B) with respect to Mexican signals, the secondary transmission is made by a cable system which received the primary transmission by means other

§111 continued   than direct interception of a free space radio wave emitted by
                      such broadcast television station, unless prior to April 15, 1976,
such cable system was actually carrying, or was specifically authorized to
carry, the signal of such foreign station on the system pursuant to the rules,
regulations, or authorizations of the Federal Communications Commission.
(d) Compulsory License for Secondary Transmissions by Cable Systems.—

(1) A cable system whose secondary transmissions have been subject to
compulsory licensing under subsection (c) shall, on a semiannual basis,
deposit with the Register of Copyrights, in accordance with requirements
that the Register shall prescribe by regulation—

(A) a statement of account, covering the six months next preceding,
specifying the number of channels on which the cable system made secondary transmissions to its subscribers, the names and locations of all primary transmitters whose transmissions were further transmitted by the
cable system, the total number of subscribers, the gross amounts paid to
the cable system for the basic service of providing secondary transmissions of primary broadcast transmitters, and such other data as the Register of Copyrights may from time to time prescribe by regulation. In
determining the total number of subscribers and the gross amounts paid
to the cable system for the basic service of providing secondary transmissions of primary broadcast transmitters, the system shall not include subscribers and amounts collected from subscribers receiving secondary transmissions for private home viewing pursuant to section 119. Such statement
shall also include a special statement of account covering any nonnetwork
television programming that was carried by the cable system in whole or in
part beyond the local service area of the primary transmitter, under rules,
regulations, or authorizations of the Federal Communications Commission
permitting the substitution or addition of signals under certain circumstances, together with logs showing the times, dates, stations, and programs
involved in such substituted or added carriage; and

(B) except in the case of a cable system whose royalty is specified in
subclause (C) or (D), a total royalty fee for the period covered by the statement, computed on the basis of specified percentages of the gross receipts
from subscribers to the cable service during said period for the basic service of providing secondary transmissions of primary broadcast transmitters, as follows:

(i) 0.675 of 1 per centum of such gross receipts for the privilege of
further transmitting any nonnetwork programming of a primary transmitter in whole or in part beyond the local service area of such primary
transmitter, such amount to be applied against the fee, if any, payable
pursuant to paragraphs (ii) through (iv);

(ii) 0.675 of 1 per centum of such gross receipts for the first distant
signal equivalent;

(iii) 0.425 of 1 per centum of such gross receipts for each of the second, third, and fourth distant signal equivalents;

(iv) 0.2 of 1 per centum of such gross receipts for the fifth distant signal equivalent and each additional distant signal equivalent thereafter; and

in computing the amounts payable under paragraph (ii) through (iv), above, any fraction of a distant signal equivalent shall be computed at its fractional value and, in the case of any cable system located partly within and partly without the local service area of a primary transmitter, gross receipts shall be limited to those gross receipts derived from subscribers located without the local service area of such primary transmitter; and

(C) if the actual gross receipts paid by subscribers to a cable system for the period covered by the statement for the basic service of providing secondary transmissions of primary broadcast transmitters total $80,000 or less, gross receipts of the cable system for the purpose of this subclause shall be computed by subtracting from such actual gross receipts the amount by which $80,000 exceeds such actual gross receipts, except that in no case shall a cable system's gross receipts be reduced to less than $3,000. The royalty fee payable under this subclause shall be 0.5 of 1 per centum, regardless of the number of distant signal equivalents, if any; and

(D) if the actual gross receipts paid by subscribers to a cable system for the period covered by the statement, for the basic service of providing secondary transmissions of primary broadcast transmitters, are more than $80,000 but less than $160,000, the royalty fee payable under this subclause shall be (i) 0.5 of 1 per centum of any gross receipts up to $80,000; and (ii) 1 per centum of any gross receipts in excess of $80,000 but less than $160,000, regardless of the number of distant signal equivalents, if any.

(2) The Register of Copyrights shall receive all fees deposited under this section and, after deducting the reasonable costs incurred by the Copyright Office under this section, shall deposit the balance in the Treasury of the United States, in such manner as the Secretary of the Treasury directs. All funds held by the Secretary of the Treasury shall be invested in interest-bearing United States securities for later distribution with interest by the Librarian of Congress in the event no controversy over distribution exists, or by a copyright arbitration royalty panel in the event a controversy over such distribution exists.

(3) The royalty fees thus deposited shall, in accordance with the procedures provided by clause (4), be distributed to those among the following copyright owners who claim that their works were the subject of secondary transmissions by cable systems during the relevant semiannual period:

(A) any such owner whose work was included in a secondary transmission

§111 continued   made by a cable system of a nonnetwork television program
in whole or in part beyond the local service area of the primary transmitter; and

(B) any such owner whose work was included in a secondary transmission identified in a special statement of account deposited under clause (1)(A); and

(C) any such owner whose work was included in nonnetwork programming consisting exclusively of aural signals carried by a cable system in whole or in part beyond the local service area of the primary transmitter of such programs.

(4) The royalty fees thus deposited shall be distributed in accordance with the following procedures:

(A) During the month of July in each year, every person claiming to be entitled to compulsory license fees for secondary transmissions shall file a claim with the Librarian of Congress, in accordance with requirements that the Librarian of Congress shall prescribe by regulation. Notwithstanding any provisions of the antitrust laws, for purposes of this clause any claimants may agree among themselves as to the proportionate division of compulsory licensing fees among them, may lump their claims together and file them jointly or as a single claim, or may designate a common agent to receive payment on their behalf.

(B) After the first day of August of each year, the Librarian of Congress shall, upon the recommendation of the Register of Copyrights, determine whether there exists a controversy concerning the distribution of royalty fees. If the Librarian determines that no such controversy exists, the Librarian shall, after deducting reasonable administrative costs under this section, distribute such fees to the copyright owners entitled to such fees, or to their designated agents. If the Librarian finds the existence of a controversy, the Librarian shall, pursuant to chapter 8 of this title, convene a copyright arbitration royalty panel to determine the distribution of royalty fees.

(C) During the pendency of any proceeding under this subsection, the Librarian of Congress shall withhold from distribution an amount sufficient to satisfy all claims with respect to which a controversy exists, but shall have discretion to proceed to distribute any amounts that are not in controversy.

(e) Nonsimultaneous Secondary Transmissions by Cable Systems.—

(1) Notwithstanding those provisions of the second paragraph of subsection (f) relating to nonsimultaneous secondary transmissions by a cable system, any such transmissions are actionable as an act of infringement under section 501, and are fully subject to the remedies provided by sections 502 through 506 and sections 509 and 510, unless—

(A) the program on the videotape is transmitted no more than one time to the cable system's subscribers; and

(B) the copyrighted program, episode, or motion picture videotape, including the commercials contained within such program, episode, or picture, is transmitted without deletion or editing; and

(C) an owner or officer of the cable system (i) prevents the duplication of the videotape while in the possession of the system, (ii) prevents unauthorized duplication while in the possession of the facility making the videotape for the system if the system owns or controls the facility, or takes reasonable precautions to prevent such duplication if it does not own or control the facility, (iii) takes adequate precautions to prevent duplication while the tape is being transported, and (iv) subject to clause (2), erases or destroys, or causes the erasure or destruction of, the videotape; and

(D) within forty-five days after the end of each calendar quarter, an owner or officer of the cable system executes an affidavit attesting (i) to the steps and precautions taken to prevent duplication of the videotape, and (ii) subject to clause (2), to the erasure or destruction of all videotapes made or used during such quarter; and

(E) such owner or officer places or causes each such affidavit, and affidavits received pursuant to clause (2)(C), to be placed in a file, open to public inspection, at such system's main office in the community where the transmission is made or in the nearest community where such system maintains an office; and

(F) the nonsimultaneous transmission is one that the cable system would be authorized to transmit under the rules, regulations, and authorizations of the Federal Communications Commission in effect at the time of the nonsimultaneous transmission if the transmission had been made simultaneously, except that this subclause shall not apply to inadvertent or accidental transmissions.

(2) If a cable system transfers to any person a videotape of a program nonsimultaneously transmitted by it, such transfer is actionable as an act of infringement under section 501, and is fully subject to the remedies provided by sections 502 through 506 and 509, except that, pursuant to a written, nonprofit contract providing for the equitable sharing of the costs of such videotape and its transfer, a videotape nonsimultaneously transmitted by it, in accordance with clause (1), may be transferred by one cable system in Alaska to another system in Alaska, by one cable system in Hawaii permitted to make such nonsimultaneous transmissions to another such cable system in Hawaii, or by one cable system in Guam, the Northern Mariana Islands, or the Trust Territory of the Pacific Islands, to another cable system in any of those three territories, if—

(A) each such contract is available for public inspection in the offices of the cable systems involved, and a copy of such contract is filed, within thirty days after such contract is entered into, with the Copyright Office (which Office shall make each such contract available for public inspection); and

§111 continued   (B) the cable system to which the videotape is transferred
complies with clause (1)(A), (B), (C)(i), (iii), and (iv), and (D)
through (F); and

(C) such system provides a copy of the affidavit required to be made
in accordance with clause (1)(D) to each cable system making a previous
nonsimultaneous transmission of the same videotape.

(3) This subsection shall not be construed to supersede the exclusivity
protection provisions of any existing agreement, or any such agreement
hereafter entered into, between a cable system and a television broadcast station in the area in which the cable system is located, or a network with
which such station is affiliated.

(4) As used in this subsection, the term "videotape," and each of its variant forms, means the reproduction of the images and sounds of a program
or programs broadcast by a television broadcast station licensed by the Federal Communications Commission, regardless of the nature of the material objects, such as tapes or films, in which the reproduction is embodied.

(f) Definitions.—As used in this section, the following terms and their variant forms mean the following:

A "primary transmission" is a transmission made to the public by the transmitting facility whose signals are being received and further transmitted by
the secondary transmission service, regardless of where or when the performance or display was first transmitted.

A "secondary transmission" is the further transmitting of a primary transmission simultaneously with the primary transmission, or nonsimultaneously
with the primary transmission if by a "cable system" not located in whole or
in part within the boundary of the forty-eight contiguous States, Hawaii, or
Puerto Rico: Provided, however, That a nonsimultaneous further transmission
by a cable system located in Hawaii of a primary transmission shall be deemed
to be a secondary transmission if the carriage of the television broadcast signal comprising such further transmission is permissible under the rules, regulations, or authorizations of the Federal Communications Commission.

A "cable system" is a facility, located in any State, Territory, Trust Territory,
or Possession, that in whole or in part receives signals transmitted or programs
broadcast by one or more television broadcast stations licensed by the Federal
Communications Commission, and makes secondary transmissions of such
signals or programs by wires, cables, microwave, or other communications
channels to subscribing members of the public who pay for such service. For
purposes of determining the royalty fee under subsection (d)(1), two or more
cable systems in contiguous communities under common ownership or control or operating from one headend shall be considered as one system.

The "local service area of a primary transmitter," in the case of a television
broadcast station, comprises the area in which such station is entitled to insist
upon its signal being retransmitted by a cable system pursuant to the rules,

regulations, and authorizations of the Federal Communications Commission in effect on April 15, 1976, or such station's television market as defined in section 76.55(e) of title 47, Code of Federal Regulations (as in effect on September 18, 1993), or any modifications to such television market made, on or after September 18, 1993, pursuant to section 76.55(e) or 76.59 of title 47 of the Code of Federal Regulations, or in the case of a television broadcast station licensed by an appropriate governmental authority of Canada or Mexico, the area in which it would be entitled to insist upon its signal being retransmitted if it were a television broadcast station subject to such rules, regulations, and authorizations. In the case of a low power television station, as defined by the rules and regulations of the Federal Communications Commission, the "local service area of a primary transmitter" comprises the area within 35 miles of the transmitter site, except that in the case of such a station located in a standard metropolitan statistical area which has one of the 50 largest populations of all standard metropolitan statistical areas (based on the 1980 decennial census of population taken by the Secretary of Commerce), the number of miles shall be 20 miles. The "local service area of a primary transmitter," in the case of a radio broadcast station, comprises the primary service area of such station, pursuant to the rules and regulations of the Federal Communications Commission.

A "distant signal equivalent" is the value assigned to the secondary transmission of any nonnetwork television programming carried by a cable system in whole or in part beyond the local service area of the primary transmitter of such programming. It is computed by assigning a value of one to each independent station and a value of one-quarter to each network station and noncommercial educational station for the nonnetwork programming so carried pursuant to the rules, regulations, and authorizations of the Federal Communications Commission. The foregoing values for independent, network, and noncommercial educational stations are subject, however, to the following exceptions and limitations. Where the rules and regulations of the Federal Communications Commission require a cable system to omit the further transmission of a particular program and such rules and regulations also permit the substitution of another program embodying a performance or display of a work in place of the omitted transmission, or where such rules and regulations in effect on the date of enactment of this Act permit a cable system, at its election, to effect such deletion and substitution of a nonlive program or to carry additional programs not transmitted by primary transmitters within whose local service area the cable system is located, no value shall be assigned for the substituted or additional program; where the rules, regulations, or authorizations of the Federal Communications Commission in effect on the date of enactment of this Act permit a cable system, at its election, to omit the further transmission of a particular program and such rules, regulations, or authorizations also permit the substitution of another program embodying a performance or display of a

§111 continued   work in place of the omitted transmission, the value assigned
for the substituted or additional program shall be, in the case
of a live program, the value of one full distant signal equivalent multiplied by
a fraction that has as its numerator the number of days in the year in which
such substitution occurs and as its denominator the number of days in the year.
In the case of a station carried pursuant to the late-night or specialty programming rules of the Federal Communications Commission, or a station carried on a part-time basis where full-time carriage is not possible because the
cable system lacks the activated channel capacity to retransmit on a full-time
basis all signals which it is authorized to carry, the values for independent, network, and noncommercial educational stations set forth above, as the case may
be, shall be multiplied by a fraction which is equal to the ratio of the broadcast hours of such station carried by the cable system to the total broadcast
hours of the station.

A "network station" is a television broadcast station that is owned or operated by, or affiliated with, one or more of the television networks in the United
States providing nationwide transmissions, and that transmits a substantial
part of the programming supplied by such networks for a substantial part of
that station's typical broadcast day.

An "independent station" is a commercial television broadcast station other
than a network station.

A "noncommercial educational station" is a television station that is a noncommercial educational broadcast station as defined in section 397 of title 47.
(PL 94-553, Title I, §101, Oct. 19, 1976, 90 Stat. 2550; PL 99-397, §§1, 2[a],
[b], Aug. 27, 1986, 100 Stat. 848; PL 100-667, Title II, §202[1], Nov. 16, 1988,
102 Stat. 3949; PL 101-318, §3[a], July 3, 1990, 104 Stat. 288; PL 103-198,
§6[a], Dec. 17, 1993, 107 Stat. 2311; PL 103-369, §3, Oct. 18, 1994, 108 Stat.
3480; PL 104-39, §5[b], Nov. 1, 1995, 109 Stat. 348.)

17 U.S.C. §112 Limitations on exclusive rights: Ephemeral recordings

(a) Notwithstanding the provisions of section 106, and except in the case
of a motion picture or other audiovisual work, it is not an infringement of
copyright for a transmitting organization entitled to transmit to the public a
performance or display of a work, under a license or transfer of the copyright
or under the limitations on exclusive rights in sound recordings specified by
section 114(a), to make no more than one copy or phonorecord of a particular
transmission program embodying the performance or display, if—

    (1) the copy or phonorecord is retained and used solely by the transmit-
ting organization that made it, and no further copies or phonorecords are
reproduced from it; and

    (2) the copy or phonorecord is used solely for the transmitting organi-
zation's own transmissions within its local service area, or for purposes of
archival preservation or security; and

(3) unless preserved exclusively for archival purposes, the copy or phonorecord is destroyed within six months from the date the transmission program was first transmitted to the public.

(b) Notwithstanding the provisions of section 106, it is not an infringement of copyright for a governmental body or other nonprofit organization entitled to transmit a performance or display of a work, under section 110(2) or under the limitations on exclusive rights in sound recordings specified by section 114(a), to make no more than thirty copies or phonorecords of a particular transmission program embodying the performance or display, if—

(1) no further copies or phonorecords are reproduced from the copies or phonorecords made under this clause; and

(2) except for one copy or phonorecord that may be preserved exclusively for archival purposes, the copies or phonorecords are destroyed within seven years from the date the transmission program was first transmitted to the public.

(c) Notwithstanding the provisions of section 106, it is not an infringement of copyright for a governmental body or other nonprofit organization to make for distribution no more than one copy or phonorecord, for each transmitting organization specified in clause (2) of this subsection, of a particular transmission program embodying a performance of a nondramatic musical work of a religious nature, or of a sound recording of such a musical work, if—

(1) there is no direct or indirect charge for making or distributing any such copies or phonorecords; and

(2) none of such copies or phonorecords is used for any performance other than a single transmission to the public by a transmitting organization entitled to transmit to the public a performance of the work under a license or transfer of the copyright; and

(3) except for one copy or phonorecord that may be preserved exclusively for archival purposes, the copies or phonorecords are all destroyed within one year from the date the transmission program was first transmitted to the public.

(d) Notwithstanding the provisions of section 106, it is not an infringement of copyright for a governmental body or other nonprofit organization entitled to transmit a performance of a work under section 110(8) to make no more than ten copies or phonorecords embodying the performance, or to permit the use of any such copy or phonorecord by any governmental body or nonprofit organization entitled to transmit a performance of a work under section 110(8), if—

(1) any such copy or phonorecord is retained and used solely by the organization that made it, or by a governmental body or nonprofit organization entitled to transmit a performance of a work under section 110(8), and no further copies or phonorecords are reproduced from it; and

(2) any such copy or phonorecord is used solely for transmissions authorized under section 110(8), or for purposes of archival preservation or security; and

§112 continued   (3) the governmental body or nonprofit organization permitting any use of any such copy or phonorecord by any governmental body or nonprofit organization under this subsection does not make any charge for such use.

(e) The transmission program embodied in a copy or phonorecord made under this section is not subject to protection as a derivative work under this title except with the express consent of the owners of copyright in the preexisting works employed in the program. (PL 94-553, Title I, §101, Oct. 19, 1976, 90 Stat. 2558.)

17 U.S.C. §113 Scope of exclusive rights in pictorial, graphic, and sculptural works

(a) Subject to the provisions of subsections (b) and (c) of this section, the exclusive right to reproduce a copyrighted pictorial, graphic, or sculptural work in copies under section 106 includes the right to reproduce the work in or on any kind of article, whether useful or otherwise.

(b) This title does not afford, to the owner of copyright in a work that portrays a useful article as such, any greater or lesser rights with respect to the making, distribution, or display of the useful article so portrayed than those afforded to such works under the law, whether title 17 or the common law or statutes of a State, in effect on December 31, 1977, as held applicable and construed by a court in an action brought under this title.

(c) In the case of a work lawfully reproduced in useful articles that have been offered for sale or other distribution to the public, copyright does not include any right to prevent the making, distribution, or display of pictures or photographs of such articles in connection with advertisements or commentaries related to the distribution or display of such articles, or in connection with news reports.

(d)(1) In a case in which—

(A) a work of visual art has been incorporated in or made part of a building in such a way that removing the work from the building will cause the destruction, distortion, mutilation, or other modification of the work as described in section 106A(a)(3), and

(B) the author consented to the installation of the work in the building either before the effective date set forth in section 610(a) of the Visual Artists Rights Act of 1990, or in a written instrument executed on or after such effective date that is signed by the owner of the building and the author and that specifies that installation of the work may subject the work to destruction, distortion, mutilation, or other modification, by reason of its removal, then the rights conferred by paragraphs (2) and (3) of section 106A(a) shall not apply.

(2) If the owner of a building wishes to remove a work of visual art which is a part of such building and which can be removed from the building without

the destruction, distortion, mutilation, or other modification of the work as described in section 106A(a)(3), the author's rights under paragraphs (2) and (3) of section 106A(a) shall apply unless—

(A) the owner has made a diligent, good faith attempt without success to notify the author of the owner's intended action affecting the work of visual art, or

(B) the owner did provide such notice in writing and the person so notified failed, within 90 days after receiving such notice, either to remove the work or to pay for its removal.

For purposes of subparagraph (A), an owner shall be presumed to have made a diligent, good faith attempt to send notice if the owner sent such notice by registered mail to the author at the most recent address of the author that was recorded with the Register of Copyrights pursuant to paragraph (3). If the work is removed at the expense of the author, title to that copy of the work shall be deemed to be in the author.

(3) The Register of Copyrights shall establish a system of records whereby any author of a work of visual art that has been incorporated in or made part of a building, may record his or her identity and address with the Copyright Office. The Register shall also establish procedures under which any such author may update the information so recorded, and procedures under which owners of buildings may record with the Copyright Office evidence of their efforts to comply with this subsection. (PL 94-553, Title I, §101, Oct. 19, 1976, 90 Stat. 2560 amended by PL 101-650, Title VI, §604, Dec. 1, 1990, 104 Stat. 5130.)

17 U.S.C. §114 Scope of exclusive rights in sound recordings

(a) The exclusive rights of the owner of copyright in a sound recording are limited to the rights specified by clauses (1), (2), (3) and (6) of section 106, and do not include any right of performance under section 106(4).

(b) The exclusive right of the owner of copyright in a sound recording under clause (1) of section 106 is limited to the right to duplicate the sound recording in the form of phonorecords or copies that directly or indirectly recapture the actual sounds fixed in the recording. The exclusive right of the owner of copyright in a sound recording under clause (2) of section 106 is limited to the right to prepare a derivative work in which the actual sounds fixed in the sound recording are rearranged, remixed, or otherwise altered in sequence or quality. The exclusive rights of the owner of copyright in a sound recording under clauses (1) and (2) of section 106 do not extend to the making or duplication of another sound recording that consists entirely of an independent fixation of other sounds, even though such sounds imitate or simulate those in the copyrighted sound recording. The exclusive rights of the owner of copyright in a sound recording under clauses (1), (2), and (3) of section 106 do not apply to sound recordings included in educational television

§114 continued and radio programs (as defined in section 397 of title 47) distributed or transmitted by or through public broadcasting entities (as defined by section 118[g]: Provided, That copies or phonorecords of said programs are not commercially distributed by or through public broadcasting entities to the general public.

(c) This section does not limit or impair the exclusive right to perform publicly, by means of a phonorecord, any of the works specified by section 106(4).

(d) Limitations on exclusive right.—Notwithstanding the provisions of section 106(6)—

(1) Exempt transmissions and retransmissions.—The performance of a sound recording publicly by means of a digital audio transmission, other than as a part of an interactive service, is not an infringement of section 106(6) if the performance is part of—

(A)(i) a nonsubscription transmission other than a retransmission;

(ii) an initial nonsubscription retransmission made for direct reception by members of the public of a prior or simultaneous incidental transmission that is not made for direct reception by members of the public; or

(iii) a nonsubscription broadcast transmission;

(B) a retransmission of a nonsubscription broadcast transmission: Provided, That, in the case of a retransmission of a radio station's broadcast transmission—

(i) the radio station's broadcast transmission is not willfully or repeatedly retransmitted more than a radius of 150 miles from the site of the radio broadcast transmitter, however—

(I) the 150 mile limitation under this clause shall not apply when a nonsubscription broadcast transmission by a radio station licensed by the Federal Communications Commission is retransmitted on a nonsubscription basis by a terrestrial broadcast station, terrestrial translator, or terrestrial repeater licensed by the Federal Communications Commission; and

(II) in the case of a subscription retransmission of a nonsubscription broadcast retransmission covered by subclause (I), the 150 mile radius shall be measured from the transmitter site of such broadcast retransmitter;

(ii) the retransmission is of radio station broadcast transmissions that are—

(I) obtained by the retransmitter over the air;

(II) not electronically processed by the retransmitter to deliver separate and discrete signals; and

(III) retransmitted only within the local communities served by the retransmitter;

(iii) the radio station's broadcast transmission was being retransmitted to cable systems (as defined in section 111[f]) by a satellite carrier on January 1, 1995, and that retransmission was being retransmitted by cable systems as a separate and discrete signal, and the satellite carrier obtains the radio station's broadcast transmission in an analog format: Provided, That the broadcast transmission being retransmitted may embody the programming of no more than one radio station; or

(iv) the radio station's broadcast transmission is made by a noncommercial educational broadcast station funded on or after January 1, 1995, under section 396(k) of the Communications Act of 1934 (47 U.S.C. 396[k]), consists solely of noncommercial educational and cultural radio programs, and the retransmission, whether or not simultaneous, is a nonsubscription terrestrial broadcast retransmission; or

(C) a transmission that comes within any of the following categories—

(i) a prior or simultaneous transmission incidental to an exempt transmission, such as a feed received by and then retransmitted by an exempt transmitter: Provided, That such incidental transmissions do not include any subscription transmission directly for reception by members of the public;

(ii) a transmission within a business establishment, confined to its premises or the immediately surrounding vicinity;

(iii) a retransmission by any retransmitter, including a multichannel video programming distributor as defined in section 602(12) of the Communications Act of 1934 (47 U.S.C. 522[12]), of a transmission by a transmitter licensed to publicly perform the sound recording as a part of that transmission, if the retransmission is simultaneous with the licensed transmission and authorized by the transmitter; or

(iv) a transmission to a business establishment for use in the ordinary course of its business: Provided, That the business recipient does not retransmit the transmission outside of its premises or the immediately surrounding vicinity, and that the transmission does not exceed the sound recording performance complement. Nothing in this clause shall limit the scope of the exemption in clause (ii).

(2) Subscription transmissions.—In the case of a subscription transmission not exempt under subsection (d)(1), the performance of a sound recording publicly by means of a digital audio transmission shall be subject to statutory licensing, in accordance with subsection (f) of this section, if—

(A) the transmission is not part of an interactive service;

(B) the transmission does not exceed the sound recording performance complement;

(C) the transmitting entity does not cause to be published by means of an advance program schedule or prior announcement the titles of the

§114 *continued*   specific sound recordings or phonorecords embodying such
sound recordings to be transmitted;

(D) except in the case of transmission to a business establishment, the transmitting entity does not automatically and intentionally cause any device receiving the transmission to switch from one program channel to another; and

(E) except as provided in section 1002(e) of this title, the transmission of the sound recording is accompanied by the information encoded in that sound recording, if any, by or under the authority of the copyright owner of that sound recording, that identifies the title of the sound recording, the featured recording artist who performs on the sound recording, and related information, including information concerning the underlying musical work and its writer.

(3) Licenses for transmissions by interactive services. —

(A) No interactive service shall be granted an exclusive license under section 106(6) for the performance of a sound recording publicly by means of digital audio transmission for a period in excess of 12 months, except that with respect to an exclusive license granted to an interactive service by a licensor that holds the copyright to 1,000 or fewer sound recordings, the period of such license shall not exceed 24 months: Provided, however, That the grantee of such exclusive license shall be ineligible to receive another exclusive license for the performance of that sound recording for a period of 13 months from the expiration of the prior exclusive license.

(B) The limitation set forth in subparagraph (A) of this paragraph shall not apply if—

(i) the licensor has granted and there remain in effect licenses under section 106(6) for the public performance of sound recordings by means of digital audio transmission by at least 5 different interactive services: Provided, however, That each such license must be for a minimum of 10 percent of the copyrighted sound recordings owned by the licensor that have been licensed to interactive services, but in no event less than 50 sound recordings; or

(ii) the exclusive license is granted to perform publicly up to 45 seconds of a sound recording and the sole purpose of the performance is to promote the distribution or performance of that sound recording.

(C) Notwithstanding the grant of an exclusive or nonexclusive license of the right of public performance under section 106(6), an interactive service may not publicly perform a sound recording unless a license has been granted for the public performance of any copyrighted musical work contained in the sound recording: Provided, That such license to publicly perform the copyrighted musical work may be granted either by a performing rights society representing the copyright owner or by the copyright owner.

(D) The performance of a sound recording by means of a retransmission of a digital audio transmission is not an infringement of section 106(6) if—

(i) the retransmission is of a transmission by an interactive service licensed to publicly perform the sound recording to a particular member of the public as part of that transmission; and

(ii) the retransmission is simultaneous with the licensed transmission, authorized by the transmitter, and limited to that particular member of the public intended by the interactive service to be the recipient of the transmission.

(E) For the purposes of this paragraph—

(i) a "licensor" shall include the licensing entity and any other entity under any material degree of common ownership, management, or control that owns copyrights in sound recordings; and

(ii) a "performing rights society" is an association or corporation that licenses the public performance of nondramatic musical works on behalf of the copyright owner, such as the American Society of Composers, Authors and Publishers, Broadcast Music, Inc., and SESAC, Inc.

(4) Rights not otherwise limited.—

(A) Except as expressly provided in this section, this section does not limit or impair the exclusive right to perform a sound recording publicly by means of a digital audio transmission under section 106(6).

(B) Nothing in this section annuls or limits in any way—

(i) the exclusive right to publicly perform a musical work, including by means of a digital audio transmission, under section 106(4);

(ii) the exclusive rights in a sound recording or the musical work embodied therein under sections 106(1), 106(2) and 106(3); or

(iii) any other rights under any other clause of section 106, or remedies available under this title, as such rights or remedies exist either before or after the date of enactment of the Digital Performance Right in Sound Recordings Act of 1995.

(C) Any limitations in this section on the exclusive right under section 106(6) apply only to the exclusive right under section 106(6) and not to any other exclusive rights under section 106. Nothing in this section shall be construed to annul, limit, impair or otherwise affect in any way the ability of the owner of a copyright in a sound recording to exercise the rights under sections 106(1), 106(2) and 106(3), or to obtain the remedies available under this title pursuant to such rights, as such rights and remedies exist either before or after the date of enactment of the Digital Performance Right in Sound Recordings Act of 1995.

(e) Authority for negotiations.—

(1) Notwithstanding any provision of the antitrust laws, in negotiating

§114 continued   statutory licenses in accordance with subsection (f), any copyright owners of sound recordings and any entities perform-
ing sound recordings affected by this section may negotiate and agree upon
the royalty rates and license terms and conditions for the performance of
such sound recordings and the proportionate division of fees paid among
copyright owners, and may designate common agents on a nonexclusive
basis to negotiate, agree to, pay, or receive payments.

(2) For licenses granted under section 106(6), other than statutory
licenses, such as for performances by interactive services or performances
that exceed the sound recording performance complement—

(A) copyright owners of sound recordings affected by this section may
designate common agents to act on their behalf to grant licenses and
receive and remit royalty payments: Provided, That each copyright owner
shall establish the royalty rates and material license terms and conditions
unilaterally, that is, not in agreement, combination, or concert with other
copyright owners of sound recordings; and

(B) entities performing sound recordings affected by this section may
designate common agents to act on their behalf to obtain licenses and collect and pay royalty fees: Provided, That each entity performing sound
recordings shall determine the royalty rates and material license terms and
conditions unilaterally, that is, not in agreement, combination, or concert
with other entities performing sound recordings.

(f) Licenses for nonexempt subscription transmissions.—

(1) No later than 30 days after the enactment of the Digital Performance
Right in Sound Recordings Act of 1995, the Librarian of Congress shall
cause notice to be published in the Federal Register of the initiation of voluntary negotiation proceedings for the purpose of determining reasonable
terms and rates of royalty payments for the activities specified by subsection (d)(2) of this section during the period beginning on the effective date
of such Act and ending on December 31, 2000. Such terms and rates shall
distinguish among the different types of digital audio transmission services
then in operation. Any copyright owners of sound recordings or any entities performing sound recordings affected by this section may submit to the
Librarian of Congress licenses covering such activities with respect to such
sound recordings. The parties to each negotiation proceeding shall bear
their own costs.

(2) In the absence of license agreements negotiated under paragraph (1),
during the 60-day period commencing 6 months after publication of the
notice specified in paragraph (1), and upon the filing of a petition in accordance with section 803(a)(1), the Librarian of Congress shall, pursuant to
chapter 8, convene a copyright arbitration royalty panel to determine and
publish in the Federal Register a schedule of rates and terms which, subject
to paragraph (3), shall be binding on all copyright owners of sound recordings

and entities performing sound recordings. In addition to the objectives set forth in section 801(b)(1), in establishing such rates and terms, the copyright arbitration royalty panel may consider the rates and terms for comparable types of digital audio transmission services and comparable circumstances under voluntary license agreements negotiated as provided in paragraph (1). The Librarian of Congress shall also establish requirements by which copyright owners may receive reasonable notice of the use of their sound recordings under this section, and under which records of such use shall be kept and made available by entities performing sound recordings.

(3) License agreements voluntarily negotiated at any time between one or more copyright owners of sound recordings and one or more entities performing sound recordings shall be given effect in lieu of any determination by a copyright arbitration royalty panel or decision by the Librarian of Congress.

(4)(A) Publication of a notice of the initiation of voluntary negotiation proceedings as specified in paragraph (1) shall be repeated, in accordance with regulations that the Librarian of Congress shall prescribe—

(i) no later than 30 days after a petition is filed by any copyright owners of sound recordings or any entities performing sound recordings affected by this section indicating that a new type of digital audio transmission service on which sound recordings are performed is or is about to become operational; and

(ii) in the first week of January 2000 and at five-year intervals thereafter.

(B)(i) The procedures specified in paragraph (2) shall be repeated, in accordance with regulations that the Librarian of Congress shall prescribe, upon the filing of a petition in accordance with section 803(a)(1) during a 60-day period commencing—

(I) six months after publication of a notice of the initiation of voluntary negotiation proceedings under paragraph (1) pursuant to a petition under paragraph (4)(A)(i); or

(II) on July 1, 2000, and at five-year intervals thereafter.

(ii) The procedures specified in paragraph (2) shall be concluded in accordance with section 802.

(5)(A) Any person who wishes to perform a sound recording publicly by means of a nonexempt subscription transmission under this subsection may do so without infringing the exclusive right of the copyright owner of the sound recording—

(i) by complying with such notice requirements as the Librarian of Congress shall prescribe by regulation and by paying royalty fees in accordance with this subsection; or

(ii) if such royalty fees have not been set, by agreeing to pay such royalty fees as shall be determined in accordance with this subsection.

(B) Any royalty payments in arrears shall be made on or before the twentieth day of the month next succeeding the month in which the royalty fees are set.

(g) Proceeds from licensing of subscription transmissions.—

(1) Except in the case of a subscription transmission licensed in accordance with subsection (f) of this section—

(A) a featured recording artist who performs on a sound recording that has been licensed for a subscription transmission shall be entitled to receive payments from the copyright owner of the sound recording in accordance with the terms of the artist's contract; and

(B) a nonfeatured recording artist who performs on a sound recording that has been licensed for a subscription transmission shall be entitled to receive payments from the copyright owner of the sound recording in accordance with the terms of the nonfeatured recording artist's applicable contract or other applicable agreement.

(2) The copyright owner of the exclusive right under section 106(6) of this title to publicly perform a sound recording by means of a digital audio transmission shall allocate to recording artists in the following manner its receipts from the statutory licensing of subscription transmission performances of the sound recording in accordance with subsection (f) of this section:

(A) 2½ percent of the receipts shall be deposited in an escrow account managed by an independent administrator jointly appointed by copyright owners of sound recordings and the American Federation of Musicians (or any successor entity) to be distributed to nonfeatured musicians (whether or not members of the American Federation of Musicians) who have performed on sound recordings.

(B) 2½ percent of the receipts shall be deposited in an escrow account managed by an independent administrator jointly appointed by copyright owners of sound recordings and the American Federation of Television and Radio Artists (or any successor entity) to be distributed to nonfeatured vocalists (whether or not members of the American Federation of Television and Radio Artists) who have performed on sound recordings.

(C) 45 percent of the receipts shall be allocated, on a per sound recording basis, to the recording artist or artists featured on such sound recording (or the persons conveying rights in the artists' performance in the sound recordings).

(h) Licensing to affiliates.—

(1) If the copyright owner of a sound recording licenses an affiliated entity the right to publicly perform a sound recording by means of a digital audio transmission under section 106(6), the copyright owner shall make the licensed sound recording available under section 106(6) on no less favorable terms and conditions to all bona fide entities that offer similar services,

except that, if there are material differences in the scope of the requested license with respect to the type of service, the particular sound recordings licensed, the frequency of use, the number of subscribers served, or the duration, then the copyright owner may establish different terms and conditions for such other services.

(2) The limitation set forth in paragraph (1) of this subsection shall not apply in the case where the copyright owner of a sound recording licenses—

(A) an interactive service; or

(B) an entity to perform publicly up to 45 seconds of the sound recording and the sole purpose of the performance is to promote the distribution or performance of that sound recording.

(i) No effect on royalties for underlying works.—License fees payable for the public performance of sound recordings under section 106(6) shall not be taken into account in any administrative, judicial, or other governmental proceeding to set or adjust the royalties payable to copyright owners of musical works for the public performance of their works. It is the intent of Congress that royalties payable to copyright owners of musical works for the public performance of their works shall not be diminished in any respect as a result of the rights granted by section 106(6).

(j) Definitions.—As used in this section, the following terms have the following meanings:

(1) An "affiliated entity" is an entity engaging in digital audio transmissions covered by section 106(6), other than an interactive service, in which the licensor has any direct or indirect partnership or any ownership interest amounting to 5 percent or more of the outstanding voting or non-voting stock.

(2) A "broadcast" transmission is a transmission made by a terrestrial broadcast station licensed as such by the Federal Communications Commission.

(3) A "digital audio transmission" is a digital transmission as defined in section 101, that embodies the transmission of a sound recording. This term does not include the transmission of any audiovisual work.

(4) An "interactive service" is one that enables a member of the public to receive, on request, a transmission of a particular sound recording chosen by or on behalf of the recipient. The ability of individuals to request that particular sound recordings be performed for reception by the public at large does not make a service interactive. If an entity offers both interactive and non-interactive services (either concurrently or at different times), the non-interactive component shall not be treated as part of an interactive service.

(5) A "nonsubscription" transmission is any transmission that is not a subscription transmission.

(6) A "retransmission" is a further transmission of an initial transmission, and includes any further retransmission of the same transmission. Except

§114 continued   as provided in this section, a transmission qualifies as a "retransmission" only if it is simultaneous with the initial transmission. Nothing in this definition shall be construed to exempt a transmission that fails to satisfy a separate element required to qualify for an exemption under section 114(d)(1).

(7) The "sound recording performance complement" is the transmission during any 3-hour period, on a particular channel used by a transmitting entity, of no more than—

(A) 3 different selections of sound recordings from any one phonorecord lawfully distributed for public performance or sale in the United States, if no more than 2 such selections are transmitted consecutively; or

(B) 4 different selections of sound recordings—

(i) by the same featured recording artist; or

(ii) from any set or compilation of phonorecords lawfully distributed together as a unit for public performance or sale in the United States, if no more than three such selections are transmitted consecutively:

Provided, That the transmission of selections in excess of the numerical limits provided for in clauses (A) and (B) from multiple phonorecords shall nonetheless qualify as a sound recording performance complement if the programming of the multiple phonorecords was not willfully intended to avoid the numerical limitations prescribed in such clauses.

(8) A "subscription" transmission is a transmission that is controlled and limited to particular recipients, and for which consideration is required to be paid or otherwise given by or on behalf of the recipient to receive the transmission or a package of transmissions including the transmission.

(9) A "transmission" includes both an initial transmission and a retransmission.

(P 94-553, Title I, §101, Oct. 19, 1976, 90 Stat. 2560; PL 104-39, §3, Nov. 1, 1995, 109 Stat. 336.)

17 U.S.C. §115 Scope of exclusive rights in nondramatic musical works: Compulsory license for making and distributing phonorecords

In the case of nondramatic musical works, the exclusive rights provided by clauses (1) and (3) of section 106, to make and to distribute phonorecords of such works, are subject to compulsory licensing under the conditions specified by this section.

(a) Availability and Scope of Compulsory License.—

(1) When phonorecords of a nondramatic musical work have been distributed to the public in the United States under the authority of the copyright owner, any other person, including those who make phonorecords or digital phonorecord deliveries, may, by complying with the provisions of this

section, obtain a compulsory license to make and distribute phonorecords of the work. A person may obtain a compulsory license only if his or her primary purpose in making phonorecords is to distribute them to the public for private use, including by means of a digital phonorecord delivery. A person may not obtain a compulsory license for use of the work in the making of phonorecords duplicating a sound recording fixed by another, unless: (i) such sound recording was fixed lawfully; and (ii) the making of the phonorecords was authorized by the owner of copyright in the sound recording or, if the sound recording was fixed before February 15, 1972, by any person who fixed the sound recording pursuant to an express license from the owner of the copyright in the musical work or pursuant to a valid compulsory license for use of such work in a sound recording.

(2) A compulsory license includes the privilege of making a musical arrangement of the work to the extent necessary to conform it to the style or manner of interpretation of the performance involved, but the arrangement shall not change the basic melody or fundamental character of the work, and shall not be subject to protection as a derivative work under this title, except with the express consent of the copyright owner.

(b) Notice of Intention to Obtain Compulsory License.—

(1) Any person who wishes to obtain a compulsory license under this section shall, before or within thirty days after making, and before distributing any phonorecords of the work, serve notice of intention to do so on the copyright owner. If the registration or other public records of the Copyright Office do not identify the copyright owner and include an address at which notice can be served, it shall be sufficient to file the notice of intention in the Copyright Office. The notice shall comply, in form, content, and manner of service, with requirements that the Register of Copyrights shall prescribe by regulation.

(2) Failure to serve or file the notice required by clause (1) forecloses the possibility of a compulsory license and, in the absence of a negotiated license, renders the making and distribution of phonorecords actionable as acts of infringement under section 501 and fully subject to the remedies provided by sections 502 through 506 and 509.

(c) Royalty Payable under Compulsory License.—

(1) To be entitled to receive royalties under a compulsory license, the copyright owner must be identified in the registration or other public records of the Copyright Office. The owner is entitled to royalties for phonorecords made and distributed after being so identified, but is not entitled to recover for any phonorecords previously made and distributed.

(2) Except as provided by clause (1), the royalty under a compulsory license shall be payable for every phonorecord made and distributed in accordance with the license. For this purpose, and other than as provided in paragraph (3), a phonorecord is considered "distributed" if the person exercising

§115 continued the compulsory license has voluntarily and permanently parted with its possession. With respect to each work embodied in the phonorecord, the royalty shall be either two and three-fourths cents, or one-half of one cent per minute of playing time or fraction thereof, whichever amount is larger.

(3)(A) A compulsory license under this section includes the right of the compulsory licensee to distribute or authorize the distribution of a phonorecord of a nondramatic musical work by means of a digital transmission which constitutes a digital phonorecord delivery, regardless of whether the digital transmission is also a public performance of the sound recording under section 106(6) of this title or of any nondramatic musical work embodied therein under section 106(4) of this title. For every digital phonorecord delivery by or under the authority of the compulsory licensee—

(i) on or before December 31, 1997, the royalty payable by the compulsory licensee shall be the royalty prescribed under paragraph (2) and chapter 8 of this title; and

(ii) on or after January 1, 1998, the royalty payable by the compulsory licensee shall be the royalty prescribed under subparagraphs (B) through (F) and chapter 8 of this title.

(B) Notwithstanding any provision of the antitrust laws, any copyright owners of nondramatic musical works and any persons entitled to obtain a compulsory license under subsection (a)(1) may negotiate and agree upon the terms and rates of royalty payments under this paragraph and the proportionate division of fees paid among copyright owners, and may designate common agents to negotiate, agree to, pay or receive such royalty payments. Such authority to negotiate the terms and rates of royalty payments includes, but is not limited to, the authority to negotiate the year during which the royalty rates prescribed under subparagraphs (B) through (F) and chapter 8 of this title shall next be determined.

(C) During the period of June 30, 1996, through December 31, 1996, the Librarian of Congress shall cause notice to be published in the Federal Register of the initiation of voluntary negotiation proceedings for the purpose of determining reasonable terms and rates of royalty payments for the activities specified by subparagraph (A) during the period beginning January 1, 1998, and ending on the effective date of any new terms and rates established pursuant to subparagraph (C), (D) or (F), or such other date (regarding digital phonorecord deliveries) as the parties may agree. Such terms and rates shall distinguish between (i) digital phonorecord deliveries where the reproduction or distribution of a phonorecord is incidental to the transmission which constitutes the digital phonorecord delivery, and (ii) digital phonorecord deliveries in general. Any copyright owners of nondramatic musical works and any persons entitled to obtain a compulsory license under subsection (a)(1) may submit to the Librarian of Congress licenses covering such activities. The parties to each negotiation proceeding shall bear their own costs.

(D) In the absence of license agreements negotiated under subparagraphs (B) and (C), upon the filing of a petition in accordance with section 803(a)(1), the Librarian of Congress shall, pursuant to chapter 8, convene a copyright arbitration royalty panel to determine and publish in the Federal Register a schedule of rates and terms which, subject to subparagraph (E), shall be binding on all copyright owners of nondramatic musical works and persons entitled to obtain a compulsory license under subsection (a)(1) during the period beginning January 1, 1998, and ending on the effective date of any new terms and rates established pursuant to subparagraph (C), (D) or (F), or such other date (regarding digital phonorecord deliveries) as may be determined pursuant to subparagraphs (B) and (C). Such terms and rates shall distinguish between (i) digital phonorecord deliveries where the reproduction or distribution of a phonorecord is incidental to the transmission which constitutes the digital phonorecord delivery, and (ii) digital phonorecord deliveries in general. In addition to the objectives set forth in section 801(b)(1), in establishing such rates and terms, the copyright arbitration royalty panel may consider rates and terms under voluntary license agreements negotiated as provided in subparagraphs (B) and (C). The royalty rates payable for a compulsory license for a digital phonorecord delivery under this section shall be established de novo and no precedential effect shall be given to the amount of the royalty payable by a compulsory licensee for digital phonorecord deliveries on or before December 31, 1997. The Librarian of Congress shall also establish requirements by which copyright owners may receive reasonable notice of the use of their works under this section, and under which records of such use shall be kept and made available by persons making digital phonorecord deliveries.

(E)(i) License agreements voluntarily negotiated at any time between one or more copyright owners of nondramatic musical works and one or more persons entitled to obtain a compulsory license under subsection (a)(1) shall be given effect in lieu of any determination by the Librarian of Congress. Subject to clause (ii), the royalty rates determined pursuant to subparagraph (C), (D) or (F) shall be given effect in lieu of any contrary royalty rates specified in a contract pursuant to which a recording artist who is the author of a nondramatic musical work grants a license under that person's exclusive rights in the musical work under sections 106(1) and (3) or commits another person to grant a license in that musical work under sections 106(1) and (3), to a person desiring to fix in a tangible medium of expression a sound recording embodying the musical work.

§115 continued (ii) The second sentence of clause (i) shall not apply to—

(I) a contract entered into on or before June 22, 1995, and not modified thereafter for the purpose of reducing the royalty rates determined pursuant to subparagraph (C), (D) or (F) or of increasing the number of musical works within the scope of the contract covered by the reduced rates, except if a contract entered into on or before June 22, 1995, is modified thereafter for the purpose of increasing the number of musical works within the scope of the contract, any contrary royalty rates specified in the contract shall be given effect in lieu of royalty rates determined pursuant to subparagraph (C), (D) or (F) for the number of musical works within the scope of the contract as of June 22, 1995; and

(II) a contract entered into after the date that the sound recording is fixed in a tangible medium of expression substantially in a form intended for commercial release, if at the time the contract is entered into, the recording artist retains the right to grant licenses as to the musical work under sections 106(1) and 106(3).

(F) The procedures specified in subparagraphs (C) and (D) shall be repeated and concluded, in accordance with regulations that the Librarian of Congress shall prescribe, in each fifth calendar year after 1997, except to the extent that different years for the repeating and concluding of such proceedings may be determined in accordance with subparagraphs (B) and (C).

(G) Except as provided in section 1002(e) of this title, a digital phonorecord delivery licensed under this paragraph shall be accompanied by the information encoded in the sound recording, if any, by or under the authority of the copyright owner of that sound recording, that identifies the title of the sound recording, the featured recording artist who performs on the sound recording, and related information, including information concerning the underlying musical work and its writer.

(H)(i) A digital phonorecord delivery of a sound recording is actionable as an act of infringement under section 501, and is fully subject to the remedies provided by sections 502 through 506 and section 509, unless—

(I) the digital phonorecord delivery has been authorized by the copyright owner of the sound recording; and

(II) the owner of the copyright in the sound recording or the entity making the digital phonorecord delivery has obtained a compulsory license under this section or has otherwise been authorized by the copyright owner of the musical work to distribute or authorize the distribution, by means of a digital phonorecord delivery, of each musical work embodied in the sound recording.

(ii) Any cause of action under this subparagraph shall be in addition to those available to the owner of the copyright in the nondramatic musical work under subsection (c)(6) and section 106(4) and the owner of the copyright in the sound recording under section 106(6).

(I) The liability of the copyright owner of a sound recording for infringement of the copyright in a nondramatic musical work embodied in the sound recording shall be determined in accordance with applicable law, except that the owner of a copyright in a sound recording shall not be liable for a digital phonorecord delivery by a third party if the owner of the copyright in the sound recording does not license the distribution of a phonorecord of the nondramatic musical work.

(J) Nothing in section 1008 shall be construed to prevent the exercise of the rights and remedies allowed by this paragraph, paragraph (6), and chapter 5 in the event of a digital phonorecord delivery, except that no action alleging infringement of copyright may be brought under this title against a manufacturer, importer or distributor of a digital audio recording device, a digital audio recording medium, an analog recording device, or an analog recording medium, or against a consumer, based on the actions described in such section.

(K) Nothing in this section annuls or limits (i) the exclusive right to publicly perform a sound recording or the musical work embodied therein, including by means of a digital transmission, under sections 106(4) and 106(6), (ii) except for compulsory licensing under the conditions specified by this section, the exclusive rights to reproduce and distribute the sound recording and the musical work embodied therein under sections 106(1) and 106(3), including by means of a digital phonorecord delivery, or (iii) any other rights under any other provision of section 106, or remedies available under this title, as such rights or remedies exist either before or after the date of enactment of the Digital Performance Right in Sound Recordings Act of 1995.

(L) The provisions of this section concerning digital phonorecord deliveries shall not apply to any exempt transmissions or retransmissions under section 114(d)(1). The exemptions created in section 114(d)(1) do not expand or reduce the rights of copyright owners under section 106(1) through (5) with respect to such transmissions and retransmissions.

(4) A compulsory license under this section includes the right of the maker of a phonorecord of a nondramatic musical work under subsection (a)(1) to distribute or authorize distribution of such phonorecord by rental, lease, or lending (or by acts or practices in the nature of rental, lease, or lending). In addition to any royalty payable under clause (2) and chapter 8 of this title, a royalty shall be payable by the compulsory licensee for every act of distribution of a phonorecord by or in the nature of rental, lease, or lending, by or under the authority of the compulsory licensee. With respect to each nondramatic musical work embodied in the phonorecord, the royalty shall be a proportion of the revenue received by the compulsory licensee from

§115 continued   every such act of distribution of the phonorecord under this
clause equal to the proportion of the revenue received by the
compulsory licensee from distribution of the phonorecord under clause (2)
that is payable by a compulsory licensee under that clause and under chapter 8. The Register of Copyrights shall issue regulations to carry out the purpose of this clause.

(5) Royalty payments shall be made on or before the twentieth day of each month and shall include all royalties for the month next preceding. Each monthly payment shall be made under oath and shall comply with requirements that the Register of Copyrights shall prescribe by regulation. The Register shall also prescribe regulations under which detailed cumulative annual statements of account, certified by a certified public accountant, shall be filed for every compulsory license under this section. The regulations covering both the monthly and the annual statements of account shall prescribe the form, content, and manner of certification with respect to the number of records made and the number of records distributed.

(6) If the copyright owner does not receive the monthly payment and the monthly and annual statements of account when due, the owner may give written notice to the licensee that, unless the default is remedied within thirty days from the date of the notice, the compulsory license will be automatically terminated. Such termination renders either the making or the distribution, or both, of all phonorecords for which the royalty has not been paid, actionable as acts of infringement under section 501 and fully subject to the remedies provided by sections 502 through 506 and 509.

(d) Definition.—As used in this section, the following term has the following meaning: A "digital phonorecord delivery" is each individual delivery of a phonorecord by digital transmission of a sound recording which results in a specifically identifiable reproduction by or for any transmission recipient of a phonorecord of that sound recording, regardless of whether the digital transmission is also a public performance of the sound recording or any nondramatic musical work embodied therein. A digital phonorecord delivery does not result from a real-time, non-interactive subscription transmission of a sound recording where no reproduction of the sound recording or the musical work embodied therein is made from the inception of the transmission through to its receipt by the transmission recipient in order to make the sound recording audible. (PL 94-553, Title I, §101, Oct. 19, 1976, 90 Stat. 2561; PL 98-450, §3, Oct. 4, 1984, 98 Stat. 1727; PL 104-39, §4, Nov. 1, 1995, 109 Stat. 344.)

17 U.S.C. §116 Negotiated licenses for public performances by means of coin-operated phonorecord players

(a) Applicability of section.—This section applies to any nondramatic musical work embodied in a phonorecord.

(b) Negotiated licenses.—

(1) Authority for negotiations.—Any owners of copyright in works to which this section applies and any operators of coin-operated phonorecord players may negotiate and agree upon the terms and rates of royalty payments for the performance of such works and the proportionate division of fees paid among copyright owners, and may designate common agents to negotiate, agree to, pay, or receive such royalty payments.

(2) Arbitration.—Parties to such a negotiation, within such time as may be specified by the Librarian of Congress by regulation, may determine the result of the negotiation by arbitration. Such arbitration shall be governed by the provisions of title 9, to the extent such title is not inconsistent with this section. The parties shall give notice to the Librarian of Congress of any determination reached by arbitration and any such determination shall, as between the parties to the arbitration, be dispositive of the issues to which it relates.

(c) License agreements superior to copyright arbitration royalty panel determinations.—License agreements between one or more copyright owners and one or more operators of coin-operated phonorecord players, which are negotiated in accordance with subsection (b), shall be given effect in lieu of any otherwise applicable determination by a copyright arbitration royalty panel.

[(d) Redesignated(c).]

[(e) to (g) Repealed.]

(PL 100-568, §4[a][4], Oct. 31, 1988, 102 Stat. 2855, §116[A]; renumbered §116 and amended, PL 103-198, §3([a)], [b][1], Dec. 17, 1993, 107 Stat. 2309.)

17 U.S.C. §117 Limitations on exclusive rights: Computer programs

Notwithstanding the provisions of section 106, it is not an infringement for the owner of a copy of a computer program to make or authorize the making of another copy or adaptation of that computer program provided:

(1) that such a new copy or adaptation is created as an essential step in the utilization of the computer program in conjunction with a machine and that it is used in no other manner, or

(2) that such new copy or adaptation is for archival purposes only and that all archival copies are destroyed in the event that continued possession of the computer program should cease to be rightful.

Any exact copies prepared in accordance with the provisions of this section may be leased, sold, or otherwise transferred, along with the copy from which such copies were prepared, only as part of the lease, sale, or other transfer of all rights in the program. Adaptations so prepared may be transferred only with the authorization of the copyright owner. (PL 96-517, §10[b], Dec. 12, 1980, 94 Stat. 3028.)

17 U.S.C. §118 Scope of exclusive rights: Use of certain works in connection with noncommercial broadcasting

(a) The exclusive rights provided by section 106 shall, with respect to the works specified by subsection (b) and the activities specified by subsection (d), be subject to the conditions and limitations prescribed by this section.

(b) Notwithstanding any provision of the antitrust laws, any owners of copyright in published nondramatic musical works and published pictorial, graphic, and sculptural works and any public broadcasting entities, respectively, may negotiate and agree upon the terms and rates of royalty payments and the proportionate division of fees paid among various copyright owners, and may designate common agents to negotiate, agree to, pay, or receive payments.

(1) Any owner of copyright in a work specified in this subsection or any public broadcasting entity may submit to the Librarian of Congress proposed licenses covering such activities with respect to such works. The Librarian of Congress shall proceed on the basis of the proposals submitted to it as well as any other relevant information. The Librarian of Congress shall permit any interested party to submit information relevant to such proceedings.

(2) License agreements voluntarily negotiated at any time between one or more copyright owners and one or more public broadcasting entities shall be given effect in lieu of any determination by the Librarian of Congress: Provided, That copies of such agreements are filed in the Copyright Office within thirty days of execution in accordance with regulations that the Register of Copyrights shall prescribe.

(3) In the absence of license agreements negotiated under paragraph (2), the Librarian of Congress shall, pursuant to chapter 8, convene a copyright arbitration royalty panel to determine and publish in the Federal Register a schedule of rates and terms which, subject to paragraph (2), shall be binding on all owners of copyright in works specified by this subsection and public broadcasting entities, regardless of whether such copyright owners have submitted proposals to the Librarian of Congress. In establishing such rates and terms the copyright arbitration royalty panel may consider the rates for comparable circumstances under voluntary license agreements negotiated as provided in paragraph (2). The Librarian of Congress shall also establish requirements by which copyright owners may receive reasonable notice of the use of their works under this section, and under which records of such use shall be kept by public broadcasting entities.

(c) The initial procedure specified in subsection (b) shall be repeated and concluded between June 30 and December 31, 1997, and at five-year intervals thereafter, in accordance with regulations that the Librarian of Congress shall prescribe.

(d) Subject to the terms of any voluntary license agreements that have been negotiated as provided by subsection (b)(2), a public broadcasting entity may, upon compliance with the provisions of this section, including the rates and terms established by a copyright arbitration royalty panel under subsection (b)(3), engage in the following activities with respect to published nondramatic musical works and published pictorial, graphic, and sculptural works:

(1) performance or display of a work by or in the course of a transmission made by a noncommercial educational broadcast station referred to in subsection (g); and

(2) production of a transmission program, reproduction of copies or phonorecords of such a transmission program, and distribution of such copies or phonorecords, where such production, reproduction, or distribution is made by a nonprofit institution or organization solely for the purpose of transmissions specified in paragraph (1); and

(3) the making of reproductions by a governmental body or a nonprofit institution of a transmission program simultaneously with its transmission as specified in paragraph (1), and the performance or display of the contents of such program under the conditions specified by paragraph (1) of section 110, but only if the reproductions are used for performances or displays for a period of no more than seven days from the date of the transmission specified in paragraph (1), and are destroyed before or at the end of such period. No person supplying, in accordance with paragraph (2), a reproduction of a transmission program to governmental bodies or nonprofit institutions under this paragraph shall have any liability as a result of failure of such body or institution to destroy such reproduction: Provided, That it shall have notified such body or institution of the requirement for such destruction pursuant to this paragraph: And provided further, That if such body or institution itself fails to destroy such reproduction it shall be deemed to have infringed.

(e) Except as expressly provided in this subsection, this section shall have no applicability to works other than those specified in subsection (b).

(1) Owners of copyright in nondramatic literary works and public broadcasting entities may, during the course of voluntary negotiations, agree among themselves, respectively, as to the terms and rates of royalty payments without liability under the antitrust laws. Any such terms and rates of royalty payments shall be effective upon filing in the Copyright Office, in accordance with regulations that the Register of Copyrights shall prescribe.

(2) On January 3, 1980, the Register of Copyrights, after consulting with authors and other owners of copyright in nondramatic literary works and their representatives, and with public broadcasting entities and their representatives, shall submit to the Congress a report setting forth the extent to which voluntary licensing arrangements have been reached with respect to the use of nondramatic literary works by such broadcast stations. The report should also describe any problems that may have arisen, and present legislative or other recommendations, if warranted.

(f) Nothing in this section shall be construed to permit, beyond the limits

§118 continued   of fair use as provided by section 107, the unauthorized
                dramatization of a nondramatic musical work, the production
of a transmission program drawn to any substantial extent from a published
compilation of pictorial, graphic, or sculptural works, or the unauthorized use
of any portion of an audiovisual work.

(g) As used in this section, the term "public broadcasting entity" means a
noncommercial educational broadcast station as defined in section 397 of title
47 and any nonprofit institution or organization engaged in the activities
described in paragraph (2) of subsection (d). (PL 94-553, Title I, §101, Oct. 19,
1976, 90 Stat. 2565; PL 103-198, §4, Dec. 17, 1993, 107 Stat. 2309.)

17 U.S.C. §1008 Prohibition on certain infringement actions

No action may be brought under this title alleging infringement of copyright based on the manufacture, importation, or distribution of a digital audio
recording device, a digital audio recording medium, an analog recording device,
or an analog recording medium, or based on the noncommercial use by a consumer of such a device or medium for making digital musical recordings or
analog musical recordings. (PL 102-563, §2, Oct. 28, 1992, 106 Stat. 4244.)

Index